Plantation Agriculture and Social Control in Northern Peru, 1875–1933

Latin American Monographs, No. 62
Institute of Latin American Studies
The University of Texas at Austin

Plantation Agriculture
and Social Control
in Northern Peru, 1875-1933

By Michael J. Gonzales

University of Texas Press, Austin

First Edition, 1985

Requests for permission to reproduce material from
this work should be sent to:
Permissions
University of Texas Press
P.O. Box 7819
Austin, Texas 78713

Library of Congress Cataloging in Publication Data

Gonzales, Michael J., 1946-
   Plantation agriculture and social control in northern Peru, 1875-1933.

   (Latin American monographs; no. 62)
   Includes index.
   1. Sugar trade—Peru—History. 2. Sugar workers—Peru—History. 3. Plantations—Peru—History. 4. Social control. I. Title. II. Series: Latin American
monographs (University of Texas at Austin. Institute of Latin American Studies);
no. 62.
HD9114.P52G66   1984   338.1'7361'09851   84-2359
ISBN 0-292-76491-X

To Gail, for helping me with every facet of this study
and giving me valuable intellectual and moral support.

Contents

Figure

Tables

Maps

Acknowledgments

Several persons assisted me in the completion of this study. In Peru, I would especially like to thank Tito Rodríguez, the former director of the Archivo del Fuero Agrario (AFA), who fought to keep his unique archive alive and who did everything possible to facilitate my research. I would also like to thank two of my fellow researchers at the AFA, Dennis Gilbert and Bill Albert, who helped make my work a pleasant and rewarding experience. And Peru would not have been the same had I not met Mariel Romero de Farfán. Research is a time-consuming process, and I was fortunate to have Kitty King Corbett as a research assistant.

Many scholars in the United States have read this work at various stages and offered salutary comments. I wish especially to thank Tulio Halperín Donghi, James F. King, Benjamin S. Orlove, Fredrick B. Pike, Susan E. Ramírez, and Ann Waltner. Professor Halperín Donghi has played a special role in my development as a historian, first as my adviser at the University of California at Berkeley, and since then as my friend.

It has taken several years to complete this book, and throughout that time I have benefited from the support and encouragement of my family and friends. I would particularly like to thank my mother, grandmother, and wife, and my close friends Steven and David Gilmartin.

The research for this work was made possible by grants from the Ford Foundation Graduate Fellowships Program, the Center for Latin American Studies of the University of California, Berkeley, and the Department of History of the same institution. Additional funding was provided by the College of Humanities Career Development Committee of the University of Utah. A David P. Gardner Fellowship gave me the time to make essential revisions in the manuscript. I must also thank Tony L. Scott for typing the manuscript, Adrienne Morgan for drawing maps 1 and 2, and James Patterson for drawing maps 3 through 6. I am also grateful to Cambridge University Press for permission to publish material from my article "Capitalist Agriculture and Labour Contracting in Northern Peru, 1880–1905," *Journal of Latin American Studies* 12, part 2 (November 1980):291–315.

Abbreviations and Conventions

The majority of information in this study comes from the Aspíllaga family's private correspondence, which is now housed in the Archivo del Fuero Agrario in Lima. The names of the principal correspondents are referred to in the notes by their initials, except in those cases where they simply signed the title of the family firm, Aspíllaga Hermanos. The following is a list of all correspondents and titles that are abbreviated.

Ramón Aspíllaga Ferrebú	RAF
Antero Aspíllaga Barrera	AAB
Ramón Aspíllaga Barrera	RAB
Baldomero Aspíllaga Barrera	BAB
Ismael Aspíllaga Barrera	IAB
Víctor Aspíllaga Taboada	VAT
Ismael Aspíllaga Anderson	IAA
Luis Aspíllaga Anderson	LAA
Gustavo Aspíllaga Anderson	GAA
Antero Aspíllaga Anderson	AAA
Aspíllaga Hermanos	AH

The Aspíllagas occasionally wrote two letters on the same day. In such cases, the first letter filed in a volume of correspondence is cited as (a) and the second as (b).

Plantation Agriculture and Social Control
in Northern Peru, 1875–1933

Introduction: Modern Peru, Plantation Agriculture, and Social Control

In 1968 General Juan Velasco Alvarado led a coup d'état that removed President Fernando Belaúnde Terry from office and installed a revolutionary junta pledged to alleviate Peru's massive social, economic, and political inequities. A focal point of the regime's policy was the nationalization of property owned by foreign corporations and the national elite. These groups controlled the most important sectors of the economy: coastal agriculture, mining, finance, and industry. The junta accused these leading capitalists of profiting unjustifiably at the expense of the rest of society and argued that only by a thorough redistribution of wealth and political power could Peru emerge as a truly independent and prosperous country. Although poor planning, political dissension, corruption, and global recession doomed the Revolutionary Government's attempts at reform, its criticism of the Peruvian reality was not without some foundation.[1]

The creation of modern Peru, the nation that Velasco sought to dismantle, can be dated from the formation of the coastal oligarchy during the mid– and late nineteenth century and its linkage with foreign capital and overseas markets. The form of economic and political control that took shape during these years was to endure, with various modifications, well into this century. A critical component of this process was the development of coastal agriculture, particularly sugarcane plantations, and the rise of a select group of planters to political and social prominence under the banner of the aristocratic Civilista party, which dominated Peruvian politics during the period known as the República Aristocrática (1899–1919).[2]

Some sugar planters envisioned themselves as heroes who would be remembered as architects of economic prosperity and political stability. They and their political allies succeeded in helping to revitalize the export economy and return the nation to civilian rule. However, their blueprint for Peru clearly favored their own interests: low taxes on exports and imports, encouragement of foreign investment, limited suffrage, and centralized government. It was a classic example of liberal economic theory and oligarchic democracy.

The rulers of the República Aristocrática were also largely unaffected by feelings of cultural nationalism. Their economic, social, and intellectual orientation was more directed toward Europe and Europeans than it was toward Peru and Peruvians. The sugar industry looked across the seas for its markets, its technology, and sometimes its capital. Planters admired their European trading partners for their business knowledge and cultural background as much as they disliked their laborers for their ignorance and lack of sophistication.

Cast in their role as agriculturalists, however, sugar planters were continually forced to deal, directly and indirectly, with laborers on their estates. Indeed, their success as businessmen largely depended on acquiring and securing large numbers of workers during labor shortages. Without laborers to work their estates, they could never have achieved wealth, social position, and political power. In their dealings with workers, planters revealed a great deal about themselves. Their notions of race, work, wealth, and power both unveil the morality of capitalist development in Peru and provide insights into the character and mentality of the national elite.

This study concerns the development of the sugarcane industry on the northern coast, the principal area of production, from the late nineteenth century to the early years of the Great Depression. Important themes include the formation of a new planter elite, sources of capital, technological innovation, land consolidation, and the recruitment, organization, and control of labor.

Another theme, interwoven throughout much of the discussion, is the development of wage-labor regimes. The mid– to late nineteenth century was the great period of transition from slave to nonslave labor on the plantations of Latin America. One by one areas that had relied on black slavery for centuries abolished that form of servitude and replaced it with a variety of labor regimes, including sharecropping, indentured servitude, and wage labor.

For laborers, this was not necessarily a transition from bondage to freedom. Historians have long recognized that coercion, violence, and intimidation were prominent features of non-slave-labor regimes on large estates in Latin America. For example, peonage, the process through which indebted laborers remained bound to estates for long periods of time, traditionally has been seen as a common practice during the nineteenth century. Paternalism has also been mentioned frequently as a method employed by estate owners to dominate laborers.

This view of labor regimes is now, however, changing. Recent studies have established that there existed great diversity in the amount of freedom laborers enjoyed on plantations, even among those plantations growing the same crops and employing similar payment methods. Such diversity, in hindsight, should not be surprising, given the regional differences that existed in, among other things, political economy, demography, seasonal labor requirements, ecology, and culture.³

This study contributes to this widening view of labor relations during a period of transition and change. It demonstrates that, for the northern coast of Peru, plantations' connections with the outside world as well as the internal historical dynamics of individual estates affected social relations of production. The complex interaction of these forces resulted in a general pattern of labor relations, with some variation in timing and context among individual plantations, that may yield areas of comparison for scholars studying plantation agriculture in other parts of the world.

The sugar industry in northern Peru traditionally had relied on servile labor, and the initial transition to wage labor had nothing to do with the marketplace. Rather, it resulted from the end in the trade in Chinese indentured servants in 1874, and from the unavailability of alternative sources of nonwage labor. Over the course of half a century, different wage-labor regimes developed in a series of stages, with laborers gradually acquiring more freedom or, put another way, with planters losing more control over labor.

This evolution reflected the growing size and social complexity of the plantation economy and community, as well as the growing stability and political complexity of the Peruvian nation. These internal and external forces made coercion a less-effective tool of social control and compelled planters to rely more heavily on accomodation and manipulation to maintain a certain dominance over workers.

Although this general trend is clearly discernible, it is also true that labor regimes were never completely homogeneous. There was always a sizable minority of workers who enjoyed relatively more or less freedom and who received different wages for the same work. The basic distinction was ability to market one's own labor, as workers enjoyed more freedom and higher wages if they could deal directly with planters, rather than through a labor broker.

There also existed some important distinctions among individual plantations. Although all major producers in the region utilized modern equipment, farmed extensive expanses of land, and employed essentially the same labor systems, some were more technologically advanced than others. On more primitive estates, planters could more successfully employ paternalistic methods of control that stemmed from preindustrial social relations of production. Besides this important structural variation, it is also true that some planters were patient, clever, and manipulative, whereas others were petulant, temperamental, and harsh. These distinctions in personality and character sometimes significantly influenced relations between owners and workers.

In part, the nature of the available documentation determined the focus of this analysis. Most studies of large estates in modern Latin America have not been based on estate records. This has, predictably, resulted in some problems of interpretation.[4] When the Velasco government seized coastal plantations under its agrarian reform program, some records of the former owners were left behind and collected by an enterprising group of scholars. They were eventually housed in the Archivo del Fuero Agrario in Lima, where I consulted them for this study. Some of the documents, particularly plantation correspondence, are rich in detail and insights into the reality of social relations of production. The material is, logically, slanted toward the interests of estate owners. Labor is discussed in great detail in terms of recruitment, control, housing, health, and work routine; however, there is extremely little information that relates directly to the views and concerns of laborers, particularly to the growth of class consciousness. This lack of data makes it impossible to deal systematically and definitively with the formation of a rural proletariat.

Not surprisingly, the records in the Archivo del Fuero Agrario are more complete for some estates than for others.[5] This is simply the luck of historical preservation. For the northern coast, there are scattered pieces of documentation from a number of sugar estates and a nearly complete set of correspondence for the plantation Cayaltí. This set of circumstances compelled me to focus my analysis on Cayaltí within a regional perspective.

Cayaltí is located in the Saña Valley in the Department of Lambayeque. The Aspíllaga family purchased it in 1859. By the turn of the century, the estate stood as one of the nation's biggest sugar producers, and the Aspíllagas had risen to a position of social and political prominence. Their history is representative of the formation of the coastal oligarchy and the República Aristocrática, and their control of sugar workers is, with some important exceptions, illustrative of general patterns within the region.

This study is divided into two general sections. The first, consisting of chapters 1 through 3, analyzes the development of the sugar industry and also provides essential background material for the study of labor. Chapter 1 covers the physical and historical setting, explains how geography and climate influenced the nature of estate agriculture, and also briefly surveys the history of sugar in the region to 1860. Chapter 2 discusses planters and capital and focuses on the rise of regional sugar planters to economic, social, and political importance and on their sources of capital, both foreign and domestic. Chapter 3 analyzes land consolidation and technological development on the northern coast and discusses important differences in the pace of technological growth for the major producers in the region.

The second part, covering chapters 4 through 9, focuses on labor. Chapter 4 analyzes the organization of labor and explains the allocation of workers to different production tasks and the impact of technological change. Chapter 5 discusses the recruitment of Chinese wage laborers following the abolition of indentured servitude. A brief history of the coolie trade is followed by a detailed look at the methods employed at Cayaltí to secure a work force during a period of crisis in the industry. This chapter is followed by an analysis of the Chinese experience at Cayaltí in terms of culture and social control. It is a brief social history of the Chinese community and the methods the Aspíllagas employed to maintain and control laborers whose experience, at times, resembled that of slaves. Chapter 7 examines the recruitment of Peruvian wage labor to replace the aging, and no longer useful, Chinese. It shows how both the marketplace and coercion played important roles in labor contracting and addresses the problem of peonage and oppression within a comparative context. The next chapter looks at the plantation community from 1890 to 1933, and shows how Cayaltí grew into a more complex society that presented management with new problems of social control. A social history of the plantation examines housing, the sale of goods, health and health care, as well as the Aspíllagas' efforts to establish a paternalistic regime. The final chapter considers the growing level of confrontation between laborers and planters from World War I into the early 1930s. It identifies the general causes of conflict in the region as well as drawing important distinctions in the pattern of confrontation on individual estates. The conclusion summarizes these findings within the context of my theoretical framework.

Part I. The Development of the Sugar Industry

1. The Physical and Historical Setting

On the northern coast of Peru, the economic and social importance of the large estate was firmly established in the colonial era, as haciendas gained control over vital land, water, and human resources. Developments during the first half of the nineteenth century, moreover, reinforced general patterns of control and established precedents that facilitated the later domination of the region by the Aspíllagas and other planters. In this sense, the modern development of the sugar industry and of a planter elite was fundamentally rooted in an earlier epoch.

The Environment

The history of agriculture in the region is closely related to the adaptation to and control of the natural environment. The Peruvian coast presents formidable barriers to agricultural development, for it averages less than thirty millimeters of rainfall a year, making it one of the driest deserts in the world.[1] The barren coastline, which extends to the south for much of the length of Chile, is the creation of the cold Peruvian Current, which passes off shore, and the Andes, which rise abruptly several miles inland. The only regular form of precipitation on the coast is a heavy mist known as the *garúa*, which has little if any practical value for agriculture. In fact, near the sea the combination of mist and heavy fog actually inhibits agriculture, as plants are shielded from the life-giving rays of the sun, and the high humidity fosters the growth of harmful fungi.[2]

What makes this area habitable is a series of river valleys that crisscross the barren landscape. Flowing down from the Andes, these life-giving currents have been used since pre-Columbian times to irrigate large expanses of land. Away from the sea, the semitropical climate and long periods of intense sunlight actually become allies of the farmer by accelerating the growing process and providing bountiful yields.

To assure year-round production, the flow of river water must be carefully channeled through a series of irrigation canals, which dissect each valley.

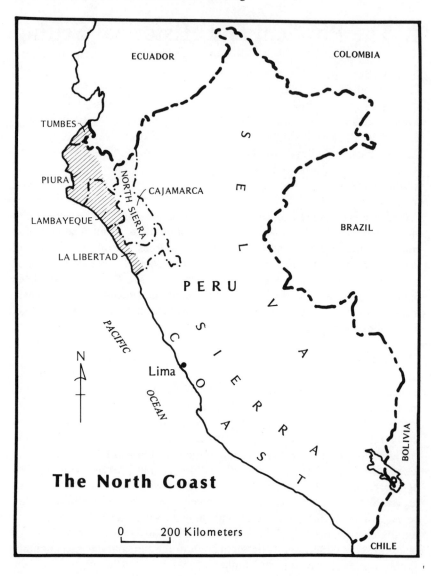

Source: Adapted from Claude Collin Delavaud, *Les Régions Côtières du Pérou Septentrional* (Lima: Institut Français D'Etudes Andines, 1968), p. 13.

During the rainy season in the Andes (January through April), sufficient water is available to meet the needs of agriculturalists; during the rest of the year, however, water must be rationed, and farmers in the foothills have a distinct advantage over those in the lower reaches.[3]

Each valley has unique features that have shaped local forms of agricultural development. On the northern portion of the coast, the principal sugar-producing valleys have been, from north to south, the Lambayeque, Saña, Chicama, and Moche (or Santa Catalina) (see map 2).

The Chicama Valley, with its broad, gently sloping landscape, is ideally suited for the irrigation of large expanses of cane, which grow to luxuriant heights in the rich bottom soils. The Chicama River is an adequate source of water, which planters have supplemented in modern times by drilling wells. Estate owners benefited from the relatively low population density in the valley, which permitted them to expand more easily and to monopolize water resources.[4]

The Lambayeque Valley is also well-suited for the cultivation of sugarcane, as soil conditions and water resources facilitated the growth of plantations. The valley was much more densely populated than the Chicama Valley, owing to the presence of the Indian communities of Reque, Ferreñafe, and Monsefú. During the course of the colonial period, however, these communes were removed from the better land, and their impoverished condition sometimes forced their members to seek work on sugar estates, thus providing planters with a handy source of labor. The trend was for estates to expand into both the fertile upper portions of the valley, which gave them first access to river water in times of scarcity, and the lower valley, where they eventually grew cane right up to the outskirts of the departmental capital, Chiclayo.[5]

The Saña and Moche valleys are comparatively small and sparsely populated. By the late nineteenth century, single sugarcane plantations dominated both valleys, with communities of small farmers clustered around the seas of sugarcane that hopelessly competed for land and water resources. The Moche Valley extends out from the important city of Trujillo. It contained the Indian community of Moche, a sad remnant of the once-powerful Mochica Empire. The Saña Valley contained the Saña Indian community as well as the town of Saña, an important ecclesiastical and administrative center during the colonial period in which the local elite maintained villas. The history of the valley was decisively altered in 1720, however, when a disastrous flood completely destroyed the town. It was only partially rebuilt and its government agencies were transferred to Lambayeque. The town was subsequently reduced to fighting a losing battle with the sugarcane plantation Cayaltí for control over its land.[6]

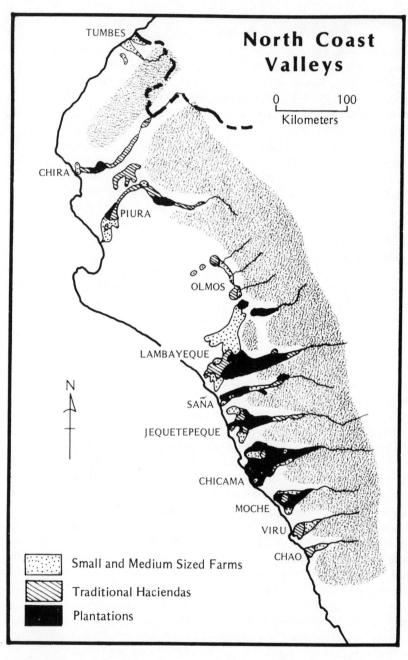

North Coast
Valleys

TUMBES

CHIRA

PIURA

OLMOS

LAMBAYEQUE

SAÑA

JEQUETEPEQUE

CHICAMA

MOCHE

VIRU

CHAO

N

0   100
Kilometers

Small and Medium Sized Farms

Traditional Haciendas

Plantations

Source: Adapted from Claude Collin Delavaud, *Les Régions Côtières du Pérou Septentrional* (Lima: Institut Français D'Etudes Andines, 1968), p. 237.

The Development of Large-Scale Agriculture

Land was cultivated on the northern coast long before the arrival of Francisco Pizarro and his band of conquistadores in 1532. Complex societies were formed on the basis of irrigation systems that linked neighboring valleys into economic, social, and political units. In the opinion of one scholar, the larger states, such as the Chimú Empire, resembled what Karl Wittfogel called "hydraulic" civilizations.[7]

The Spanish conquest of the region thoroughly disrupted traditional society and initiated a long period of colonial rule. However, irrigated agriculture remained the principal economic activity. The first phase of Iberian colonization, dominated by conquistadores and *encomenderos*,[8] soon gave way to a more stable economy and society led by *hacendados*. The rise of the great estate in the region was linked to the decline of the *encomienda* and the founding of Spanish towns on the coast. These became markets for traditional Spanish foods, such as bread, beef, mutton, wine, and sugar. The first commercial farms began as medium-sized enterprises called *chacras*, which then expanded into large estates capable of exporting products to northern South America and other distant regions of the Viceroyalty of Peru.[9]

On the coast, the Spaniards acquired land in several ways, most commonly through royal land grants administered by town councils, viceroys, and tribunals, and by purchases from Indian nobles and communities. Land grants were fairly easy to obtain and averaged around 300 acres, although some were as large as 2,000 acres. Under Spanish law, Indian nobles and commoners could sell community land, despite the fact that the Inca did not recognize private property as defined by Europeans. Many natives in this region and elsewhere were forced to divest land to meet burdensome tribute obligations imposed by the Crown and *encomenderos*. The payment of tribute, in fact, frequently made farming unprofitable for Indians, because it absorbed their surplus capital.[10]

The Saña Valley became the center of agricultural development in the region. In 1563 the Crown ordered the founding of the town of Santiago de Miraflores de Saña. It quickly attracted both *encomenderos* and new settlers anxious to develop estates. Significantly, in this frontier region agriculturalists found all of the capital resources necessary to succeed. Loans could be obtained from the church as well as from the general treasuries of Indian communities and from trusts established to carry out acts of charity and other good works. These early bankers considered real estate safe collateral and charged a yearly interest rate of 7.14 percent.

Estate owners were also able to acquire Indian labor from at least two sources. The colonial labor draft (*mita*) regularly supplied allotments of adult males to growers, who were only required to pay *mitayos* a modest wage. *Hacendados* also hired wage laborers from a growing pool of Indians (called *forasteros*) who had fled their villages to escape labor and tribute obligations.

New Crown policies further facilitated agricultural growth. Beginning in 1569, the Viceroyalty of Peru underwent a thorough administrative reorganization under the direction of Francisco de Toledo. One of Toledo's most important actions was the resettlement of much of the Indian population into new villages constructed on European models (*reducciones*). The rationale for the policy was to facilitate religious indoctrination, segregate the Indian population from the evil influences of the colonists, and expedite royal tax collection and control. However, on the northern coast, resettlement also removed Indians from the better lands, which then became available for Spanish occupation. These lands, which were located farther inland, also had first access to irrigation water. Several of the estates that took shape on former Indian property expanded in later years and still existed at the time of the agrarian reform of 1969.

By the late sixteenth century, Spaniards were engaged in a variety of agricultural activities. North of the Lambayeque River, farmers specialized in stock raising and the production of hides, soap, and other livestock by-products, and in the Saña Valley enterprising agriculturalists were already cultivating sugarcane.

The production of sugar represented a major change in the history of the region. Wheat farmers and stock raisers received most of the land and labor they required from the Crown, and neither activity demanded sophisticated tools. Although sugar planters benefited from the same land policies, they had to make substantial investments in labor and technology, for example, wooden mills to grind the cane, copper cauldrons for boiling the cane juice into syrup, iron tools for planting, cultivation, and harvesting, as well as oxen and mules. Labor also became an expensive item, because of the need to purchase African slaves.[11]

Sugar planters would have used Indian labor happily, but the Crown had discouraged it. Critics of Spanish labor practices in the Indies, led by Bartolomé de Las Casas, had convinced the king of the dangers inherent in the cultivation and processing of sugarcane and noted that serious accidents were disturbingly commonplace. Since the stated purpose of the conquest had been to convert natives to Christianity, not to exterminate them, Africans slaves were generally exploited in their place. Blacks were subsequently imported into the region from Africa as well as from the Caribbean and northern South America.[12] This was one of the few areas where the Indians were actually spared, as Crown policies generally accelerated their loss of land and water rights.

During the first half of the seventeenth century, Spanish landowners consolidated their estates into larger enterprises, mostly at the expense of the Indian population. The critical component of the process was a review of land titles in the Spanish colonies, a *visita de la tierra*, ordered by Philip II in 1589 to earn money for the depleted royal treasury. Under the law, Spaniards could legally acquire land that they had previously stolen from Indians by paying a fee to the Crown. The law also permitted officials to confiscate Indian communal land considered to be in excess of what the natives actually needed. These surplus lands were then sold at public auction. Both of these procedures directly benefited Spanish landowners and helped to impoverish the natives.[13]

Land titles established the hacienda as a permanent institution in the region. However, estate owners increasingly complained of labor shortages, as drafted Indian and local wage labor simply could not meet their needs. They tried recruiting Indians from the nearby highlands, but they were unable to convince or compel significant numbers of highlanders to migrate. The labor shortage on the coast, which was to be a recurring problem, eventually forced the Crown to import more black slaves into the region.[14]

Frederick Bowser has studied the slave trade to Peru and the role of the African in colonial society. His work shows that blacks played a vital role in the development of coastal agriculture, including in the northern region.[15] There, the increased reliance on slave labor made possible the expansion of sugarcane cultivation. In the years to follow, sugar growers participated in the general trend toward land consolidation and specialization of production.

One result of this growth was increased demand for irrigation water. The problem was not one of quantity but of accessibility: enough water existed to meet everyone's needs, but irrigation canals were insufficient in number to handle the increased demand. In general, *hacendados* found it easier to acquire more land and steal irrigation water from Indian communities than to dig new canals. As usual, local officials supported or covered up their actions.

These steps laid the foundation for the unprecedented expansion of large-scale agriculture in the Lambayeque and Saña valleys from 1650 to 1719. The skyrocketing price of sugar, which increased profits and resulted in a new round of land consolidation and capital investments, initially caused the boom. Sugarcane cultivation spread from the Saña to the Lambayeque Valley, where it placed new demands on labor and water resources.

To alleviate the labor shortage, the Crown deregulated the slave trade, thus increasing the number of Africans arriving in Saña and lowering the average price per slave. As a result, the slave population on several estates doubled or tripled after 1650. During this period, landowners were also able to recruit more wage labor because of the gradual demographic recovery among Indians, mulattos, and mestizos, who now constituted a supplementary labor pool.[16] *Hacendados* still received small numbers of drafted Indian laborers, but this labor source became less significant as the century advanced, and was abolished locally in 1720.

It was also during this period that peonage became an important method of control on regional estates. To prevent transitory laborers from leaving, landowners advanced them goods and cash with the proviso that they remain until their debt had been repaid. On one estate, debts ranged from 30 to 100 pesos, which must have been difficult to repay, considering that wages only ranged from 2 to 6 reales a day (12.5 to 13.5 reales per peso).

As the number of wage earners increased, a racial division of labor began to appear on many estates. In general, planters preferred to use slaves in the more technically difficult tasks of sugar refining, which required specialized training, and for feeding cane into the mill. They preferred Indians and mestizos, on the other hand, for heavy field work, evidently to avoid attrition among the expensive slave population.

The experience of the estate Cayaltí illustrates the expansion of sugarcane cultivation during this period. Already an important hacienda in 1622, Cayaltí produced sugar, alfalfa, and livestock. Twenty slaves operated two wooden grinding mills, and five hundred head of livestock grazed on fields not planted in cane. During the second half of the century, the estate owners purchased more slaves and processing equipment. By 1705, fifty-four slaves manned three bronze crushing mills, and a variety of hand tools, carts, draft animals, and other equipment had been acquired. Over the next twelve years, the estate continued to plant more cane and to increase its production of sugar and molasses.

The history of Cayaltí during these years illustrates a more general tendency in the region: the combination of sugarcane cultivation with stock raising. The two activities complemented one another, because land left fallow after recent cane harvests could be used as pasture. The success of such mixed estates led to another round of land consolidation, and gradually to the solidification of a smaller, more exclusive regional elite.

As before, more land under cultivation led directly to increased demand for irrigation water. This time, *hacendados* and Indian communities responded by building reservoirs to trap water during times of plenty, by digging new irrigation canals, and by more thoroughly cleaning existing systems. These measures, however, still fell short of *hacendados'* needs.

The surest means of acquiring additional water was to purchase more land, as all property, no matter how unproductive, had irrigation rights. Estates were bought for the sole purpose of acquiring their water rights and, once again, *hacendados* laid claim to Indian land. The royal *visita* of 1711–1712, which readjusted the property of Indian communities to meet current population levels, greatly facilitated the latter effort. In all, the royal *visitador* reduced the property owned by communities in the Lambayeque region by 30 percent. Spaniards had already illegally occupied much of this land, and now, for a fee, they received legal title to it. It was also during this *visita* that the Crown, for the first time, permitted the sale of common pastureland. Previously, these lands had been designated for the use of the community, but they were now placed on the market as a means of earning money for the depleted royal treasury.

Through the process of land consolidation, Indians lost both land and water. Over the years, some communities were deprived of literally all of their irrigation water, and others were left near the subsistence level. As life became impossible, many natives left their homes to seek work as wage laborers on neighboring estates. This, too, benefited *hacendados*.[17]

The era of agricultural prosperity that began in the mid-seventeenth century, with such disastrous results for the Indian population, began to subside in the early 1700s. A sharp fall in sugar prices caused by a dramatic increase in production and the saturation of local, regional, and international markets was the initial impetus. In the Lambayeque region, a number of small-scale producers appeared during the late seventeenth and early eighteenth centuries, to supply local markets with molasses, sugar cake (*chancaca*), and cane alcohol. More important, dozens of sugar estates were established at the same time in practically every coastal valley between Lambayeque and Lima. In the Trujillo area alone, there were eighteen sugar plantations, and the Jesuits, who were known for their efficiency, operated thirteen estates in the valleys of Ilo, Pisco, Chincha, Rímac, Chancay, Huaura, and Santa. Sugar plantations even appeared in sheltered highland valleys in Cajamarca and Huamachuco in the north, and in Abancay, Aymaraez, and Urubamba in the south. The increased production generated by these new growers oversupplied markets within highland and coastal Peru and sent prices plummeting.[18]

An important international market for sugar planters on the northern coast had been northern South America, especially the Panama region. During the second half of the seventeenth century, however, sugar estates expanded rapidly in the Caribbean and gradually captured this lucrative market. Lambayeque producers suffered a similar fate in the Rio de la Plata region, where the growing port of Buenos Aires was supplied with cheaper contraband Brazilian sugar.[19]

The policies of the Spanish Bourbons also hurt Peruvian agriculturalists. The Crown initiated a series of reforms in the Indies designed to increase income, improve defenses, and generally strengthen the imperial presence. Increases in sales and head taxes were purposely designed to hurt Peruvian sugar producers and favor sugar growers in southern Spain and wine makers in Peru, whose product competed with cane alcohol. Moreover, under Charles III (1759–1788), the Crown took the extreme step of prohibiting the production of any alcoholic beverage in Peru except wine, a measure that hamstrung sugar growers until the Constitution of 1812 removed it from the books.[20]

The creation of the viceroyalty in La Plata in 1776 also temporarily damaged the fabric of the Peruvian economy. The new viceroyalty included the most prosperous regions of the old Viceroyalty of Peru, including silver-rich Upper Peru and the bustling harbor of Buenos Aires. Moreover, as the trans-Atlantic trade route grew in importance, it became increasingly difficult for Peruvian sugar planters to obtain new slaves and other supplies.[21] Although the mining economy of Peru made a significant recovery,[22] agriculture continued to stagnate.

The situation was particularly dreary on the northern coast of Peru, where floods twice inundated sugar plantations during the early eighteenth century. In 1720 the Saña and Lambayeque rivers overflowed, drowning herds of livestock, uprooting sugarcane, leveling buildings, clogging irrigation canals with debris and mud, and completely destroying the town of Saña. One of the worst victims of the flood was the plantation Cayaltí, which lay in complete ruin.

Recovery proved to be a slow, difficult, and expensive process for sugar planters. Additional laborers had to be hired to effect the necessary repairs, which cost growers considerable sums for wages and provisions. Moreover, new cane had to be planted and then allowed to ripen for approximately eighteen months before it could be harvested, which left planters without an income for two seasons. Irrigation canals also proved difficult to clean, thereby causing water shortages and disruption of production schedules. In all, the flood was a major disaster from which growers never completely recovered.

Hardly had planters gotten their estates back in operating order, moreover, when a second major flood struck in 1728. Many residents of Saña permanently abandoned the town, and planters once again underwent a series of difficult and costly repairs.[23]

The combination of natural disasters, falling sugar prices, general agricultural depression, and increased taxes worked to force many sugar planters into heavy debt and eventual bankruptcy. Foreclosures occurred on a number of estates during the eighteenth century, including Cayaltí in 1785, and brought financial ruin to many members of the regional elite. Socially ambitious members of the middle sectors of colonial society, particularly professionals, public administrators, and merchants, frequently purchased the former estates of the elite and went on to establish themselves as new members of the local aristocracy.[24]

Moreover, a similar pattern occurred in the neighboring Jequetepeque Valley, where the Augustinian Order rented out most of its land to a group of ambitious Spaniards of local birth (criollos).[25]

In the Lambayeque region, newcomers faced the formidable task of revitalizing their estates. A return to sugar production would necessitate extensive capital investments in refining equipment and slave labor during a period of tight money and saturated markets. A more viable alternative appeared to be stock raising, an activity that required very little labor and equipment, and that provided a safer return on capital investment because of the less elastic demand for meat and livestock by-products. Therefore, during the late eighteenth and early nineteenth centuries, the number of livestock estates increased while sugar production declined.[26]

The expansion of the livestock industry necessitated the acquisition of additional land for grazing. *Hacendados* could have expanded their irrigation networks and brought barren lands into pasture, but that would have required extensive capital investment. A cheaper alternative was, once again, to acquire Indian land and water.

Here, many new *hacendados* benefited from their posts as public officials: they could ignore legislation protecting Indians and communal property, or interpret it in a way favorable to their own interests. For example, the local *corregidor de indios* and protector of the Indians generally approved the sale of communal land, against the general interests of the community, when individuals fell behind on tribute payments or needed money to meet extraordinary expenses, such as funerals or baptisms. Outright theft of Indian land and water also occurred, sometimes at the hands of priests and official protectors.

Indians sometimes appealed to royal authorities in Lima to regain stolen land and water, but their claims were generally rejected or reduced. The Spanish bureaucracy moved too slowly and imperfectly to protect the interests of people who were technically wards of the Crown, and frustration over loss of land and water twice led the Indians of the Chiclayo area to riot against local *hacendados*. Such rebellious actions elicited a quicker response from authorities, who lost no time in suppressing the Indians and protecting the interests of landowners.[27]

By the end of the colonial period the Indians of the Lambayeque region had lost much of their land and water to large estates, which were firmly entrenched as the dominant economic and social institutions. Sugarcane cultivation had been the greatest source of wealth, but by the early nineteenth century the livestock industry had superseded it in importance. In addition, *hacendados* had begun to plant tobacco, cotton, and rice. The economy was slowly recovering and diversifying when the wars of independence expelled the Spanish from South America and initiated a new period of economic decline.[28]

The economic and political chaos that followed in the wake of the fighting presented sugar planters with a new set of problems. Their chief concerns were the loss of physical capital and large numbers of slaves, who were impressed by both royalist and rebel forces and could not be readily replaced. The slave trade to Peru (which was already petering out in the late eighteenth century) was almost completely shut off by Great Britain after

1810 and, despite improved working and living conditions, slaves failed to reproduce in large numbers. Consequently, the slave population declined from 40,337 in 1792 to 25,505 in 1854, the year of abolition.[29]

The achievement of independence upset the economy and polity of the region, but not everyone suffered equally. Large landowners may have lost money for several years, but many of them, at least, had the option of retrenching and taking advantage of political alliances to improve their position. During the first few decades after independence much of the economic gain realized by sugar planters came at the expense of peasants and large landowners who had backed the losing side. In this context, *hacendados* owed a great deal to Simón Bolívar's ignorance of Peruvian rural society and misguided sense of social justice. During his brief tenure as president of Peru, Bolívar sought to elevate the Peruvian peasantry to a class of yeoman farmers by disentailing Indian communal land. Blinded by a liberal vision of rural prosperity based on a European model, Bolívar helped to destroy one of the few buffers peasants had against economic domination by large landowners. The bulk of the communal land that was auctioned off went to those with the capital to pay for it, namely *hacendados*, who subsequently found it easier to exploit an increasingly landless peasantry.[30] Continuing to follow a liberal blueprint, Bolívar confiscated all property belonging to convents with less than eight resident clergy as well as many estates owned by royalists. Future presidents, particularly Agustín Gamarra, then used this new state land as a means of rewarding political allies and financial supporters. Some sugar planters on the north coast, notably Dionisio and Casimiro Rázuri in the Jequetepeque Valley, benefited from this form of political payoff.[31]

Immediately following the wars of independence, sugar production decreased as a result of the razing of cane fields, the diminishing slave population, and the loss of processing machinery. As life began to return to normal, production could not keep pace with demand, so the price of sugar rose fivefold from 1825 to 1829. This allowed those planters who could still produce to realize substantial profits, which they subsequently invested in water-powered mills and other technological improvements.[32]

The period of prosperity was, however, short-lived. As more plantations returned to operation, production once again surpassed demand, causing the price of sugar to return to its 1825 level. Planters also had to face the temporary loss of the Chilean market and soaring interest rates, both of which combined to keep the industry depressed until the 1840s.

The importance of the Chilean market dates from the late seventeenth century, when Peru was having trouble finding markets for its sugar and growing enough wheat to feed its people. A symbiotic trade relationship subsequently developed, whereby Chile exchanged wheat for Peruvian sugar. This relationship was upset after independence, however, when Peru placed a new tariff on imported wheat of 3 pesos per fanega (157 pounds) and imposed new technical restrictions on the unloading of wheat at Callao. The Chileans retaliated in 1832 by slapping an impost of 3 pesos per arroba (25 pounds) on Peruvian sugar imported into the country, which effectively priced Peruvian producers out of the Chilean market.[33]

The Chilean market was not recaptured until three years later, when both countries did away with their various restrictions on trade by granting each other most-favored-nation status. However, geopolitical rivalry soon disrupted the agreement, as the Peruvian-Bolivian Confederation was created and war broke out with Chile. Only with the defeat of the confederation in 1839 did Chile once again become the principal overseas market for Peruvian sugar.[34]

Producers were also shackled during the 1830s by high interest rates. During the late colonial period sugar planters could obtain credit from a number of sources, including private loans (especially from the church), commercial accounts, and cash advances from merchants in lieu of the sale of a shipment of sugar. The wars upset the financial structure, however, by driving capital out of the region and forcing interest rates upwards. When the government removed all restrictions on interest rates in 1832, they rose to 24 percent per annum, where they remained for another decade.[35]

The financial revival of the sugar industry began in the 1840s as a spinoff of the guano boom, which injected millions of pesos into the sagging economy. European farmers struggling with soil exhaustion and shortages of animal fertilizers enthusiastically greeted the discovery of massive quantities of guano on the offshore islands of Peru. European merchants struck deals with the Peruvian government to sell guano abroad on consignment, which generated substantial profits for both over the years.[36]

The chief beneficiaries of the boom were British merchants, who hauled profits out of the country by the boat load. Although the Peruvian government earned over 250 million soles from guano, most of the money went to pay off foreign creditors and to construct a series of railroads that had comparatively little long-term benefit for the economy. Still, enough of the guano revenues were channeled into the hands of local capitalists to have a positive effect on the coastal economy.[37]

Among local agriculturalists, sugar planters benefited most from increased government revenues. The sugar industry represented one of the better hopes for the development of the economy, and planters were, by and large, respected members of the coastal elite, with effective political alliances. Therefore, their pleas for government assistance to help revive their industry were frequently answered. In the 1840s and 1850s the government directly or indirectly aided the sugar industry by consolidating the internal debt, indemnifying slaveholders after the abolition of slavery, and paying bonuses to planters for importing nonslave laborers into the country.

The consolidation of the internal debt was a windfall for many Peruvians with good political connections. Since independence, Peruvian political leaders had regularly borrowed money from regional strongmen and the affluent to finance revolutions, pet programs, and personal expenditures. Before the guano boom, some of these loans were repaid with state land, but during the administration of José Echenique (1851–1854) the decision was made to repay the internal debt in cash. Echenique quickly came under criticism for awarding his friends and associates large sums of money with little or no proof of an outstanding loan. He was eventually overthrown by his former mentor Ramón Castilla, but not before he had paid out between 13 million and 16 million pesos to Peruvian bondholders and his cronies. According to Pablo Macera, about one-half of this money was later invested in coastal agriculture.[38]

During his campaign to overthrow Echenique, Castilla sought black recruits for his cause by declaring the abolition of slavery. Nevertheless, he did not want to alienate slaveholders, so he arranged to indemnify them with 300 pesos for each slave or *liberto* freed.[39] In all, slaveowners received over 7 million pesos.

Abolition with indemnification greatly benefited sugarcane planters, who owned the majority of slaves. As stated earlier, the slave trade had been effectively shut off in 1810, and slaves had not reproduced in large numbers. Planters realized that they would have to find alternative sources of labor, and by the 1840s they had already begun to replace slaves with Chinese indentured servants and other foreign workers. The government had encouraged such labor substitution by granting planters premiums for every nonslave laborer imported into the country. Between 1839 and 1851, some 450,000 pesos in premiums were paid out.[40] According to Macera, two-thirds of the money expended for indemnification, consolidation, and premiums was directly invested in sugarcane plantations.[41]

The Peruvian government would not have been able to lay out such sums, of course, without the millions of pesos of income the guano boom generated. This great infusion of capital also helped sugar planters by lowering interest rates to 12 percent per annum by 1854, and by bringing planters into closer contact with European merchants who would later become their business partners and creditors.[42]

It should not be surprising that sugar planters were willing to invest so much money in their plantations during the mid-nineteenth century. By the 1840s, the Chilean market had been recaptured and the introduction of steamship navigation to Peru foreshadowed the opening up of new overseas markets.[43] Moreover, there were not that many investment opportunities available. The mining boom had not yet begun, and agriculture was an established business long associated with social prestige.

The revival of the sugarcane industry on the northern coast would mark a turning point in Peruvian history. A new planter class with access to foreign markets and capital would begin another round of land consolidation and technological improvements and would emerge as political power brokers on the national level.

A pattern of agricultural development going back to the sixteenth century had paved the way for these changes. Large estates had developed to supply expanding markets, and with their growth came control over local land and water resources. Indian communities were reduced to subsisting on marginal lands with inadequate water sources, and in this desert climate water was the critical ingredient for agricultural prosperity.

Plantations would grow even more rapidly during the nineteenth and twentieth centuries, pushing Indian communities as well as small farmers even closer to the edge of the economic abyss. Green cane stalks carpeted coastal valleys, and the smokestacks of the powerful mills signaled to the surrounding countryside the plantations' total domination.

2. Planters and Capital, 1860–1933

During the 1860s and 1870s important steps were taken in the economic and political transformation of Peru. The guano boom was entering its final phase, and the time was approaching when capitalists would have to look elsewhere for financial gain. Many of the merchants and speculators who had profited from the guano trade chose to invest their gains in coastal agriculture over the course of the nineteenth century. Some of them belonged to old colonial families, but many were recently arrived immigrants who combined considerable business skill with a driving ambition to get ahead economically, socially, and politically. By turning their investments into fortunes, they eventually gained entrance into the national elite and the aristocratic Civilista party.[1]

The Civilista party had been founded in 1871 by disgruntled guano consignees, led by Manuel Pardo, who were upset with the government's abolition of the consignment system. Pardo's election in 1872 as Peru's first civilian president was an important landmark in national history. However, his assassination in 1878 and Peru's subsequent defeat by Chile during the War of the Pacific (1879–1883), plunged the nation into chaos and another decade of military rule.[2]

It was not until 1895 that the Civilista party reemerged as an important political force on the national level. In that year it supported the successful presidential candidacy of Nicolás de Piérola, an old political adversary of the Civilista party, who was the only civilian politician popular enough to win the election. The party's strategy was subsequently vindicated, as Piérola's four-year administration served as an important transitional phase to a longer period of Civilista control.[3] Piérola and the Civilistas in the past had differed over who was to rule, rather than over actual policies. Both sides were in general agreement over the value of liberal economic theory, centralized administration, and an ordered society designed to protect the interests of the elite against the unruly masses.[4] In the area of economic policy, the abolition of export taxes on sugar and cotton and import taxes on industrial goods were among Piérola's most important actions. The president also established the Ministry of Development and encouraged the founding of the important information-gathering and pressure groups, the National Societies of Agriculture, Mining, and Industry. Such policies directly benefited the Civilistas, whose membership included large landowners, important merchants, leading lawyers, owners of large blocks of urban real estate, and other prosperous businessmen.[5]

In 1899 the Civilistas won the presidential election and remained in power, except from 1912 to 1915, until 1919. Historians have called this period in Peruvian history the República Aristocrática because of the importance of elites in the party leadership.[6] Sugar planters assumed an unusually important role in the political history of Peru during these years, with two growers being elected to the nation's highest office under the Civilista banner, Eduardo López de Romaña (1899–1903) and José Pardo (1904–1908; 1915–1919). The Aspíllagas were another sugar family that produced prominent Civilista politicians, and their history encapsulates many important features of the political, economic, and social history of the period.

Throughout the República Aristocrática the Civilistas stood at the pinnacle of power. They were never a completely homogeneous group of politicians, however, as divisions existed among leaders, members of pressure groups with divergent interests, and officials in the executive and legislative branches of government. These divisions eventually contributed to the dissolution of the Civilista party and the dictatorship of Augusto B. Leguía, a leader of one of the party's factions and a former president.[7]

Leguía succeeded in seizing the presidency again in 1919 and establishing an independent political base that permitted him to remain in power until 1930, when the Great Depression forced him from office. During this eleven-year period, commonly referred to as the Oncenio, the Civilistas were kept out of positions of political authority but were allowed to retain their extensive economic interests. Leguía's fight with the coastal oligarchy, from whose ranks he came, was more personal and political than philosophical. As with his predecessors, he welcomed foreign investment, favored the export sector, and suppressed popular participation in government and trade unionism.[8]

The economic transformation of Peru during the República Aristocrática and the Oncenio was closely associated with the development of coastal agriculture, particularly the sugarcane industry. The nature of the business logically tied sugar planters to foreign capital and overseas markets. Peru had become more fully integrated into the world capitalist economy during the guano boom, and trading networks and mercantile capital were subsequently available to handle new products. During the second half of the nineteenth century, the demand for sugar greatly increased in Western Europe and the United States, with per capita consumption in the United

Kingdom alone rising from 16.32 pounds in the 1840 to 1844 period to 82.05 pounds in the 1895 to 1899 period.[9] This resulted in a tremendous increase in world sugar production, which transformed local economies wherever sugar was grown.

Peruvian producers successfully gained a foothold in the large British market while maintaining their virtual monopoly over the expanding Chilean market. Peruvian sugar was marketed abroad primarily by British import-export houses, which sold sugar to refiners in Liverpool and Chile and earned a commission on total sales. British merchants also helped to finance the sugar industry by extending credit to planters, particularly during periods of political and financial turmoil, when domestic sources of capital were scarce. However, Peruvian planters were far from dependent on foreign merchants for their livelihood. They had considerable managerial and political skills of their own, and after the turn of the century they could draw more on domestic sources of credit as well as profits.

Planters

The mid-nineteenth century was a period when ambitious men could earn fortunes in Peru. Large amounts of capital flowed in and out of the country to the benefit of merchants, financiers, politicians, and others with nothing more than social and political connections. This led to speculation and incautious spending by the government, particularly in railroad construction, and to a great deal of high living by individuals who could afford to import luxuries from Europe. The most ambitious, however, looked to the future and invested their money prudently. Among this group were several who became sugarcane planters.

On the northern coast, a surprising number of new sugarcane planters were immigrants. Among the most important families were the Larcos and the Gildemeisters, who acquired vast landholdings in the Chicama Valley. In 1862 Andrés and Rafael Larco left Italy to join their brother, who had established a prosperous retail trade in Lima. Within three years the brothers had accumulated enough capital to purchase the estate San Ildefonso in the Virú Valley, where they produced cochineal. They turned a profit for several years, but when chemical dyes appeared on the market in 1870 they sold out and began acquiring estates in the Chicama Valley for the purpose of producing sugar.[10]

Between 1872 and 1878 the Larcos rented the estates Chiquitoy and Mocollope and purchased Tulape, which they renamed Roma, and Cepeda. Family members continued to purchase estates in the valley, with Rafael's son Víctor becoming the largest landowner in the valley shortly before the outbreak of World War I.[11] Like other north coast sugar planters, members of the family served as Civilista congressmen and gained entrance into the national elite.[12] The Larcos remained prominent landholders in the Chicama Valley until their property was expropriated during the agrarian reform of 1969.

Another important landholder in the Chicama Valley was Juan Gildemeister. Gildemeister was a German immigrant who had come to Peru via Brazil in the mid-nineteenth century. He began as an importer in Lima, but soon invested heavily in nitrates in the south, becoming one of the most important nitrate producers in Tarapacá by the 1870s. He remained there until 1889 when, judging that the industry might enter into a period of decline, he sold his holdings to an English firm for 1 million pounds sterling.[13]

At that juncture, Gildemeister began to purchase estates in the Chicama Valley, beginning with Casa Grande and Sausal, which he acquired from fellow countryman Luis Albrecht. By the time of his death in 1898, he had purchased six additional estates, making him the second-largest landholder in the valley, behind the Larcos. The following year his heirs formed the Sociedad Agrícola Casa Grande Ltd., with capital shares valued at 270,000 pounds sterling. Between 1903 and 1910 the firm acquired four more estates in the valley and in 1910 merged with a German corporation to form Casa Grande Zuckerplantagen A.G.[14] The Gildemeisters later surpassed the Larcos as the largest landowners in the valley, a position they enjoyed until the agrarian reform in 1969.[15]

Unlike the Larcos, the Gildemeisters did not become completely assimilated into Peruvian society, nor did they limit their investments to Peru. This has led Ernesto Yepes del Castillo to characterize them as foreigners and to lump them together with United States and British corporations with property in Peru.[16] Peter Klarén, on the other hand, is more cautious, referring to Casa Grande as a German-Peruvian enterprise.[17] The family clearly bridges simple categories of national and foreign, exhibiting some characteristics of a multinational firm but with most of its investments and influence in Peru. Casa Grande Zuckerplantagen A.G. had been chartered in Germany and the majority of its stockholders were residents of Bremen, the birthplace of Juan Gildemeister. Family members also spoke both German and Spanish, seldom married Peruvians, and maintained considerable business interests in Europe and Chile. Nevertheless, after the First World War the German company was dissolved and replaced by a firm registered in Peru, the Empresa Agrícola Chicama Ltd., with capital shares totaling $14,760,000. Later, the family diversified its investments in Peru by purchasing huge tracts of land in the northern sierra to raise livestock. The Gildemeisters also developed close social ties with members of the national elite and, although they were never politicians themselves, actively supported political organizations, pressure groups, and newspapers that favored the interests of exporters.[18]

The third major landowner in the Chicama Valley was clearly a foreign firm, W. R. Grace & Co. of the United States. Grace became one of the most important corporations in Peru, acquiring ownership of steamship lines, textile factories, and sugarcane plantations in other valleys. The founder of this corporate giant was William R. Grace, an Irish immigrant who got his start in Lima as a merchant. By 1862 Grace had expanded his scope of operation by establishing an export-import house in New York City, which became the home base for the corporation. In 1882 W. R. Grace & Co. entered the sugar business when it was awarded the estate Cartavio in payment for an outstanding debt owed by Guillermo Alzamora. Nine years later, the company chartered the Cartavio Sugar Co. in London, with a share capital of 200,000 pounds sterling.[19] In contrast to other north coast planters, members of the Grace family never became actively involved in Peruvian politics nor in Lima society.[20] The corporation retained ownership of Cartavio and other plantations until the agrarian reform.

In the neighboring Moche Valley, the most important landholder was Manuel A. Chopitea, a Basque immigrant and former muleteer. By 1876 he had already acquired the estates Laredo, which became the center of the family's holdings, Santo Domingo, and Huambos. In 1881 Manuel rented Laredo to his son, José Ignacio, who proceeded to make improvements and to purchase and rent other estates in the valley. The Chopitea family remained the principal landholders in the area until 1937, when they sold out to the Gildemeisters.[21] Following the general pattern, José Ignacio Chopitea served as a Civilista congressman, and the family entered the upper rung of Lima society.[22]

Farther north in the Lambayeque Valley, planters came from equally diverse backgrounds. The plantation Tumán was acquired by Manuel Pardo in 1872, the same year in which, as the Civilista candidate, he was elected president of Peru. Pardo and his father-in-law, Felipe Barreda y Aguilar, had been the two most prominent figures in the Compañía Nacional de Consignación del Guano and the Banco de Lima. The Pardos took an interest in the administration of the estate, but delegated administrative responsibilities to trusted employees more frequently than did other north coast planters.[23] The Pardo family was one of the most respected members of the national elite and produced two presidents, Manuel (1872–1876) and José (1904–1908; 1915–1919). Like other planters, the Pardos lost their estate to the agrarian reform.

Spaniard Vincente Gutiérrez acquired the plantation Pomalca-Collud in 1869, and his heirs maintained ownership until 1920, when they sold out to the de la Piedra family. The de la Piedras were originally from Ecuador and had been involved in several business concerns in the Chiclayo area since the mid-nineteenth century. Their holdings included an export-import house, the Molino de Pilar Arroz "Santa Rosa," and the Fábrica de Chocolate "Santa Rosa." They were also important stockholders in the

Compañía del Ferrocarril y Muelle de Pimentel. Their purchase of Pomalca-Collud for $3,672,000 coincided with their entry into national politics and elite society. Both Enrique and Julio de la Piedra Castillo served as senators from Lambayeque during the Oncenio, and Enrique was an important adviser to Leguía.[24] The de la Piedras retained ownership of Pomalca-Collud until the agrarian reform. Pátapo was another important sugar plantation in the Lambayeque Valley. The Chilean Tomás Ramos Font purchased it in 1861. Ramos Font died in 1891, and fifteen years later his heirs formed the Compañía Azucarera de Chiclayo in Chile with a share capital of 125,000 pounds sterling. Sometime between 1925 and 1930 Juan Pardo y Miguel, a cousin of the owners of Tumán, acquired Pátapo. José María Izaga acquired the other major sugar plantation in the valley, Pucalá, in 1850, and it remained in the family until the agrarian reform. The Izagas were generally recognized as members of the national elite.[25]

One of the most striking examples of the direct investment of fortunes earned during the guano boom into sugar plantations came in the Jequetepeque Valley. Throughout the nineteenth century, the most important sugar plantation in the valley was Lurifico. In 1866 Colonel José Balta (president, 1868–1872) purchased Lurifico for 150,000 pesos. Five years later he sold it to Henry Meiggs, the American railroad builder, for 300,000 soles. Meiggs made several improvements on the estate, but in 1874, when faced with his political and financial denouement, he sold out to Federico Ford, an associate of Auguste Dreyfus, the famous guano merchant. In 1895 the owners formed the Peruvian Sugar Estates Company Limited in London, with a share capital of 500,000 pounds sterling. After the drastic fall in sugar prices in 1902, the company converted the estate to rice.[26]

The Aspíllagas, like many prominent north coast planters, were of immigrant origin. Catalina Ferrebú de Aspíllaga left Chile for Peru in the 1820s, apparently after being deserted by her husband. She brought with her a small son, Ramón, and shortly after her arrival gave birth to another child, Antonio.[27]

By the time Ramón had become an adult, the family was making a good living by hauling freight between Lima and Callao. In the early 1850s, Ramón Aspíllaga Ferrebú expanded the scope of the family's investments by purchasing an eighty-five-ton ship licensed to engage in commercial shipping,[28] and by buying a small cotton plantation (Palto) located near Pisco, south of Lima.[29]

When war broke out with Spain in 1866, Ramón felt affluent enough to make a quiet 2,000-peso donation to the war treasury, accompanied by a guarantee of another 200 pesos in credit each month until the end of hostilities. In a letter to the minister of the interior, he explained, "I have formed a small fortune in Peru and having passed my youth [here] since

Independence was declared and having a wife and children born on this soil, I cannot do enough for Peru [at this time of peril]."[30]

Despite his financial success, Aspíllaga's social status was apparently hampered by his having been a wagoner. In countering criticism of the appointment of a former silversmith to a diplomatic position in May of 1862, *El Comercio* remarked, "Just a few years ago they said to the worthy and honorable Don Ramón Aspíllaga, 'You are a wagoner and therefore worthless.' "[31]

Ramón's financial dealings brought him into association with Julián de Zaracóndegui, "one of the most outstanding representatives of capitalism of the time" and a man with "great political connections." Zaracóndegui owned one of the most important import-export businesses in Lima, and at one time or another was a guano consignee, general director of the Banco de Lima, a deputy, prior of the Tribunal del Consulado, and member of the Beneficiencia de Lima.[32] In 1859 Zaracóndegui and Aspíllaga purchased the plantation Cayaltí as equal partners, with the former putting up $119,860 for Aspíllaga (the exact purchase price is not known). Ramón agreed to repay the loan at 12 percent interest and to manage the estate for a salary.[33]

Over the next fifteen years, Aspíllaga's finances became increasingly intertwined with those of Zaracóndegui. In September of 1871 Aspíllaga owed Zaracóndegui some 60,000 pesos. But as the latter began to invest more heavily in nitrates, he borrowed as much as 120,000 soles from Aspíllaga. The financial fate of the one was affected by the other, and with the crash of 1873 both men suffered greatly. In late 1873, they took out a mortgage of $338,700 on Cayaltí. Aspíllaga agreed to repay the entire mortgage in return for Zaracóndegui's share in the plantation. Shortly thereafter, Zaracóndegui declared bankruptcy and committed suicide, an event that startled polite society in Lima and was recorded in a *tradición* of Ricardo Palma.[34]

In 1875 Ramón Aspíllaga Ferrebú died and left Cayaltí to his four sons, Antero, Ramón, Baldomero, and Ismael. Antero and Ramón, who were 26 and 25, respectively, had been actively involved in managing Cayaltí for several years. With the estate, they also inherited their father's debts. Over the course of the next twenty-four years they were continually hounded by creditors, threatened with law suits and the imminent loss of Cayaltí through forced public auction. It is a credit to their tenacity, business sense, and political tact that they finally gained clear title to the plantation in 1899.[35]

From 1875 into the 1920s, Cayaltí was managed principally by Antero and Ramón Aspíllaga Barrera. During these years they amassed a fortune that gained them and their relatives entrance into the national oligarchy and a place of political prominence for Antero.[36] From the beginning, both brothers had set very high goals for themselves, getting from their father the

Table 1
Cayaltí's Creditors, 1879

Creditor	Company Type	Nationality	Debt (Soles)
Prevost & Co.	Import/Export	U.S.	170,000
Manuel Elguera	Import/Export	Peruvian	97,000
Vda. de Figuerola	Private Loan	Peruvian	16,000
Menchaca & Cia.	Import/Export	Peruvian	10,000
Unspecified			5,000
Total			298,000

Source: AH to AH, 18 November 1879, AFA. Elguera and Menchaca & Cia. are identified as operators of commercial houses in Yepes del Castillo (pp. 161–162). I have found no conversion for soles to dollars for 1879; however, in 1873 the rate was $1.044 per sol (Dennis Gilbert, "The Oligarchy and the Old Regime in Peru [Ph.D. diss., Cornell University, 1977], app. A).

belief that through hard work they could become national heroes. Thus, in September of 1875 Ramón reminded Antero of their father's words: "Economy dear sons, only with economy can we pay our debts and become heroes."[37] Three years later, one brother rejected the criticism that their Chinese workers were being subjected to virtual slavery:

It is not necessary to think of slavery, since it exists for but short periods of time; besides, we are not the only ones, although they say that to follow the bad example of several is to take the advice of fools. But some need others, and this brings us forward as heroes who search for a sure death in order to live eternally in the pages of history.[38]

In the difficult years from the 1870s into the 1890s, the young Aspíllagas overcame many problems that would have overwhelmed less ambitious and clever individuals. Antero was the guiding spirit during this period. He read widely in sugar journals, kept pace with current technology, personally selected a new mill for Cayaltí, and on one occasion took over a post in the mill and made sugar with his own hands. This particularly impressed Ramón, who wrote to Ismael, "Antero with his tenacious character and clear intelligence has succeeded in making, with his own hands, sugar in the vacuum pan, which should bring justifiable pride and satisfaction to him and to us, I too will learn."[39]

The Aspíllagas, like many planters, were threatened with the total loss of their estate during the War of the Pacific. The Chilean army of occupation, led by General Lynch, put many estates to the torch and levied tribute on all producers. Many estates lost all or most of their Chinese workers, who, in some cases, welcomed the Chileans as liberators and helped them to destroy property.[40] At Cayaltí, however, the Aspíllagas prevented significant loss of property and manpower primarily because of Antero's organizational ability and foresight. As the Chileans were sweeping through the northern valleys, Antero noticed that they tended to inflict less damage on estates owned by foreigners. He quickly arranged to have a document drawn up showing Cayaltí to be owned by a major creditor, Prevost & Co. of the United States. In addition, he hid all cane alcohol and much of the food, items that the Chileans were certain to want. Then, to help keep order on the estate, he paid the Chinese ahead of time and tightened plantation security. As a result of these precautions, when one hundred Chilean cavalry occupied Cayaltí in October of 1880, damage was kept to a minimum. The Chileans stole some food and oxen, three Chinese escaped, and the Aspíllagas were required to pay tribute, but production continued, and Cayaltí survived without physical damage.[41]

By the end of hostilities, the Aspíllagas were beginning to attain the political and social advancement that they desired:

In the years after the War of the Pacific the Aspíllaga Barrera brothers were conspicuous participants in the social, economic and political elite that was emerging in Lima. They had been educated in Lima's best private schools, such as La Recoleta where they could mix with children from such prestigious families as the Pardos, the Beltráns, the Riva Agüeros, and the Ortiz de Zevallos. By 1890 all four brothers had been admitted to Lima's Club Nacional [the social center of the national elite].[42]

The Aspíllaga Barreras' interest in politics probably came from their father, who had actively participated in many of the political struggles of the time. For example, he had opposed the revolt against General Vivanco in 1854, had supported the 1867 revolution and Manuel Pardo's successful bid for the presidency in 1872.[43] Nevertheless, Aspíllaga Ferrebú was never an important politician himself; that distinction was reserved for his sons.

All four of the Aspíllaga Barrera brothers served at one time or another as Civilista congressmen during the so-called República Aristocrática. However, Antero was the family politician. In the course of his career, he served as minister of the treasury (under General Cáceres), four times as president of the Senate, and stood unsuccessfully as Civilista candidate for president in 1912 and 1919, the second time losing to Leguía.[44]

In addition, in 1896 both Antero and Ramón were instrumental in the foundation of the Sociedad Nacional Agraria (SNA), an important interest group for large-scale agriculture. During the República Aristocrática, the SNA played a major role in the formulation of government policy toward agriculture. Members of the Aspíllaga family remained active in the organization, frequently serving as officers or on the board of directors, until its forced dissolution under the Velasco government.[45]

The political careers of Antero and Ramón Aspíllaga Barrera did not prevent them from playing active roles in the management of Cayaltí. When Leguía ordered Antero's deportation in 1923, however, he sold out his interest in Cayaltí to Ramón, who gradually turned over the management of the estate to his sons, the Aspíllaga Andersons.[46]

In 1928 a new family firm was founded under the rubric of Aspíllaga Anderson Hermanos, S. A., to operate Cayaltí and Palto, with total capital placed at $2.64 million. The eldest son, Ramón, took over as chief executive officer. Day-to-day management of Cayaltí was generally entrusted to either Luis or Ismael, either separately or together, and Ramón ran the company from Lima. The remaining brothers, although occasionally serving as members of the board of directors, never held positions of operating responsibility for significant periods of time, nor, in keeping with traditional business practices, did any of the sisters.[47] The Aspíllaga Andersons retained ownership of Cayaltí until 1968, when they sold out to a Cuban exile shortly before the agrarian reform.[48]

Capital

The success of the Aspíllagas and other north coast planters depended on a number of variables, but none more important than capital. The development of the sugar industry was based in the guano era and sustained by foreign capital and accumulated profits. In general, the industry relied more heavily on foreign credit during periods of economic and political turmoil, and benefited from domestic resources during times of prosperity and stability.

An important spinoff of the guano boom was the creation of Peru's first banks. On the strength of increased capital resources, between 1862 and 1873 the nation experienced something of a banking boom. Many different types of banking institutions were founded during these years, including the first branch of the British Banco de Londres, Méjico y Sud América (1863), and the domestically chartered Banco del Perú (1863), which was associated with the Compañía Nacional del Guano and the Pardo family. Several banks were also established that specialized in specific industries, such as railroads, nitrates, or gas. Of particular importance for the sugar industry were Peru's first two mortgage banks, the Banco de Crédito Hipotecario (1866) and the Banco Territorial Hipotecario (1870), which issued short-term loans at 6 to 8 percent interest and long-term loans at 10.5 to 12 percent interest.[49] Among the planters who borrowed from banks were the Aspíllagas, who in August of 1875 owed 45,000 soles to the Banco de Lima.[50]

The endurance of the newly created banks depended on the viability of the export economy, the strength of the sol, and public confidence. Unfortunately, the end of the guano boom, the Panic of 1873, and the War of the Pacific undermined all. By the early 1870s guano deposits had been severely depleted, and the Peruvian government had run up a substantial debt.[51] When the worldwide depression of 1873 struck Peru, exports declined much more rapidly than imports. According to the leading authority on Peruvian banks, Carlos Camprubi, the result was an increase in exchange rates, a shortage of metal currency, and a depreciation of paper money.[52]

The economy, which had been wavering, collapsed. Inflation ran out of control, government income declined so rapidly that public employees went unpaid for three to four months, commercial houses went bankrupt (e.g., Zaracóndegui), and stocks drastically declined in value. Banks were given a brief respite when the government assumed control over all currency for one year. But the following year all banks went under, except for the Banco de Londres, Méjico y Sud América and the Banco del Callao.[53]

Nevertheless, the Peruvian economy still had not reached bottom. That came in the following years as the result of the War of the Pacific. Government revenues, which might have been used to help restore the economy, went to equip an army that suffered total defeat. Moreover, the Chilean army of occupation destroyed considerable physical capital, including railroads and sugar plantations, and forced capitalists to pay tribute. Public finance lay vanquished, as government revenues fell from 35,190,169.96 soles in 1879 to 1,197,546.08 soles in 1883.[54]

It took Peru several years to recover from its defeat, and during the interlude many sugar planters depended on foreign capital to remain in operation. By the turn of the century, however, the economy was showing clear signs of recovery. In the area of finance, three new banks were founded, the Banco Italiano, the Banco Internacional, and the Banco Popular. Several other banks were chartered in subsequent years, and many of them made loans to planters.[55] This is not surprising, since planters frequently served on the boards of directors of the leading banks. For example, Antero Aspíllaga Barrera and Ismael Aspíllaga Barrera served as directors of the Banco Internacional, and Carlos Gildemeister and Juan Pardo as directors of the Banco Popular, the latter apparently from 1908 to 1923.[56] In 1927, moreover, 60 percent of the substantial financial portfolio of Ramón Aspíllaga Barrera was invested in banks and insurance companies.[57] There is no way of calculating how much credit planters received from Peruvian banks. However, from 1906 to 1914 money lent by the five mortgage banks increased tenfold, from $423,720 to $4,149,790, and some of it undoubtedly went to the sugar industry.[58]

Import-export houses, most of which were foreign, were another important source of credit for sugar planters. The number of commercial houses, both foreign and domestic, had significantly increased during the guano boom, and once this resource became depleted merchants looked for other products to export.[59] In some cases, they aggressively recruited potential clients, as in August of 1876, when a representative of Graham, Rowe & Co. of England unexpectedly appeared at Cayaltí with an offer to market its sugar. The Aspíllagas declined, but only because they already had a satisfactory arrangement with Prevost & Co. of the United States.[60]

It is not surprising that merchant houses emerged as important creditors during the crisis period from the mid-1870s into the 1890s. They had been important sources of credit in Peru before the development of banks (see table 1),[61] and when most banks failed in the 1870s, they moved in to fill the void. They lent money to planters to earn interest and also because much of their income came from marketing plantation products.Thus, it was in the import-export houses' own best interests to keep the plantation economy going.

British merchants, in particular, made large loans to north coast planters. In 1895, for example, the Larcos owed Graham, Rowe & Co. some 200,000 pounds sterling.[62] Moreover, in the 1880s the Aspíllagas had arranged to market their sugar through the firm of Henry Kendall & Sons of Liverpool, England, and Kendall quickly became Cayaltí's principal creditor, underwriting three mortgages on the estate from 1884 to 1910.[63] The Aspíllagas also worked closely with Kendall & Sons during these years on other matters, often receiving advice from the British firm on management and technological development. Sometimes advice turned to criticism, which the Aspíllagas welcomed:

They [Kendall & Sons] are correct because they say it very clearly: your business is not established with clarity nor with vision, and a business of blind men cannot but adversely affect the confidence that one should have in the business. . . . They are very correct, they lend us their money, their credit, their capital, and our duty is to reciprocate [by] removing all bad . . . and giving good . . . results.[64]

In the area of finance, plantations owned by international conglomerates, such as Casa Grande and Cartavio, could, of course, draw on overseas revenues of their own. For example, when Casa Grande merged with a German syndicate in 1910, it received capital needed for expansion and modernization as well as the services of German technicians to improve the management of the estate.[65] Thereafter, the Gildemeisters continued to maintain extensive investments in Europe and Chile and could have drawn on overseas profits to develop Casa Grande in later years.[66] W. R. Grace & Co. was in a similar position. The New York-based firm ran a prosperous shipping line in South America and owned several businesses in Peru, including a major textile mill, which could have provided capital for the development of Cartavio.[67]

Table 2
Price of Raw Sugar in London
(Shillings per Cwt.)

Year	Price	Year	Price	Year	Price	Year	Price
1860	24/0	1879	19/0	1898	9/6	1917	31/6
1861	22/0	1880	20/6	1899	10/6	1918	33/0
1862	20/0	1881	21/3	1900	11/3	1919	38/5
1863	21/0	1882	20/0	1901	9/3	1920	58/0
1864	26/0	1883	19/0	1902	7/3	1921	18/3
1865	22/0	1884	13/3	1903	8/6	1922	15/3
1866	21/0	1885	13/6	1904	10/3	1923	25/9
1867	22/0	1886	11/9	1905	11/0	1924	21/9
1868	22/0	1887	11/9	1906	8/6	1925	12/9
1869	24/0	1888	13/0	1907	9/3	1926	12/3
1870	23/0	1889	16/0	1908	9/9	1927	13/9
1871	25/6	1890	13/0	1909	10/3	1928	11/7
1872	25/6	1891	13/6	1910	11/0	1929	9/0
1873	22/6	1892	13/6	1911	11/6	1930	6/7
1874	21/6	1893	14/3	1912	11/0	1931	6/4
1875	20/0	1894	11/3	1913	9/6	1932	5/9
1876	21/6	1895	10/0	1914	11/7	1933	5/3
1877	24/6	1896	10/9	1915	14/4		
1878	20/0	1897	9/3	1916	24/3		

Source: Noel Deerr, *The History of Sugar*, vol. 2 (New York: American Book, 1949), p. 531.
Note: Price includes cost, insurance, freight.

Plantations, of course, did not always have to rely on outside sources of credit. After the turn of the twentieth century, profits began to accumulate, thereby releasing planters from their dependency on foreign capital and allowing some of them to invest in other sectors of the national economy.[68]

The profitability of sugar in Peru hinged on a number of variables, including the cost of labor, the pace of technological improvements, and the security of markets.[69] But the most important variable was the price of sugar (see table 2).

In the absence of price controls and quota systems, the price of sugar basically reflected supply and demand on the world market. During the 1860s and 1870s world production grew slowly (averaging 4 percent a year, 1860-1880) while demand increased in Great Britain and elsewhere. As a result, prices remained relatively high and stable.[70]

This situation changed significantly in the 1880s, however, as production began to outstrip demand. Production increased most dramatically in Europe (beet sugar) and in Cuba, and the result was to drive prices downward, where they remained until the outbreak of World War I.

With the eruption of hostilities in Europe, however, sugar beet production came to a virtual halt. The worldwide supply of sugar fell below current levels of demand, causing prices to soar to record highs and ushering in a period of record profit-taking for Peruvian planters.

Profits remained high until the early 1920s, when European sugar beet producers re-entered the market, increasing supplies and forcing prices downward until they reached record lows with the onset of the Great Depression.[71]

Profits and losses for plantations closely reflected the ebb and flow of sugar prices on the world market. The amount of profit or loss for individual estates varied, of course, owing to differences in scale, overall efficiency, and other intangibles, such as floods, strikes, and political considerations.[72] Although yearly balance sheets for all major north coast producers are not available, the data in tables 3 through 6 show that sugar was generally profitable in Peru, especially between 1914 and 1921.

The high profits Casa Grande earned deserve a special word of explanation (table 9). Because of their German origin and business connections, Great Britain blacklisted the Gildemeisters during World War I. Although this caused them some temporary problems, it also allowed them to stockpile a tremendous amount of sugar, which they were able to sell at peak market prices following the war.[73] This accounts for their enormous gains for the period 1919 to 1922. On the other hand, Casa Grande's profits during the difficult period from 1927 to 1934 resulted from cuts in the cost of production and special marketing advantages. Remarkably, the Gilde-meisters reduced the cost of producing one quintal of sugar (FOB) from

Table 3
Profit and Loss at Laredo, Pomalca, and Cartavio, Available Years

Plantation	Year	Profits	Loss
Cartavio	1904	$50,194.50	
Laredo	1932		$202,349.39
Pomalca	1926		81,250.27
Pomalca	1930		Unspecified

Sources: *Cartavio*—William Bollinger, "The Rise of U.S. Influence in the Peruvian Economy, 1869- 921" (M.A. thesis, UCLA, 1971), p. 128.
Laredo—Deloitte, Plender, Sydney-Merrit & Co., *Informe sobre los libros y cuentas por el año terminado el 30 de junio de 1932,* 14 December 1932, AFA.
Pomalca—Gerencia to Administración de Contabilidad, 11 February 1928, Cartas Pomalca, AFA; Gerencia to Oficina en Chiclayo, 11 February 1931, AFA.

Table 4
Profit and Loss at Chiclín

Year	Profit	Year	Profit
1909	$ 26,667.24	1916	$312,882.10
1910	28,487.76	1917	339,220.59
1911	26,161.74	1918	364,388.33
1912	50,680.01	1919	575,311.54
1913	73,729.22	1920	901,414.17
1914	51,385.75	1921	n.a.
1915	283,645.14	1922	88,665.65

Source: Bill Albert, *An Essay on the Peruvian Sugar Industry, 1880–1920 and the Letters of Ronald Gordon, Administrator of the British Sugar Company in Cañete, 1914–1920* (Norwich: School of Social Studies, University of East Anglia, 1976), p. 126a.
Note: Chiclín was owned by Rafael Larco.

Table 5
Profit and Loss at Casa Grande

Year	Previous Balance	Yearly Gains	Total	Dividends	Balance
1919–1922		$4,024,612.10	$4,024,612.10	$3,712,187.50	$ 312,424.60
1923–1927	312,424.60	992,124.80	1,304,549.40	588,300.00	716,249.40
1927–1934	692,647.35	1,194,641.30	1,887,288.65		1,871,570.75

Source: Gildemeister folder, AFA; from a balance prepared in July 1941.

Table 6
Profit and Loss at Cayalti

Year	Profit	Loss	Comment
1877			Balance of 200,000 soles
1879			Yearly profit of 20,000 soles by October
1891			Losing money following War of the Pacific
1893	$ 73,420.20		
1894	21,182.32		
1897	96,608.52		13 percent return on capital invested
1898			Making a profit
1907	5,876.77		
1911	195,031.47		New mill
1912	240,138.93		
1913		$ 75,557.05	Unusually long mill shutdown
1914	338,485.81		World War I begins
1915	322,801.40		
1921	360,840.16		
1922	219,936.40		
1923	774,569.90		
1924	441,068.97		
1925		111,899.90	Flood
1926	20,832.00		
1927			About the same profit as in 1926
1928		133,848.04	Six-month shutdown, poor-quality sugar
1931			Making a slight profit
1932		93,014.33	Depression

Source: Cayalti correspondence, 1877–1933.

14.11.5 pounds sterling in 1924 to 4.1.80 pounds sterling in 1932. According to the Aspíllagas, because the Gildemeisters owned stock in the Viña del Mar sugar refinery, they also enjoyed marketing advantages over their Peruvian competitors in the important Chilean market. This proved particularly advantageous to them during the Depression.[74]

Profits and losses at Cayalti are more easily explained, because they closely follow the rise and fall of the value of sugar on the world market (table 6). Thus, the largest profits came during the period from 1914 to 1924, and the severest losses from 1928 to 1932. However, there were some additional variables. For example, the loss suffered during 1925 was the direct result of a disastrous flood in that year, which also hurt other north coast producers. Moreover, the data for 1911, 1913, and 1928 also show the importance of technological development and efficiency. Clearly, those producers with the largest production capacities and the best management benefited the most during periods of high prices. On this score, the Aspíllagas received mixed results, for reasons that I shall discuss in the following chapter.

Conclusion

Writing in the 1920s, the famous Peruvian Marxist José Carlos Mariátegui characterized the sugar industry as dominated by foreign capital, and Peruvian planters as lacking in capitalist initiative.[75] Peter Klarén has accepted this interpretation in general terms. He views foreign capital as the "motor force" behind the development of the sugar industry, and groups sugar together with other export industries, such as copper and petroleum, that were directly controlled by foreign multinational corporations.[76]

Nevertheless, Peruvians of considerable entrepreneurial skill, such as the Aspíllagas, Pardos, Chopiteas, Izagas, and de la Piedras, owned and operated the vast majority of plantations on the northern coast. W. R. Grace & Co. was the only undisputedly foreign corporation that owned a major sugar estate. It is true that all planters depended on the foreign market and received considerable credit from British export houses. However, they also borrowed from Peruvian banks and merchants and accumulated capital reserves of their own. Contrary to the traditional image of Third World countries, Peru generated substantial portions of the capital needed for the development of its sugar industry.

Most of these sugar families acquired their properties during a period of political and economic turmoil. They needed considerable managerial skill to survive these conditions and to become prosperous exporters. They set high goals for themselves, and their spirit is captured in the young Aspíllaga brothers' heroic image of themselves.

North coast planters used their success in business as a stepping-stone to political and social prominence. Almost all of them became important Civilista politicians during the República Aristocrática. Success came rapidly for those who combined plantation agriculture with the political power to implement policies that favored foreign investment, low export and import taxes, centralized government, and suppression of popular participation in politics. Such policies did not change even with the rise to power of the dictator Augusto B. Leguía in 1919, who also believed in the importance of export agriculture and centralized government.

Equally startling was the ability of many families of recent immigrant origin, such as the Aspíllagas, to gain such rapid acceptance into the national elite. It seems clear that Peru, following a period of economic collapse and military humiliation, underwent something of a national regeneration under the direction of a largely new bourgeoisie.

3. Land and Technology, 1860–1933

With their extensive resources, sugarcane planters were in a position to become leading capitalists, not merely gentlemen farmers. The path to economic success lay in achieving a scale of operation large enough and efficient enough to produce vast quantities of unrefined sugar at acceptable costs. The pace and extent of technological development was the crucial variable, as continuous extension of the area in sugarcane was useless without the means to process it into sugar.

All major north coast plantations began to make extensive technological improvements during the late nineteenth century. This not only began their essential transformation into modern enterprises, but by automating production, helped them to combat low sugar prices and periodic labor shortages. These estates also expanded in size during this period, frequently growing substantially larger than was necessary to supply mills with sufficient amounts of cane for processing. The desire for additional access to irrigation water and the elimination of competition may explain this seemingly unwarranted expansion.

North coast planters purchased technology and land at different paces, depending on their individual capital resources and strategy for development. As the twentieth century advanced, the Gildemeisters at Casa Grande and W. R. Grace & Co. at Cartavio took the technological lead. Both had extensive outside capital resources and progressive managers dedicated to transforming their estates into model factories in the field. Prior to its expropriation by the state in 1969, Casa Grande achieved a level of technological development unmatched in the world, according to knowledgeable Peruvians.

Under the direction of Antero and Ramón Aspíllaga Barrera, Cayaltí kept pace with other major producers for many years. Major technological innovations were made in cultivation, transportation, and refining. Cayaltí began to lag behind the largest producers in the 1920s, however, when the estate suffered from poor management by the sons of Ramón Aspíllaga Barrera, the Aspíllaga Andersons.

As later chapters will show, the different levels of technological development individual estates achieved directly affected relations between planters and workers and the relative pace of working-class organization and agitation. Therefore, the basic economic changes discussed here will be pivotal in later analyses of social and political developments.

Land

Many north coast sugar estates had been formed during the colonial period through land grants and purchases from native communities. Some of them expanded during the early nineteenth century by means of additional land grants, given in exchange for political and financial favors, and by means of further acquisitions of Indian communal property.[1]

In the 1870s the end of the guano boom led many merchants to seek alternative investments in coastal agriculture, and some of them at least found real bargains from *hacendados* eager to sell out following the tumultuous War of the Pacific. By the turn of the century, a new group of sugar planters had formed on the north coast, and many of them began to expand their plantations by buying out smaller producers. They did so on the strength of their financial resources as well as of their political influence, particularly their control over local irrigation districts.

Throughout the colonial period, *hacendados* in the region acquired irrigation water through a variety of legal and illegal means, almost always to the detriment of local Indian communities. The demand for water significantly increased during the nineteenth century because of the expansion of sugarcane, which requires extensive irrigation, and the growth in population. However, for decades the central government—overwhelmed with problems of finance and war—did not nothing to address the problem. A new water code was finally written in 1902 during the administration of Eduardo López de Romaña, owner of the largest sugarcane plantation in southern Peru (Chucarapi). Not surprisingly, the code did not compromise the interests of sugar planters.

Under the new code the final authority over water rights rested with the Ministry of Development. However, water districts composed of no fewer than three landowners exercised power at the local level. Each district elected an administrator to ensure that water regulations were followed, a three-man executive board to oversee the administrator and to punish violators, and a president who had the sole authority to call meetings and to preside over them. A special judge appointed by the central government resolved all formal legal disputes over water rights.[2]

Although all of the important officers of the local water districts were elected, votes were weighted in accordance to the amount of land owned and water received. Thus, large landowners controlled elections, and chose themselves or their cronies to serve in key positions. Their control over the administration of irrigation water sometimes facilitated their acquisition of land.[3]

The Comité Interamericano de Desarrollo Agrícola (CIDA) of the OAS has done an extensive compilation on land consolidation in the Chicama Valley, and Peter Klarén has placed it in historical perspective. Klarén tells the story of how three plantations—Casa Grande, Cartavio, and Roma— came to control most of the valley by absorbing other plantations and small farms (see table 7). The discussion logically focuses on Casa Grande, for it became the largest sugarcane plantation in the department.[4]

Casa Grande grew at a frantic pace during the first three decades of the twentieth century by acquiring both small farms and adjoining estates. The most intense consolidation occurred from 1910 to 1927 when, on the strength of increased capital resources created via a merger with a powerful German corporation, the Gildemeisters purchased twenty-five estates in the valley. The owners of Casa Grande were also busy acquiring numerous small plots of land, some from members of Indian communities. In this endeavor, they benefited from their positions as officers of local irrigation boards. For example, a petition signed by six hundred *comuneros* from the local community of Paiján, and published in the Trujillo newspaper *La Reforma*, claimed that the Gildemeisters had forced many of them into selling out by denying them water.[5]

Casa Grande expanded to a staggering size, growing from a modest 724.50 hectares in 1850 to 40,848 hectares in 1927. Moreover, in 1937 the Gildemeisters purchased the sugarcane plantation Laredo in the Moche Valley and after 1940 began acquiring numerous haciendas in the northern sierra. According to Carlos Malpica, by 1964 the family owned 557,344 hectares of land in Peru.[6]

Until the late 1920s, the plantation Roma, owned by Víctor Larco, approached Casa Grande in size. Víctor was one of the heirs of Andrés and Rafael Larco, who had originally purchased a series of plantations in the Chicama Valley during the mid-nineteenth century. Members of the family also owned the estates Chiclín and Chiquitoy, but Roma was the largest. Between 1850 and 1927 it expanded from 1,449 hectares to 19,777 hectares through the acquisition of twenty-seven adjoining estates.[7]

Víctor Larco passed from the scene as a major sugarcane planter in 1927, however, when he sold out to the Gildemeisters. Larco was forced into the sale because of financial difficulties stemming from strikes, severe flood damage, and falling sugar prices. With the purchase of Roma, the Gildemeisters achieved undisputed agricultural preeminence in the Chicama Valley.[8]

The plantation Cartavio was another large producer in the valley. W. R. Grace & Co. of New York acquired it in 1882. The Grace corporation later

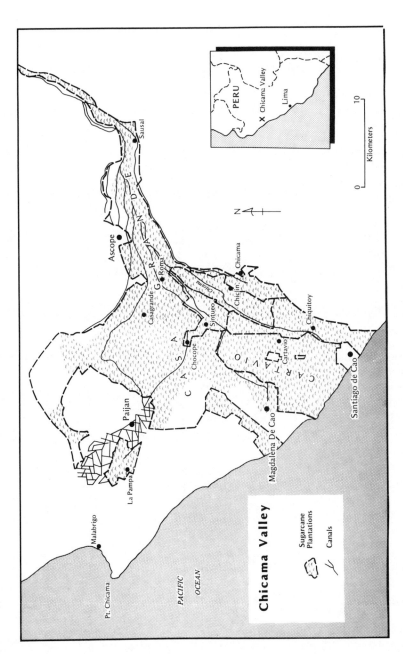

Chicama Valley

- Sugarcane Plantations
- Canals

Source: Adapted from Claude Collin Delavaud, *Les Régions Côtières du Pérou Septentrional* (Lima: Institut Français D'Etudes Andines, 1968), pp. 334-335.

Table 7
Land Consolidation in the Chicama Valley
(Hectares)

Estate	1850	1918	1927
Mocán	3,478		
Comunidad (Tierra de)	2,579		
Facalá	2,174		
Gasnape	1,730		
Sausal	1,687		
Santa Clara	1,130		
Chicamita	1,101		
Licapa	869		
Santa Rosa	869		
Casa Grande	725		
Lache	580		
Pampas	562		
Vizcaíno	464	Casa Grande	
La Viña	435	(21,071)	
Cañal	406		
La Pampa	406		
Churín and Estancia	377		
Potrero	290		
Cereaga	232		
Mayal, Bazarrate, and Terraplán	232		
Veracruz	232		
Ingenio Lazo	229		
Aljovín	145		
Lucas González	116		
Chacarilla	23		
Mocollope	4,376		Casa Grande
La Fortuna	1,449		(40,848)
Roma (Tulape)	1,449		
San José Alto	1,159		
Bazán	1,043		
La Constancia	869		
San José Bajo (I)	869		
San José Bajo (II)	869		
Tesoro	869		
Molino Galindo	623		
Molino Larco	614		
Cajenleque	580		
Palmillo	522		
Las Gavidias	464	Roma	
Montejo	435	(19,777)	

Table 7 (continued)

Estate	1850	1918	1927
La Viñita	435		
Cepeda	348		
Las Viudas	348		
La Comunidad (Ascope)	319		
Farias	290		
Pampas de Ventura	290		
El Porvenir	290		
Troche	290		
Tutumal	290		
La Libertad	261		
Garrapón	232		
La Virgen	162		
La Victoria	32		
Cartavio Viejo, Yacutinamo, and			
Nepén	1,942		
Sonolipe	1,159		
Cartavio	1,043		Cartavio
Sintuco	869		(5,610)
Hacienda Arribe	336		
Comunidad	261		
Chiquitoy	3,623		
Salamanca	2,898		Chiclín
Chiclín	1,942		(8,941)
Molino de Bracamonte	348		
Toquen	130		

Source: Peter Klarén, *Modernization, Dislocation, and Aprismo: Origins of the Peruvian Aprista Party, 1870-1932*, Latin American Monographs, no. 32 (Austin, Tex.: University of Texas Press, 1973), pp. 17-18.

48   Land and Technology

Table 8
Moche Valley Estates Owned by the Chopitea Family

Estate	Size (hectares)	Date Acquired	Purchase Price
Laredo		Before 1881	
Bambas	580	1888	$ 8,730
Menochuco	710	1895	129,417
Galindo	1,884	1903	44,014
Quirihuac	435	1910	72,750
San Blas		Before 1926	
La Esperancita		Before 1926	
El Cortijo (El Dean)	3,063	1927	194,000
La Pampa	290	Before 1926	
La Merced	464	Before 1926	
Huambos		Before 1926	
Santo Domingo		Before 1926	

Source: Testimonio de la Escritura, Constitución de Sociedad Anónima, otorgada por la Negociación Azucarera Laredo Ltd., Lima, 9 January 1926, AFA; Sesión de directorio celebrada el catorce de mayo de mil novecientos veinte i ocho, AFA; Fundos y propietarios en el Valle de Santa Catalina, 1943, Documentos Sueltos, Negociación Azucarera Laredo Ltd., AFA.

purchased several neighboring estates, but never embarked on an expansionist scheme equal to that of the Gildemeisters or the Larcos. From 1850 to 1927 Cartavio grew from 1,043 hectares to 5,610 hectares.[9]

Directly south of the Chicama Valley lies the smaller Moche, or Santa Catalina, Valley. At the western end of the valley is the capital of the Department of La Libertad, Trujillo, but beyond Trujillo's confines the valley turns into a sea of sugarcane. After the War of the Pacific, most of this area came under the control of the plantation Laredo. José Ignacio Chopitea, who systematically purchased or rented most of the estates in the valley, directed expansion and arranged to mill the cane grown by remaining producers.

Farther up the coast, in the Department of Lambayeque are found the two remaining sugar-producing valleys of the region. The largest is the Lambayeque Valley, site of the departmental capital and commercial center of Chiclayo. Several large sugarcane plantations developed in this valley during the colonial period, competing favorably with relatively large Indian communities for land and water resources. Although the information on land consolidation during the nineteenth and twentieth centuries is scarce, it is clear that the major producers grew in size after independence.

Table 9
Moche Valley Estates Rented by the Chopitea Family, 1926

Estate	Size (hectares)
La Compañia	162
Sacachique	122
Trapiche	417
El Conde and Santa Rosa	522
Palomar	206
Total	1,429

Source: Testimonio de la Escritura, Constitución de Sociedad Anónima, otorgada por la Negociación Azucarera Laredo Ltd., Lima, 9 January 1926, AFA; Sesión de directorio celebrada el catorce de mayo de mil novecientos veinte i ocho, AFA; Fundos y propietarios en el Valle de Santa Catalina, 1943, Documentos Sueltos, Negociación Azucarera Laredo Ltd., AFA.

Table 10
Growth of Lambayeque Valley Sugar Plantations
(Hectares)

Estate	Year	Size	Year	Size	Year	Size
Pomalca	1869–1877	2,300–2,465	1896	1,912	1924	7,267
Pucalá			1903	1,124		
Tumán			1907	3,734	1924	6,632

Source: Personal communication from Susan E. Ramírez.

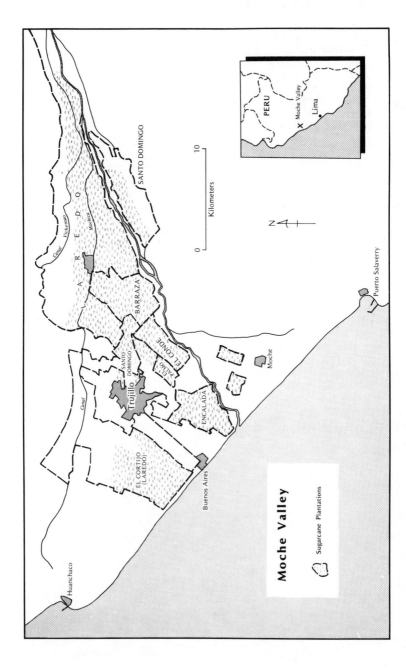

Moche Valley

Sugarcane Plantations

Huanchaco

Buenos Aires

EL CORTIJO
(LAREDO)

ENCALADA

Trujillo

SANTO
DOMINGO

EL
PALMO

EL CONDE

Moche

Puerto Salaverry

BARRAZA

Canal

Canal

Canal Pichernau

Moché

A R E D O Q

SANTO DOMINGO

0   10
⊢————————⊣
Kilometers

N

PERU

Moche Valley

Lima

Source: Adapted from Claude Collin Delavaud, *Les Régions Côtières du Pérou Septentrional* (Lima: Institut Français D'Etudes Andines, 1968), pp. 328-329.

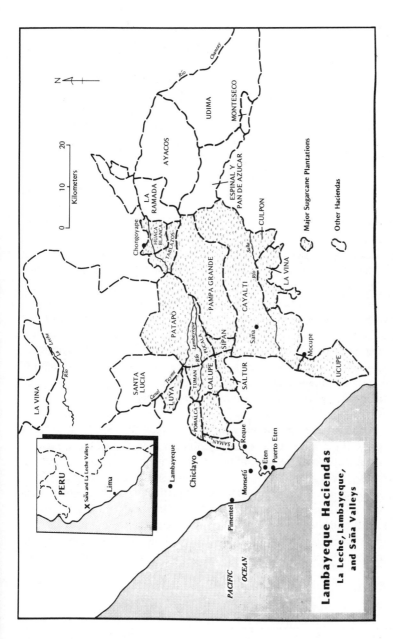

Source: Adapted from *Plano de los Fundos en Proceso de Afectación e Adjudicación en el Departamento de Lambayeque, 1970* (Lima: Ministerio de Agricultura, Zona Agraria, 1970), in Douglas E. Horton, *Haciendas and Cooperatives: A Preliminary Study of Latifundist Agriculture and Agrarian Reform in Northern Peru*, Research Paper no. 53 (Madison, Wis.: Land Tenure Center, 1973), p. vi.

Lambayeque Haciendas
La Leche, Lambayeque,
and Saña Valleys

Major Sugarcane Plantations

Other Haciendas

South of the Lambayeque Valley, near the border between the Departments of Lambayeque and Libertad, lies the Saña Valley (map 5). During the late nineteenth and early twentieth centuries, this fertile region came increasingly under the control of the sugarcane plantation Cayaltí. The estate owners, the Aspíllagas, pursued a policy of purchasing adjoining estates and occupying land previously controlled by the town of Saña.

   In their quest to acquire land the Aspíllagas clearly benefited from their political influence. For example, they, as the Gildemeisters in the Chicama Valley, were in a position to use their posts as officers on local irrigation boards to force neighboring agriculturalists to sell out.[10] Moreover, the Aspíllagas' political connections on the national level proved useful in settling disputes over land ownership. An incident that arose in 1913, after Cayaltí had won a long-standing suit with the town of Saña over title to a section of land, best illustrates this. Residents of Saña were so outraged at the verdict that they rioted, attacking property owned by the Aspíllagas within the town and burning part of the disputed land. The owners of Cayaltí retaliated by requesting the presence of the army, which brutally suppressed the riot, killed two townsmen, and injured several others. Troops then occupied the town, enforced a curfew, prohibited public meetings, and prevented the sale of liquor and the possession of firearms.[11] Such violent tactics, however, caused concern among local officials, who were not under the control of the Aspíllagas. The prefect of Lambayeque reported to Lima that neighboring estates, principally Cayaltí, had stolen all of the hills surrounding Saña and that, in suppressing the riot, the army had committed what could only be called a "massacre." A copy of the report reached the desk of Antero Aspíllaga Barrera, who was able to have the prefect removed from office and replaced with someone more to his liking in less than a week.[12]

   Such political power undoubtedly made it difficult for local towns, small farmers and estates to compete with Cayaltí over land and water resources. The Aspíllagas also had the advantage of extensive capital reserves, which they used to purchase and rent a number of estates through the years.

   By expanding the size of their estates, the Aspíllagas and other north coast planters assured themselves of control over the majority of land and water resources in the fertile river valleys that lay in between the commercial and administrative centers of Trujillo and Chiclayo. This gave them the capacity to grow thousands of additional acres of sugarcane and eliminated many competitors.

Technology

Nevertheless, once an estate had grown to several thousand hectares in size and had acquired an adequate supply of irrigation water, the level of

Table 11
Saña Valley Estates Owned or Rented by the Aspíllaga Family

Estate	Status	When Acquired
Cayaltí	Owned	1859
La Viña	Rented	1911
Chumbenique	Owned	1928
Otra Banda	Owned	After 1920
Songoy	Owned	Before 1920
Cojal	Owned	Before 1920
San Cristóbal	Owned	Before 1920
San Juan	Owned	Before 1920
Corbacho	Owned	Before 1920
Chacarilla	Owned	Before 1920
San Nicolás	Owned	Before 1920
Popancillo	Owned	Before 1920
Popán	Owned	Before 1920

Source: Certificación de los títulos de la hacienda Cayaltí con sus anexos, 17 November 1920, AFA; Enrique Espinoza, "Estadística agro-pecuaria de la República—Informe relativo al Departamento de Lambayeque," *Boletín del Ministerio de Fomento* 3, no. 9 (September 1905): 52; VAT to AH, 17 January 1912, AFA; IAA to RAB ("Muy Querido Papá"), 21 August 1928, AFA; IAA to Señor Ing. Administrador del Río de Zaña, 10 August 1931, AFA. Note: Cayaltí comprised 11,113 hectares.

technological development primarily determined production capacity. All planters realized this, but they developed their estates at varying paces, owing to differences in capital resources and entrepreneurial initiative.

Largely on the strength of foreign capital, planters began to make technological improvements during the late nineteenth century. Such innovations as larger mills, steam-powered tractors, and railroads increased production at a time of periodic labor shortages and falling sugar prices.

Mule trains had been a common mode of transportation throughout Latin America since the sixteenth century. By the late nineteenth century, however, they had become inadequate to the needs of expanding plantation economies. Railroad construction in many countries, including Cuba, Mexico, Brazil, and Peru, resulted.

The Aspíllagas provide ample testimony to the dissatisfaction of sugar planters in northern Peru with mule trains. The owners of Cayaltí viewed muleteers as little better than thieves, accused them of charging exorbitant rates and stealing sugar, and frequently complained that they were not always available when needed, especially during the rice harvest on nearby farms. Muleteers were also known to refuse to haul particularly heavy and bulky loads, such as machinery, which forced planters into organizing their own convoys with inexperienced sugar workers. The most serious problem with mule trains, however, was that they limited export capacity.[13] An Aspíllaga explained the problem this way in 1896:

I know that they [importers] will tell us that if you shipped 100,000 quintales [1 quintal equals 100 pounds] you can ship 20,000 more, but I am not totally certain, because some years we have more muleteers than others. It is also necessary to consider the condition of the livestock, which carry such a great quantity of merchandise, without counting [the weight of] the alcohol and the future expense of replacing those bulls that die. . . . It is [therefore] necessary to abandon this insecure system of transport.[14]

By the time this letter was written, planters in the Lambayeque Valley had already commissioned the construction of a series of railroads linking the plantations Pátapo, Puculá, Tumán, and Pomalca with the ports of Pimentel and Eten. Around the turn of the century, the Aspíllagas also financed the building of a line connecting Cayaltí with Eten, and by 1905 railroads had been built joining the estates Casa Grande, Cartavio, and Laredo with the port of Salaverry, and the plantations Roma and Chiquitoy with the harbor of Huanchaco. All of these railroads, with the exception of the Casa Grande-Cartavio line, were privately owned and operated.[15]

In 1915, apparently in exchange for a 44,000-pounds sterling loan, the Benavides government granted the Gildemeisters the right to construct a railroad linking Casa Grande with the nearby port of Malabrigo. The government also gave permission to renovate the port's dock facilities and to import large quantities of goods to sell at the plantation's bazaar. Rival planters and merchants in the Chicama Valley complained to the government and in the press that these concessions gave the Gildemeisters unfair advantages in exporting sugar and merchandising goods in the department. However, neither the Benavides government nor subsequent administrators rescinded the grants.[16]

The construction of larger, better-equipped mills on all of the major north coast plantations coincided with the improvement of transportation networks. This not only increased production capacity but potentially reduced labor costs and improved the overall efficiency of the estates. In many cases, new mills were constructed during a period of falling sugar prices, particularly around the turn of the century and during the 1920s.

The construction of modern mills began in the 1860s with the installation of a steam-powered facility at Facalá in the Chicama Valley.[17] The following decade, ground-breaking began for the construction of new mills at Pomalca (1873) and at Cayaltí (1877).[18] More estates might have begun the construction of mills at this time except for Peru's adherence to the silver standard, which increased the cost of machinery made in industrial nations whose currencies were backed by gold. Moreover, because Peruvian planters sold much of their sugar to these same nations, profits were stretched, which alleviated the urgency of making technological improvements. Only when Peru went onto the gold standard in 1897 did the pace of mill construction significantly increase.[19]

During the late nineteenth and early twentieth centuries, Víctor Aspíllaga toured several sugarcane plantations in the Chicama and Moche valleys. In 1899 he favorably compared the mill at Cartavio to Cayaltí's, and in 1907 wrote that Casa Grande had installed a new three-roller mill the previous year.[20] In 1908, Cayaltí's chief engineer, the Englishman Thomas Colston, visited Laredo and judged its mill superior to any in the Chicama Valley. He noted that, although it was smaller than Casa Grande's, it was more efficiently run.[21] By 1915, however, both Casa Grande and Cartavio had constructed four-roller mills, with the highest production capacities in Peru. Víctor Aspíllaga considered the mill at Casa Grande to be "the most important in Peru, since it is designed to produce one million quintales yearly,"[22] but was equally impressed with Cartavio's facility. It had a production capacity 80 percent that of Casa Grande's, produced the highest-quality sugar in Peru, and was equal in design and efficiency to any mill in Java or Hawaii.[23] Aspíllaga also praised the new mill at Laredo, which, although not as large as the mammoth facilities in the Chicama Valley, nevertheless produced the second-highest quality sugar in the country.[24]

In 1917 Víctor Aspíllaga also had the opportunity to inspect the sugar mills in the Lambayeque Valley. He observed that both Pomalca and Tumán were operating three-roller mills with the same dimensions as Cayaltí's, but with more complete facilities and consequently higher production capacities.[25]

As the following observations indicate, the Aspíllaga estate was falling behind other major north coast producers in milling capacity. Such had not been always he case, however. Antero Aspíllaga Barrera judged the steam-powered mill constructed at Cayaltí in the late 1870s the finest in the country, a view shared in 1887 by a group of dignitaries who had just toured most coastal sugarcane plantations.[26]

The Aspíllagas continued to make technological improvements in the mill throughout the early twentieth century. Between 1889 and 1901 they increased the load capacity of the conveyor system that fed cane into the mill. This permitted the crushing of larger quantities of cane, and directly led to a 30 percent increase in production and a reduction in the number of workers needed in this area.[27] In 1906 the rollers that crushed the cane were modified to increase juice extraction capacity from 57 to 68 percent, which increased the amount of sugar produced per hectare of cane planted.[28] Five years later, with money borrowed from Kendall, the Aspíllagas systematically rebuilt the entire mill. The renovated facility had three rollers with a juice extraction capacity of 78 percent. On the first day of operation the new mill produced 18 percent more sugar with 22 percent less cane. This allowed management to lay off twenty mill workers and to reduce the number of hands needed in the field. Thus, to produce 480 quintales of sugar now required sixty fewer cane cutters and twenty fewer cane loaders.[29]

These were real and long-term benefits for the Aspíllagas. However, the installation of new machinery in the mill did occasionally cause some problems. For example, sometimes manufacturers sent the wrong parts, or machinery was damaged in transit or improperly installed. If new parts had to be shipped from Europe or the United States, long delays in production could be averted only through mechanical improvisations. Such minor catastrophes were what planters had to endure for operating so far from the countries that produced their equipment.[30]

With increased crushing capacity in the mill, there was a simultaneous need to cultivate more cane and get it to the mill faster. This necessitated a series of technological improvements in the field, especially the installation of portable railroads and the increased use of steam- and gasoline-powered tractors.

Before the installation of portable railroads, cane was transported to the mill in ox-driven carts. This mode of transportation presented management with several problems. As more cane was planted in outlying areas, distances from the mill grew correspondingly longer and more time lapsed between harvesting and processing. This resulted in a lower sucrose content, the key variable in determining the quality of unrefined sugar. Moreover, harvested cane was damaged during the bumpy trip to the mill, which reduced the output of sugar produced per hectare of cane planted. Cane hauling was also extremely arduous and dangerous, sometimes resulting in fatal accidents when drivers tripped or collided with one another and were then crushed under their three-ton carts. Between 1878 and 1889 at least eleven workers at Cayaltí died while hauling cane, and many more were seriously injured. This caused delays in the field and made it difficult for management to find willing workers.[31]

Portable railroads eased many of these problems. Based on the principle of moving track from one harvested field to another, this sytem reduced much of the time lag involved in transporting cane to the mill. It also made possible the use of larger carts, thereby increasing hauling capacity, and, through the use of a more secure surface, practically eliminated serious accidents.[32]

By the late 1880s portable railroads were commonplace on north coast sugarcane plantations.[33] Cayaltí's system was introduced in 1888, and a sample of the savings it produced is shown in the following experiment conducted by the Aspíllagas:

We have weighted a cart pulled by oxen from the zone Los Angeles . . . [and] compared [it] with what the train carts carry. You will see that they do much more and

Table 12
Machinery Exports from Great Britain and the United States to Peru

Year	Great Britain Machinery and Mill Work (pounds sterling)	Sugar-Making and Refining Machinery (not including centrifuges)	United States Sugar-Milling Machinery (dollars)
1911	138,121		11,144
1912	121,877		16,652
1913	153,503		20,531
1914	146,051		19,004
1915	61,637		13,154
1916	118,952		12,419
1917	97,210		49,400
1918	91,849		77,999
1919	136,504		187,358
1920	321,195	46,504	238,097
1921	368,569	88,614	493,882
1922	118,243	19,459	66,445
1923	210,890	52,756	211,333

Source: Bill Albert, *An Essay on the Peruvian Sugar Industry, 1880–1920 and the Letters of Ronald Gordon, Administrator of the British Sugar Company in Cañete, 1914–1920* (Norwich: School of Social Studies, University of East Anglia, 1976), table 36, p. 141a.

Table 13
Regional Distribution of Sugar Production, Selected Years
(Percentages)

Year	North Coast	Central Coast	South Coast	Sierra
1894	49.9	41.5	5.9	2.8
1912	66.8	29.4	1.1	2.7
1916	70.0	27.2	1.2	1.6
1922	73.4	23.7	1.6	1.3
1927	76.8	20.3	1.8	1.2
1937	88.4	6.9	2.1	2.6
1941	90.0	5.6	1.7	2.6

Source: Rosemary Thorp and Geoffrey Bertram, *Peru 1890–1977: Growth and Policy in an Open Economy* (New York: Columbia University Press, 1978), table 4.2, p. 44.

at less cost because, although they required fifteen oxen, thirty-seven men and twelve mules, on the other hand they transport[ed] 1,680 quintales of cane. . . . This converted into the old transport system would come to . . . 550 quintales . . . plus two extra men.[34]

The new system also resulted in a considerable savings in manpower, as the Aspíllagas were able to remove 120 men from cane hauling over the course of the following year.[35]

As in the mill, however, the installation of new technology in the field caused some initial problems. With the introduction of portable railroads, the coordination of harvesting, loading, and hauling became more complex. For example, at first not enough cane was cut to operate the system at capacity. But when more workers were assigned to harvesting, more cane was cut than could be processed. To untangle the mess, the Aspíllagas finally hired someone experienced in managing portable railroads. He succeeded in making the operation run more smoothly by assigning more overseers to hauling and by orderng the laying of additional track.[36]

The ability to transport and process greater quantities of cane put pressure on the Aspíllagas and other planters to improve cultivation techniques. The principal innovation in this area was mechanized ploughing. Although ploughing never became completely mechanized during this period, several different types of steam- and gasoline-powered tractors were introduced at Cayaltí and elsewhere, from heavy models to lighter-weight, "Cuban" designs. With the tractors, ploughing could be done more rapidly and efficiently and with fewer workers. For example, to plough a field at Cayaltí required thirty men with oxen, but only eighteen with tractors.[37] This was a particularly important consideration because, during the late nineteenth century, experienced Chinese workers were being replaced, out of necessity, with inexperienced Peruvians. At Cayaltí enough men could be found to operate tractors, but not enough for oxen-driven ploughs:

With regard to the tractor, you know how profitable its use would be, but its importance is even greater because of better and more rapid cultivation. . . . The system of ploughing with oxen each day becomes more difficult and painful because the oxen are not dexterous, because there is a shortage of Chinese, because the peon from the sierra does not know how to plough, and because the peon from the coast is insufferable in ploughing for cane. All of this would make ploughing with tractors much more important.[38]

In addition to mechanizing their operations in the mill and in the field, planters began to pay greater attention to seed choice, fertilizers, use of underground streams for irrigation, and techniques for simplifying harvesting. Part of the process involved hiring agronomists and equipping them with laboratories on the plantations. The central government also proved useful in these matters by authorizing the Ministry of Development to establish

agricultural testing stations and by publishing the results of their experiments.[39]
One controversial innovation was the burning of cane before harvesting. Planters in the Cañete Valley in the late nineteenth century introduced the practice, and north coast producers soon adopted it. Initially it was considered a great labor-saving device because, once the foliage was removed from the cane stalk, cane could be harvested more rapidly and in greater quantities.[40] The Aspíllagas expressed their enthusiasm for the practice in 1898:

We have appreciated the advantages of burning before cutting. The cane cutters who hardly cut 70 arm loads per row now cut 150 arm loads, and we hope that the cane loaders will do 8 cars instead of 5. Those who transport the cane to the mill work more quickly and in general everything is going to represent a savings in labor that will not go below 4 percent; with the added advantage of being able to mill more and with regularity.[41]

Planters soon discovered, however, that burnt cane yielded 3 percent to 5 percent less sugar and tended to clog up machinery in the mill, thereby necessitating shutdowns for cleaning and repairs. For the Aspíllagas and some other planters this more than offset what they saved on labor, and they discontinued the practice. Nevertheless, planters were not in universal agreement on this point,[42] as witnessed by the fact that as late as 1975 some sugar cooperatives in the Lambayeque Valley were still burning before harvesting.
The series of technological innovations just discussed were of enormous benefit to the Aspíllagas and other planters in increasing production. Differences in production levels, in fact, closely paralleled the degree of technological development a plantation had achieved. It is important to explain, therefore, why the Aspíllagas chose to invest less in technological improvements after the major renovation of their mill in 1911.
This is not an easy question to answer, but there are a number of possible reasons. The Aspíllaga Barreras appear to have lost some of the entrepreneurial dynamism so apparent during the late nineteenth century, when they solved the financial problems inherited from their father and guided the technological development of Cayaltí. Antero, the eldest, was dedicating more time to his political career, so, although Cayaltí remained a family-run plantation, the ablest member of the family invested less time in its operation.[43]
Moreover, the First World War created conditions that made technological innovation temporarily less essential and more difficult to achieve. The fighting had forced European sugar beet producers out of the market, thereby decreasing supplies and driving the price of sugar to record highs. This resulted in high profits for sugarcane producers, which undoubtedly relieved the pressure to innovate. In addition, planters probably found it

more difficult to purchase farm machinery now that European factories had retooled to produce armaments. And finally, growers had to consider the risk of importing expensive equipment while ships were being attacked on the high seas.

The end to hostilities, however, opened up the sea lanes and returned European factories to normal production schedules. European sugar beet growers were also able to resume production, thus increasing the supply of sugar and driving prices and profit margins downward. These changes encouraged further technological innovation on many Peruvian sugarcane plantations, but not at Cayaltí.[44]

Managerial atrophy caused Cayaltí's failure to innovate during the 1920s. It was during this period that the direction of the estate was passed on to the sons of Ramón Aspíllaga Barrera, the Aspíllaga Andersons. Some of the brothers, notably Ismael and Luis, showed some enthusiasm for administration, but they never displayed the entrepreneurial drive of their father and uncle. All of the brothers had been raised in luxury in Lima; they were accustomed to spending, not making, money. Their lack of character was manifested in family quarrels, lack of leadership, and financial uncertainty. Dennis Gilbert, an expert on the Aspíllaga family, elaborates on this point:

The management of the plantation may also have been affected by deep personal enmities among certain of the brothers, mental health problems, and a lack of leadership within the family. Ismael, perhaps the most talented of his generation, was haunted for years by severe depression and finally committed suicide. He was not the only member of his generation to experience psychological difficulties. Ramón did not provide the family leadership that his father had. In Lima he was regarded as something of a *bon vivant*.

This sort of succession problem in wealthy families has been noted frequently. It is difficult for a generation born to great wealth to duplicate the ambitions and attitudes of those who established the family fortune. Granick concluded on the basis of a study of business enterprises in four European countries that family firms face severe succession problems and relatively few are able to survive three generations.[45]

Production

Despite Cayaltí's decline, it remained one of the largest sugarcane plantations in the region until the agrarian reform. Moreover, it had played an important part in the unprecedented development of the sugar industry during the late nineteenth and early twentieth centuries. During these years, north coast planters consolidated their estates and introduced technological innovations that transformed the Departments of Lambayeque and La Libertad into the nation's leading sugar-producing region and made sugar one of Peru's leading exports (see tables 13 and 14).

Differences in production among the northern valleys primarily reflected surface area and the level of technological development of individual estates

Table 14
Percentage Shares of Some Major Peruvian Exports

Year	Sugar	Cotton	Rubber	Wool	Petroleum	Copper
1900	32	7	n.a.	7	—	14
1901	24	9	n.a.	6	—	22
1902	33	8	10	6	—	8
1903	27	8	11	11	1	7
1904	25	7	16	8	—	9
1905	32	7	16	8	—	10
1906	25	8	17	9	—	14
1907	14	8	17	7	1	31
1908	19	15	11	5	2	22
1909	18	19	17	6	2	19
1910	20	14	18	7	2	13
1911	20	14	8	5	5	22
1912	15	11	14	4	8	25
1913	15	16	9	6	10	22
1914	30	16	5	6	10	19
1915	26	11	5	5	10	29
1916	24	10	4	6	8	36
1917	22	15	3	9	6	34
1918	21	19	2	14	7	19
1919	31	25	2	6	9	18
1920	42	30	1	2	5	12
1921	29	22	—	2	17	21
1922	24	25	1	3	18	17
1923	27	22	1	3	18	17
1924	21	22	1	4	23	14
1925	11	32	1	4	24	18
1926	17	22	1	3	28	16
1927	16	23	1	3	27	18
1928	13	21	—	4	28	20
1929	12	18	—	4	30	23
1930	11	18	—	3	30	19

Source: I. G. Bertram, "Development Problems in an Export Economy: A Study of Domestic Capitalists, Foreign Firms and Government in Peru, 1919–1930" (Ph.D. diss., Oxford University, 1974), p. 31.
Note: n.a. means data not available; — means no share.

Table 15
Sugar Production in North Coast Valleys
(Metric Tons)

Year	Chicama	Lambayeque	Valley Moche	Saña	Total
1912	73,148	23,385	9,978	9,317	115,828
1913	70,919	22,438	13,440	5,170	111,967
1914	75,882	32,749	19,642	11,408	139,681
1915	96,348	33,500	18,012	11,803	159,663
1916	109,505	36,414	20,486	12,510	178,915
1917	99,531	34,774	20,234	12,000	166,539
1918	122,505	38,448	18,744	14,260	193,957
1919	105,966	38,017	22,642	14,650	181,275
1920	126,097	43,770	26,164	16,923	212,954
1921	97,334	39,272	19,393	13,804	169,803
1922	129,906	44,657	23,958	18,658	217,179
1923	114,143	50,586	23,276	20,449	208,454
1924	115,866	42,100	22,108	18,775	198,849
1925	101,136	37,387	22,359	9,385	170,267
1926	162,728	47,478	29,620	14,373	254,199
1927	164,673	55,833	24,598	16,611	261,715
1928	163,009	62,377	23,155	11,477	260,018

Sources: Peru, Ministerio de Fomento, *Estadística de la industria azucarera en el Perú* (Lima, 1912–1917); Peru, Ministerio de Fomento, *Estadística de la producción de caña de azúcar en el Perú* (Lima, 1918–1929).
Note: No production data by valley were found before 1912 or after 1928.

Table 16
Sugar Production on Chicama Valleys Estates, Available Years
(Quintales)

Estate	Year	Production
Cartavio	1898	175,000
	1916	800,000
Chiquitoy	1896	100,000
	1900	250,000
Roma	1927	400,000

Source: Roma's production is an estimate based on the increase in production for Casa Grande in 1928. The remaining totals are from AH to AH, 26 February 1898, AFA; AAB to RAB and BAB, 6 March 1917, AFA; BAB to AAB, October 1900 (day not given). A quintal equals 100 pounds.

(table 15). However, additional variables included the availability of river water, soil conditions, and such intangibles as flooding, mechanical breakdowns, severe labor shortages, and strikes.

The strip of coastal land that produced the most sugar in Peru was the Chicama Valley. The largest of the northern valleys, it contained the nation's most technologically advanced plantations, Casa Grande and Cartavio (tables 16 and 17). Next in size and production totals was the Lambayeque Valley, which counted four large plantations: Tumán, Pomalca, Pátapo, and Pucalá (tables 18 and 19). It was followed in output by the significantly smaller Moche and Saña valleys. Both of these valleys were dominated by single plantations: Laredo in Moche, and Cayaltí in Saña (table 20).

Exports

Most of the millions of tons of sugar produced during the late nineteenth and early twentieth centuries were exported to sweeten the diets of the British, North Americans, and Chileans (table 21). The sugar industry played a major role in the overall development of Peru's export economy, by supplying capital for investment in other areas as well as by creating family fortunes and political dynasties.

During the late colonial and early republican periods, Chile was the principal market for Peruvian sugar (see table 22). By the 1870s, however, the United Kingdom had emerged as the leading importer, in response to a dramatic increase in the consumption of sugar. Britain remained Peru's chief market until the turn of the century, by which time it had become

Table 17
Sugar Production at Casa Grande

Year	Production (quintales)	Metric Tons/Hectare
1916	1,000,000.000	n.a
1923	1,185,802.420	112.847
1924	1,465,324.355	97.523
1925	1,371,273.198	113.690
1926	1,528,482.199	117.272
1927	1,829,283.471	97.397
1928	2,241,347.430*	121.101
1929	2,697,747.830	126.461
1930	2,481,770.345	112.011
1931	2,660,926.735	106.048
1932	3,037,167.850	111.383
1933	3,040,439.675	107.773

Source: Balance of July 1941, Gildemeister folder, AFA; BAB to ABB, RAB, and his mother ("Querida Mamá y Hermanos"), 10 April 1916, AFA.
*Roma was purchased by Casa Grande in 1927.

Table 18
Sugar Production at Tumán

Year	Total Production (quintales)
1916	200,000
1919	350,000*
1920	396,737
1923	443,000
1924	359,637*
1925	298,468*
1926	350,000
1927	468,683
1928	472,823
1929	558,963
1930	549,963
1931	600,861

Source: AAB to RAB and BAB, 23 December 1916, AFA; Administrador General to Gerente, 26 November 1919, Correspondencia Tumán, AFA; Administrador General to Gerente, 24 December 1925, Correspondencia Tumán, AFA; Administrador General to Gerente, 31 December 1925, Correspondencia Tumán, AFA; Administrador General to Gerente, 24 December 1926, Correspondencia Tumán, AFA.
*In 1917 Tumán built a new mill. In 1924 there was a drought, followed by a flood the next year.

Table 19
Sugar Production at Pomalca

Year	Total Production (quintales)
1914	168,962
1915	166,917
1921	231,000
1923	390,000*
1924	300,000
1929	572,286
1930	585,000

Source: Douglas Horton, *Haciendas and Cooperatives: A Preliminary Study of Latifundist Agriculture and Agrarian Reform in Northern Peru*, research paper, no. 53 (Madison, Wis.: Land Tenure Center, 1973), p. 21; Libro de Contabilidad de la Hacienda Pomalca, 1914–1917, AFA; Gerente to Administrador, 7 January 1930, Cartas Pomalca, AFA; IAA to RAA, 20 December 1924, AFA.
*Total given is "casi 400,000 qq."

Table 20
Sugar and Alcohol Production at Cayaltí

Year	Area in Cane (fanegadas)*	Production (quintales)	Quintales/ Fanegada	Alcohol (gallons)
1880	n.a.	23,203		n.a.
1881	107	36,437	341	34,090
1882	120	50,054	417	57,155
1883	153	39,145	256	49,319
1884	125	37,010	296	56,236
1885	n.a.	n.a.		n.a.
1886	n.a.	n.a.		n.a.
1887	211	31,168	148	36,649
1888	n.a.	34,409		55,055
1889	n.a.	52,000		60,000
1890	n.a.	50,000		84,000
1891	n.a.	50,513		96,170
1892	212	58,000	274	97,500
1893	246	78,000	317	96,023
1894	370	67,000	181	n.a.
1895	540	100,000	185	111,775
1896	n.a.	106,560		130,775
1897	n.a.	123,000		121,566
1898	n.a.	118,016		134,251
1899		113,911	249	94,833
1900	588	102,198		80,689

Table 20 (continued)

Year	Area in Cane (fanegadas)*	Production (quintales)	Quintales/ Fanegada	Alcohol (gallons)
1901	n.a.	n.a.		n.a.
1902	n.a.	108,000		n.a.
1903	n.a.	123,000		n.a.
1904	n.a.	116,000		50,000
1905	620	104,791	169	n.a.
1906	n.a.	n.a.		n.a.
1907	516	89,000	172	74,000
1908	n.a.	161,000		n.a.
1909	n.a.	151,332		63,852
1910	n.a.	126,408		n.a.
1911	n.a.	150,310		n.a.
1912	n.a.	202,539		n.a.
1913	556	112,495	202	n.a.
1914	857	248,309	289	80,780
1915	463	256,595	569	n.a.
1916	472	271,685	576	n.a.
1917	n.a.	258,016		n.a.
1918	n.a.	305,211		n.a.
1919	n.a.	323,395		n.a.
1920	n.a.	367,000		n.a.
1921	655	300,000	458	n.a.
1922	695	370,000	532	n.a.
1923		331,000	648	n.a.
1924		303,000	488	n.a.
1925		203,000	553	n.a.
1926	695	305,000	439	n.a.
1927	664	361,000	543	n.a.
1928	n.a.	249,504		n.a.
1929	n.a.	314,658		n.a.
1930	n.a.	388,780		n.a.
1931	n.a.	n.a.		n.a.
1932	n.a.	305,000		n.a.

Source: Cayaltí correspondence, 1880–1933, AFA.
*A fanegada equals 2.898 hectares.

Table 21
Peruvian Sugar Exports to Chile, the United Kingdom,
and the United States
(Metric Tons)

Year	To Chile	To the United Kingdom	To the United States
1868		969	
1869		840	
1870		2,552	
1871		4,420	
1872		6,651	
1873		16,215	
1874	7,367	24,017	
1875	9,180	46,024	
1876	9,082	46,033	
1877	7,408	56,312	
1878	8,361	56,351	
1879	12,322		
1880	5,798		
1881	11,838	32,632	
1882	11,283	33,057	
1883	10,997	23,517	
1884	15,225	19,038	
1885	14,754	31,084	
1886	19,553	24,407	
1887	13,916	22,302	
1888	15,194	25,270	
1889	17,113	35,383	
1890	8,217	30,842	
1891	16,756	21,448	
1892	11,486	36,489	
1893	17,796	26,572	
1894	17,613	16,841	
1895	21,954	37,226	
1896	22,353	42,535	
1897	28,511	43,061	1,299
1898	40,497	50,912	3,876
1899	35,479	16,734	22,716
1900	48,235	12,197	34,091
1901	33,602	4,893	58,731
1902	41,537	8,173	46,561
1903	51,238	19,555	40,301
1904	55,454	51,706	22,077
1905	32,117	57,797	21,677

Table 21 (continued)

Year	To Chile	To the United Kingdom	To the United States
1906	43,645	27,322	16,498
1907	49,686	30,057	15,967
1908	n.a.	54,789	8,496
1909	62,291	40,244	9,238
1910	64,915	46,972	8,850
1911	66,637	27,611	4,145
1912	61,631	63,190	5,968
1913	74,972	27,926	6,202
1914	72,503	47,627	4,074
1915	69,063	33,089	32,258
1916	74,684	56,503	37,556
1917	87,541	51,708	36,427
1918	87,259	42,363	2,504
1919	88,117	78,818	7,695
1920	73,386	49,665	

Source: Bill Albert, *An Essay on the Peruvian Sugar Industry, 1880–1920 and the Letters of Ronald Gordon, Administrator of the British Sugar Company in Cañete, 1914–1920* (Norwich: School of Social Studies, University of East Anglia, 1976), pp. 20a, 22a, 24a.

Table 22
Destination of Peruvian Sugar Exports,
Late Eighteenth Century

Destination	Amount (arrobas)
Chile	80,000–100,000
Buenos Aires	35,000– 40,000
Guayaquil	10,000
Total	150,000

Source: C. D. Scott, "The Political Economy of Sugar in Peru" (unpublished, 1974), p. 2. An arroba equals twenty-five pounds.

saturated with sugar imported from all parts of the globe. More exports were then diverted to Chile and the United States. Sugar exports to North America increased during World War I, but decreased dramatically with the end to hostilities (see table 21).

The growth of the sugar industry, so clearly illustrated in the production and export statistics, was an important chapter in the historical development of modern Peru. A small group of planters used their substantial resources and foreign capital to transform their estates into large and efficient agricultural enterprises. In the process of land consolidation, medium-sized producers as well as Indian communities were absorbed, continuing a historical process that had begun shortly after the arrival of the Spanish conquistadores.

More than the size of their estates, however, levels of technology dictated production capacity. Those estates with the most sophisticated machinery, such as Casa Grande and Cartavio, produced larger quantities of sugar more efficiently, and thus made larger profits. The history of Cayaltí, an estate that lagged in technology, illustrates the importance of managerial leadership. The decision of the Aspíllagas to invest less in machinery after 1911 condemned Cayaltí to a more archaic system of production, and, consequently, to lower production levels and profit margins. Nevertheless, Cayaltí did remain a highly mechanized plantation that continued to produce enormous quantities of sugar.

As a generalization, all regional estates were transformed into what could be called factories in the field. Significantly, this affected other aspects of plantation life, especially patterns of labor organization and the texture of labor relations.

Part II. The Organization, Recruitment, and Control of Labor

4. The Organization of Labor at Cayaltí

Sugar production on modern plantations required the services of a large number of workers engaged in a series of interrelated jobs. Owing to the size and complexity of operation, the organization of labor more closely resembled a factory model than peasant agriculture. Most important, sugar workers labored for a wage in closely supervised groups, as opposed to growing crops for market and paying rent for land. In addition, several jobs were highly mechanized, especially in the mill, and others were directly linked to mechanical processes.

The organization and supervision of workers was the responsibility of several overseers and administrators. At the top was the general administrator, assisted by the field boss and first mechanic, who were responsible for all field and mill work, respectively. Their principal lieutenants were the *mayordomos* and mechanics who supervised field hands and mill workers and served as the main links between the administration and the workers.

The organization of labor is an especially significant topic, because it helps to define the parameters of worker-planter relations. The regimented work routine, necessary for a scale of operation this size, created a factorylike environment that could lead to tensions between labor and management over wages and other concerns. This put pressure on planters to devise methods to avoid open confrontation.

Administrative and Supervisory Personnel

Much of the work involved in the running of Cayaltí concerned the organization and supervision of labor. In addition to solving problems of labor supply and controlling the plantation community, management had to organize workers to produce a steady stream of cane for processing. This involved both the long-term allocation of human resources and the daily assembling of work gangs.

The ultimate responsibility for labor policy and management rested with the general administrator, who was almost always an Aspíllaga. He had authority over the disbursement of money, including wages, and was the source of all authority exercised by other administrative personnel. If he was an active and able administrator, like Antero and Ramón Aspíllaga Barrera, he kept a close watch over the running of the estate down to the smallest details. For major policy-decisions, however, the general administrator always consulted with the manager of the family business (also an Aspíllaga) in Lima, with whom he corresponded on a daily basis.[1]

Because of the complexity of managing an estate as large as Cayaltí, with a work force of over one thousand men after the turn of the century, the general administrator required a large staff. Numbering forty-one in April of 1882, it involved clerical workers, mechanics, engineers, foremen, and administrative assistants. All employees resided on the plantation and were expected to live up to a special code of ethics called the "Dirección general para los empleados de esta Hacienda, en las oficinas y en el campo," as well as to maintain a comportment of "dignity and composure . . . so that the superiority that should exist over the laborers is not diluted."[2]

Among the most important employees were the field boss and the first mechanic. They were the right-hand men of the general administrator, with broad administrative responsibilities over work in their areas. If they were highly competent, the general administrator could delegate much of the responsibility for the daily operation of the estate to them and concern himself with larger problems. Throughout most of the latter part of the nineteenth century, the field boss was a Spaniard named Pedro Leivas y Rodríguez. Leivas was a good administrator who frequently earned the praise of the Aspíllagas. His retirement in 1896 left a major vacuum in the administrative apparatus of Cayaltí, and for a while the Aspíllagas experimented with a clumsy system consisting of a coordinator of mayordomos and six head mayordomos. After several months, however, they returned to a more streamlined bureaucracy, and field work ran more smoothly, although not as well as it had under Leivas.[3]

Throughout most of the late nineteenth and early twentieth centuries, a period spanning over forty years, the first mechanic was Thomas Colston, a British subject. Throughout his career, Colston proved to be an important ingredient in the efficient operation of Cayaltí. He initiated most of the important technological improvements and had the uncanny ability to keep the mill running at times when proper parts were not immediately available. Officially, he was directly responsible for all operations in the mill, distillery, workshops, railroads (both portable and permanent), and mechanized ploughing.[4]

Colston was assisted in the mill by several mechanics, thirteen in 1882 and surely more later on, who had both technical and supervisory responsibilities. Most of the mechanics appear to have been Peruvians,

Table 23
Instructions Issued to Staff at Cayaltí, January 1882

—Ensure that all workers begin work exactly on time and that they carry out their assignments precisely as given.
—Display optimal order and respect in your duties and ensure that workers do likewise.
—Never mistreat workers, either verbally or physically, and report any problem to a superior immediately.
—Never leave your post until the workday has been completed.
—Prohibit any stranger from entering the estate during working hours.
—Take maximum precautions to avoid any damage or loss to the interests of the estate.
—Intercede immediately in any argument or fight between workers, and, if necessary,seek the assistance of other employees and the owners.
—Report on the amount of work done each day to either the general administrator or one of his assistants, and receive instructions for the following day from one of these superiors.
—Present a separate report at the end of the day showing how much each worker has completed.
—Keep a worksheet (*planilla*) showing how much each worker has completed over a two-week period.
—Assume responsibility for all losses of or damages to iron tools distributed to workers under your supervision.
—Bring to the attention of the general administrator any unauthorized absence by a worker.
—Be willing, energetic, and vigilant in the obedience of the orders of the estate.
—Never be absent from your post without the special permission of the general administrator.
—Be prepared to lose pay due to illness caused by carelessness.
—Pay for any damage to or loss of items lent by the estate.
—Accept without question any assignment given by the estate.
—Carry out all orders, or be fired.
—Agree to uphold all of the above instructions.

Source: Dirección general para los empleados de esta Hacienda, en las oficinas y en el campo, January 1882, AFA.

although when the new mill was constructed in 1877 thirteen of the fifteen mechanics hired temporarily were foreigners, mostly British and American.[5]

Without question, the most important supervisory personnel were the *mayordomos*, who supervised all field-workers. They were the link between the administration and field-workers and bore responsibility for the maintenance of order and discipline in the field and the completion of daily work assignments. There were three *mayordomos* specifically responsible for all work in weeding and one each for harvesting, planting, irrigation, and transporting cane to the mill. There were in addition four *mayordomos* with general responsibilities over the organization of labor in specific fields. All *mayordomos* were directly answerable to the field boss.[6]

The Aspíllagas always watched *mayordomos* closely because they were a crucial link in the organization of labor.[7] In fact, the code of ethics for the general staff primarily concerns the responsibilities of *mayordomos*. The code demonstrates the respect and discipline that the Aspíllagas demanded of their employees and also elucidates the regimentation of labor at Cayaltí (see table 23).

Wages

Wages generally reflect the importance of the position, with the highest salaries going to the general administrator, first mechanic, and field boss (see table 24). Real wages are, however, impossible to calculate with the available data. As a generalization, because this was a period of inflation, most wage increases simply worked to catch up with rising prices. Wages included not only cash remunerations but housing and a modest pension of five to seven soles per month, as calculated in 1882.[8] The one glimpse there is of the purchasing power of employees' wages is food prices, the most important item in their budget. Note in table 25 the increase in the price of rice, the chief staple of the coastal diet.

Workers

Each morning before dawn, *mayordomos* would assemble field workers and give them work assignments. Almost all work in the field was piecework (*tarea*), theoretically just enough to keep workers busy for a ten- to twelve-hour day, beginning at 6:00 a.m. and lasting until sunset (with an hour lunch break at 11:00 a.m.).[9] The general administrator determined the size of the *tarea*, and it was the job of *mayordomos* to assure that everyone completed his assignments. Workers were given an incentive to finish their tasks, because anything less meant that they would be docked half their pay. Some workers, generally older men, adolescents, or cripples, were only given half *tareas* at half pay.[10] Mill workers worked twelve-hour shifts, which was the maximum most were physically capable of.[11] Regardless of the job, workers were expected to complete a six-day week (table 26).[12]

For most jobs in the field, there was little specialization of labor. In other words, most workers could transfer from weeding to planting to harvesting without any difficulty. There were, of course, exceptions. Certain jobs required more strength than others, which eliminated frail workers from consideration, and other jobs called for dexterity. For these, teenagers, or

Table 24
Monthly Wages at Cayaltí, Available Years
(Soles)

Employee	Monthly Wage			
	1882	1889	1912	1917
General administrator	100		600	800
First mechanic	280	267		
Field boss	100		200	
Head accountant	100			
Treasurer	60	95		
Clerk	60			
Mechanic	20–35	70		
		(with ration)		
		75		
		(without ration)		
Supervisor of				
mayordomos		90		
Mayordomos	15–30	15–30		45
Tractor guard	60	40		
Tools guard	70	75		
Butcher	50	60		

Sources: Presupuesto de los gastos mensuales de la Hacienda Cayaltí, 1 April 1882, AFA;
AH to AH, 11 July 1889 (a), AFA; AAB to AH, 26 December 1912, AFA; AAB to RAB and
BAB, 15 May 1917, AFA; RAB to AAB, 18 August 1917, AFA.
Notes: Colston, who became first mechanic in 1889, always received his wage in pounds
sterling. Differences in wages among mayordomos probably reflect seniority and the number of
men they supervised.

Table 25
Prices of Some Food Items, Available Years

Item	Year	Price/Pound (centavos)
Beef	1882	.06
Rice	1882	.05
Rice	1922–23	.10
Flour	1882	.07
Butter	1882	.40
Lard	1922–23	.55
Potatoes	1922–23	.08–.10

Source: Presupuesto de los gastos mensuales de la Hacienda Cayaltí, 1 April 1882, AFA;
VAT to Señor Gerente Negociaciones Agrícolas Cayaltí y Palto, 27 January 1923, AFA; IAA
to RAB, 22 October 1923, AFA.

other nimble workers, were favored. Workers from the coast were generally preferred in irrigation simply because they had more experience. Tractor and mill operators required special training, which they received from Colston.[13]

A sugar mill was not very different from an industrial plant. Most workers worked directly with machinery, whether they manned a conveyor belt or operated complicated processing equipment. The division of labor was calculated to produce a finished product with maximum labor productivity (table 27). The mill generally ran for ten to eleven months of the year, with a shutdown scheduled for cleaning and repairs during the summer, when water was scarce and labor sometimes more difficult to recruit because of the extreme heat and the increased incidence of communicable disease.[14]

The cultivation of sugarcane was a labor-intensive process. Seventy percent or more of the workers were assigned to jobs in the field while milling was in progress, and when the mill shut down, many mill workers took up shovels and machetes.[15]

Table 26
Division of Labor at Cayaltí

Job	No. of Workers 1877	% Total Work Force	No. of Workers 1892	% Total Work Force
Mill	81	19.1	94	19.2
Harvesting	89	21.0	115	23.5
Irrigation	19	4.5	41	8.3
Ploughing and planting	15	3.5	44	8.8
Weeding	36	8.5	40	8.1
Portable railroad			30	6.0
Loading	n.a.		40	8.1
Hauling	n.a.		17	3.4
Muleteer	14	3.3	25	5.8
Livestock tender	2	.5	14	2.8
Cultivation of grain for livestock	15	3.5	16	3.3
Artisan	25	5.9	12	2.5
Burning cane			1	.2
Mill construction	110	26.0		
Wood cutting	4	.9		
Servant	10	2.4	n.a.	
Miscellaneous	4	.9		
Total	424		489	

Source: AH to AH, 11 September 1877, AFA; AH to AH, 27 September 1892, AFA.

Table 27
Division of Labor in the Mill at Cayaltí, April 1890

Job	No. of Workers
Conductor	18
Wastes	26
Interior	26
Centrifugal and depository	3
Still	5
Total	78

Source: AH to AH, 1 May 1890, AFA.
Notes: Data from May 1890 and September 1892 show approximately the same number of workers in each position. One exception, however, is in the centrifugal and depository, where as many as thirteen persons worked: AH to AH, 15 May 1890, AFA; AH to AH, 27 September 1892, AFA.

All jobs in the field had to be coordinated to supply the mill with a steady stream of ripened cane. Sugarcane was planted in plots of 215 to 285 acres, called *suertes*, which were further subdivided into fourths, or *cuarteles*. Before planting began, furrows were cut within each *cuartel* and interconnected with a network of irrigation canals.[16]

Ploughing was done either with ox-driven ploughs or tractors. The first tractors arrived at Cayaltí in 1878 and were modified through the years to cut deeper into the soil as it became exhausted or compacted. Around the turn of the century, the estate also purchased some lighter tractors, "Cuban tractors," which were easier to handle. Nevertheless, Cayaltí never relied exclusively on tractors, which were expensive to buy and to repair.[17]

Once furrows and irrigation canals were ready, planting could commence. For seed, all estates used cane shoots (*cogollo*), which were carefully planted eight inches apart with a sharpened edge facing the flow of water. Each planting was good for three harvests, as cane was generally allowed to grow back twice before being uprooted. Six workers were assigned to plant each *cuartel*, and, because the work did not require brawn, teenagers, older, and injured workers were sometimes used.[18]

Once the new shoots were planted, they had to be irrigated at regular intervals until maturity. Irrigation workers were also responsible for maintaining canals and closing off sluice gates prior to the burning of a *cuartel* before harvesting. In addition, they were the only workers required to work without compensation on Sunday mornings, from 6:00 a.m. to 10:00 a.m.[19]

All north coast agriculturalists drew irrigation water from huge canals called *acequias madres*, which were regulated by local water districts.[20]

Permission was given to take set amounts of water from these canals into a series of smaller canals on estates, called *jirones*, which then fed water into *cuarteles*.[21]

About once every two years, it was the responsibility of all users to clean *acequias madres*. Each farm had to contribute a number of workers commensurate with the amount of water it consumed, so plantations had the largest obligation. On such occasions, Cayaltí had to contribute its entire work force, or hire large numbers of additional workers, for three to four days.[22]

The Aspíllagas referred to this use of communal labor as a *minga*, no doubt in reference to the ancient Peruvian *minga*.[23] George R. Fitz-Roy Cole observed the cleaning of an *acequia madre* in 1873:

At the appointed time, the peones assemble at the head of the acequia of their district, and divide themselves into two bands, the first of which cleans away canes, rushes, and other tropical weeds, with the help of long curved hatchets [machetes] furnished to them. The task of the second party, closely following the rear of the first, is to deepen and make even the banks of the watercourse. The whole party proceeds with their work, stimulated by the music of the drum and fife, the strokes of axes and shovels keeping time with the musicians. They work quickly and eagerly . . . and it is indeed surprising to watch with what speed a party of *limpiadores* [cleaners] will descend a watercourse, cleaning away all obstructions and leaving its bed and sides clean and smooth as if newly cut.[24]

Shortly after cane shoots received their first water, weeds began to grow. Needless to say, regular weeding of furrows and canals was necessary to conserve precious space and water. At Cayaltí, there were three types of weeding, each done by a different group of workers with its own *mayordomo*. One section of field hands periodically weeded furrows and canals and cleaned up debris around the fields and roads.[25] Another group only weeded furrows and canals after the cane had reached full maturity. This was considered particularly hard work because of the large *tarea* involved and the difficulty of working in the tall cane. The number of workers here was generally limited to thirty.[26] A third group of weeders worked alongside cane harvesters and collected stubble from around cut cane, which was then used in the mill as fuel. When Cayaltí introduced burning before harvest in 1884, the work force in this section was halved.[27]

To assure the best results, cane should have been fertilized at least twice before harvesting, but Cayaltí did not fertilize on a regular basis because of the cost.[28] Even without fertilizing, newly planted cane reached maturity after eighteen months, and once- and twice-planted cane (*soca* and *resoca*), between fifteen and eighteen months. Cayaltí, however, generally harvested its cane somewhat earlier, sacrificing sugar quality for higher production yields.[29]

Many cane cutters were required to supply the mill with a steady flow of cane. Workers cut a *suerte* at a time, about 250 acres, striking the cane low on the stalk and leaving it to be gathered by other workers. Before Cayaltí began burning before harvest, the size of the *tarea* varied according to the condition of the cane. Thus, the *tarea* for newly planted cane that was thick and clean was 200 yards, but if bent and tangled, only 180 yards. On the other hand, the *tarea* for *socas* and *resocas*, which were smaller and easier to cut, varied from 300 to 500 yards. When burning before harvest was initiated, foliage and weeds were removed so that more cane could be cut in the same amount of time. This allowed the estate to increase the *tarea* to an average of 458 yards for all types of cane, thus reducing the cost of harvesting by 40 percent. Nevertheless, as mentioned in chapter 3, burning before harvest was eventually discontinued, as burnt cane yielded from 3 to 5 percent less sugar and tended to gum up machinery.[30]

Once cane had been harvested, it was essential to get it to the mill as quickly as possible, because each minute of delay meant a drop in sucrose content. Cane loading and hauling required large numbers of workers and presented the estate with more problems than any other jobs in the field.[31]

After harvesting, cane was loaded into huge carts with a capacity of three metric tons. The traditional *tarea* was five cart loads, which was difficult enough, but with the installation of the portable railroad in 1888 (and the subsequent capacity to haul more cane), the *tarea* was increased to seven cart loads. This brought cries of protest from workers, but to no avail.[32]

Cane hauling was equally difficult and considerably more dangerous. Before the installation of the portable railroad, cane was hauled in ox-driven carts over uneven roads. In 1882 Antero Aspíllaga Barrera characterized cane hauling as back-breaking work, which workers "feared" and went to great extremes to avoid.[33]

All of these problems, plus the desire to increase production, compelled the estate to install the portable railroad. Initially, mismanagement of the railroad caused some production bottlenecks, but his problem was eventually overcome. By 1890, harvesting, loading, and hauling were well-synchronized, with 250 carts in daily operation taking freshly cut cane to the mill.[34]

Once the cane reached the mill it was processed into unrefined sugar, packaged, and shipped to Eten for export abroad. The processing of cane was an assembly line operation, entailing several different jobs.

Cane haulers ended their journey at a huge conveyor belt that fed cane into the interior of the mill. Several workers were stationed on both sides of the belt to prevent cane from spilling over and to guide it into the crushers, where it was mashed, and juice separated from fiber. The juice was then poured into vacuum pans, which (through evaporation) separated out the saccharin solution. The fiber (*bagazo*) was collected and used as fuel in the boilers.[35] From the vacuum pans, the sugar was taken to the mixer, where it was pulverized and mixed with chemicals. It was then transported in carts to the centrifugal, which purified the saccharin crystals. From there it only remained to dry the sugar and to separate it by quality for packing.[36]

An important by-product of sugar processing was alcohol, which required the operation of a distillery. In 1893, this facility had a modest work force of ten to eleven men: one distiller, one preparer of must, one funnel operator, three disposers of waste, one filler of tin cans, and three or four packers.[37]

In addition to field and mill workers, Cayaltí employed several artisans and livestock tenders.[38] The most numerous were carpenters, who built and repaired houses, corrals, stores, fences, and other structures. The estate also needed a fair number of metalworkers to forge and repair iron tools and ploughs. All artisans received higher wages than field hands or mill workers.[39]

Accidents

Plantation workers were exposed to the risk of fatal or serious injury, especially in cane hauling and mill work. As noted earlier, until the portable railroad was installed, several workers were killed or seriously injured in cane hauling.[40] Fatal accidents also occurred in the mill. For example, in 1888 a mill worker was decapitated by machinery, and six years later a man's hand was crushed between two meshing gears.[41]

Until the 1920s, planters were not required by law to compensate families of workers killed or injured on the job. However, the Aspíllagas occasionally reassigned crippled workers to easy jobs or gave them some gratuity before dismissing them.[42]

Worker Productivity

Whatever the job, the estate was concerned with maximizing worker productivity. Although absenteeism was a serious problem (to be discussed in chapters 5 and 7), the available data suggest that those workers who reported for duty generally completed their assignments (see table 28). This suggests that *tareas* were not overly burdensome, that *mayordomos* were vigilant (as the Aspíllagas demanded), and that the threat of losing half a day's wage for failure to complete assignments was a strong incentive.[43]

Conclusion

The production of sugar at Cayaltí required the careful organization of large numbers of men into work gangs in the field, and assembly line and machine operators in the mill. For an agricultural enterprise, Cayaltí retained little of the image of pastoral production, with its seasonal work

Table 28
Work Output at Cayalti

Date	No. of Workers	Assignments Completed	% of Total Tarea
25 August 1884	332	322.5	97.1
27 August 1884	347	337.5	97.3
30 August 1884	346	339.5	98.1
1 September 1884	332	334.5	100.8
3 September 1884	378	371.0	98.1
6 September 1884	375	384.5	102.5
26 August 1885	426	420.0	98.6
28 August 1885	410	408.5	99.6
30 August 1885	392	376.5	96.0
2 September 1885	469	465.0	99.1
5 September 1885	459	455.0	99.1

Source: Resumen diario del trabajo de la peonada en al 15[a] del 25 de agosto al 7 de setiembre del 1884, in letter dated 7 September 1884, AFA; Resumen por dias del trabajo de la peonada en la presente quincena, in letter dated 6 September 1885, AFA.

assignments and family participation. This was an enterprise in which men sold their labor throughout the year and planters produced for an international market.

The scale of operation necessitated hiring a large number of employees to help manage the estate. In the organization of labor, the most important were *mayordomos* and mechanics. The former were responsible for the organization and supervision of field-workers, who constituted over 70 percent of the work force. Workers were assigned to specific tasks, such as planting, irrigation, and harvesting, that were coordinated to provide a steady supply of sugarcane to the mill. Mechanics were then responsible for supervising the processing of cane, from its initial crushing to its transformation into unrefined sugar. Mill workers were more skilled than field hands because they had to operate machinery.

The organization of labor was, of course, only one aspect of the larger problem of labor management. The necessity of employing hundreds of men required secure systems of labor supply and effective methods of controlling a large population. Overcoming these problems was critical to the successful operation of all sugarcane plantations in the area.

5. The Chinese Worker, 1875–1900

Plantation agriculture in the Americas was notorious for its exploitation of servile labor. For over three centuries, black slaves provided the back-breaking labor required to produce tropical food for European and North American tables and fibers for clothing woven on both sides of the Atlantic. The end of slavery in the New World during the nineteenth century presented planters with the dilemma of finding alternative sources of labor. As is well known, in the United States and in parts of the Caribbean and Brazil, blacks continued to work on plantations as sharecroppers, tenants, and wage laborers. Precisely how they were retained remains a subject of debate in the historical literature.[1]

New sources of labor were also introduced after the abolition of slavery. For example, large numbers of Italian emigrants flocked to Brazil to work on coffee plantations and, for the first time since the Ice Age, the flow of immigration also came from the other side of the world. Planters in Peru, Panama, and Cuba, as well as railroad builders in the United States and sheep ranchers in Australia, benefited from the tragedy of the Taiping Rebellion (1851–1864), which created over 1.5 million Chinese refugees, whose survival hinged on finding work outside of the country. Between 1849 and 1874 over 100,000 indentured servants emigrated to Peru alone, where they replaced blacks on sugarcane plantations.[2]

The Chinese were crucial to the economic recovery and expansion of the Peruvian sugar industry during the mid-nineteenth century. It is not surprising, therefore, that the end of the coolie trade in 1874 contributed to the decline of the industry and of the export economy in general. Planters were faced with the problem, as they had been twenty years before, of finding an alternative source of labor. The extremely chaotic political and economic conditions of the period made it impossible for them to switch over to Peruvian wage labor, and there was considerable opposition both within the country and outside to further importation of indentured servants from other parts of the globe.

Therefore, planters did everything they could to hold onto their Chinese workers. At first they simply extended the length of indentured servants' contracts and hired small numbers of noncontracted Chinese laborers (*chinos libres*). The Chilean invasion of 1880, however, disrupted the coastal economy and patterns of labor supply. The fighting resulted in the destruction of several estates and the creation of a large pool of unemployed Chinese laborers. Many of these subsequently came under the control of Chinese contractors, who hired them out to planters.

All of these workers helped to keep the sagging sugar industry alive during the tumultuous 1870s and 1880s. However, they were clearly only a stopgap to the labor needs of the industry. As the productivity of the Chinese declined with age, planters began to replace them with Peruvian wage laborers from the nearby highlands, a process facilitated by the general economic recovery of the 1890s.

Chinese Emigration to Peru, 1849–1874

As the sugar industry expanded after 1840, planters began to search for alternative sources of labor. By the end of the decade the Congress, in which planters were well represented, had passed an immigration law tailored to encourage the importation of large numbers of contract laborers. The law stipulated that anyone who could import at least fifty such workers between the ages of ten and forty would receive 30 pesos per immigrant. The law also gave one of the bill's principal backers, the Inqueño planter Domingo Elías (with his associate Juan Rodríguez), the exclusive right to import Chinese contract laborers into the Departments of Lima and La Libertad for a period of four years.[3]

Some planters, however, initially shunned the Chinese in favor of Europeans, whom they considered racially superior and better agricultural-ists.[4] Europeans, however, were unenthusiastic about a country that offered them fewer economic opportunities than the United States and southern South America. As a result, from 1850 to 1860 only some 320 Irish, 370 Germans, and 200 Spaniards emigrated to Peru as contract laborers, although millions of Europeans would soon flock to the Río de la Plata and the cities and agricultural heartland of North America.[5]

In Peru, most of the Germans settled at Pozuzo in the central highlands and never worked as plantation laborers. The Spaniards went to the estate Talambo near Chiclayo, and a majority of the Irish to the plantation Villegas, owned by a Mr. Gallagher. Neither immigrant group, however, proved good plantation workers. The Irish left abruptly after a short tenure, and it was the Spaniards' claims of mistreatment that sparked the outbreak of the Spanish-Peruvian War of 1864-1866.[6]

In the meantime, other planters were experiencing greater success with the Chinese, who entered the country in ever-increasing numbers.[7] There were several reasons for this impressive immigration. The old imperial kingdom was ravaged by famine, weakened politically and economically by its ignominious defeat in the Opium War (1839–1842), torn by internal political feuds, and then nearly toppled during the Taiping Rebellion, in which perhaps as many as 30 million persons were killed and millions more left homeless and desperate. Between 1847 and 1874, over a million Chinese emigrated abroad, despite imperial prohibitions against emigration and deep-seated religious and cultural attachments to the homeland.[8]

Most Chinese were recruited from the coastal provinces of Fukien and Kwangtung and departed via the Portuguese port of Macao. Professional Chinese contractors, who received a fee for everyone they delivered, did the recruiting. As the demand for labor increased, this fee grew from 3 to 35 pesos per head. With rare exceptions, only males were contracted.[9]

Recruitment frequently involved entrapment. Most commonly, contractors promised recruits jobs that did not exist or that would last for only a short while. In the meantime, workers accepted food and lodging on credit from contractors, who later suggested that they be repaid through the signing of contracts of indentureship. In addition to this technique, contractors acquired indentured servants through kidnapping, by purchasing prisoners from warlords, and by insisting that refugees repay their gambling debts with labor. It should also be noted that many Chinese signed contracts of indentureship of their own volition. However, judging from a report on the coolie trade in Cuba written by a special Chinese commission in 1874, they were in the minority. A full 80 percent of those interviewed claimed to have been kidnapped or duped into signing contracts.[10]

Once on Macao, contractors turned recruits over to agents who herded them into large dormitories to await shipment abroad. A typical contract of indentureship from the 1850s promised the laborer an advance on his wages, a monthly salary of 4 pesos, free food and medical care, and passage to Peru. In return, the laborer agreed to repay his advance at the rate of 1 peso per month, to work for five years (not counting periods of illness), and not to travel without his employer's permission.[11] Once indentured servants reached Peru, planters typically paid agents from $300 to $450 per worker. This amounted to a substantial profit for agents who, for a shipment of three hundred Chinese, could net anywhere from $43,975 to $84,475.[12]

The voyage between Macao and Callao took approximately 120 days. Ships of nineteen different national registries participated in the coolie trade, with the most active being, respectively, France, Peru, Great Britain, and Spain.[13] Arnold Meagher has compared the coolie trade with the slave trade, as the combination of crowded quarters, poor food, and an extremely long voyage resulted in high mortality rates and a general atmosphere of desperation, which occasionally led to mutinies.[14]

Dr. Ernst Middendorf, a German physician residing in Peru, has left us with an eyewitness account of the conditions on board a coolie ship that landed at Arica in 1856. The voyage had taken an unusually long time (180 days), during which over half of the Chinese had died. Of the survivors, eighteen had gone blind and many others were suffering from advanced eye disease. None of the ill had been treated, because the ship's doctor had sold his medicine on Macao. As soon as the ship had docked, five of the stricken Chinese had attempted suicide by throwing themselves into the ocean, and only two could be retrieved. The captain of the vessel thereupon ordered that any attempt at suicide be punished with one hundred lashes, which were immediately administered to the survivors.[15]

Mortality rates were especially high during the first fourteen years of the trade. They declined thereafter, as new provisions between trading partners stipulated that there should be no more than one passenger per two tons of registry.[16] In addition, agents and shippers probably began to provide coolies with better food and lodging as the demand for labor increased and it became more difficult to find recruits.[17] Table 29 contains the most detailed figures available on mortality rates and yearly immigration statistics. The totals are from a sample of approximately 90 percent of all Chinese imported into Peru.

Table 29
Chinese Emigration to Peru

Year	No. Embarked at Macao	No. Dead during Voyage	% of Total Embarked	No. Disembarked at Callao
1850				
1860	15,000	2,000	13.33	13,000
1860	2,007	594	29.60	1,413
1861	1,860	420	22.58	1,440
1862	1,726	718	41.60	1,008
1863	2,301	673	29.25	1,628
1864	7,010	600	8.56	6,410
1865	4,794	254	5.30	4,540
1866	6,543	614	9.38	5,929
1867	2,400	216	9.00	2,184
1868	4,732	466	9.85	4,266
1869	3,006	75	2.50	2,931
1870	7,917	373	4.71	7,544
1871	12,526	741	5.92	11,785
1872	14,505	1,114	7.68	13,391
1873	7,303	732	10.02	6,571
1874	3,939	114	2.89	3,825
Total	97,529	9,704	9.91	87,825

Source: J. B. H. Martinet, *L'agriculture au Pérou, Résumé du mémoire présenté au Congrés International de l'agriculture* (Paris: Au Siège de la Société, 1878), p. 32.

Angry debate at the national and international levels characterized the history of the coolie trade to Peru. Only a few years after the trade had begun, members of Congress, concerned over the oppressive working conditions on the guano islands, called for a halt to further importation. It was difficult to counter their claims of poor working and living conditions, but a persuasive argument based on economic necessity was made in favor of continuing the trade. The principal spokesmen in favor of the trade were, not surprisingly, Domingo Elías and Juan Rodríguez. They published a pamphlet entitled *Inmigración de los Chinos, ventajas que proporciona al país* and presented it to the Senate for consideration in 1851.[18]

The thesis of their presentation was that the Chinese represented the cheapest solution to the labor shortage and that any problems associated with the trade could be alleviated. They pointed out that the Chinese received a wage of only 4 pesos per month and could basically live on rice, but that Europeans expected to be paid 20 centavos a day and to be fed meat. Moreover, conversion to Peruvian free wage labor would be an even costlier alternative entailing additional risks, such as dealing with the military draft and the payment of *contribución personal*, a head tax on Indians and free blacks that had its origins in the colonial period. Elías and Rodríguez admitted that many Chinese had arrived in poor physical condition, but they insisted, somewhat naively, that this could be avoided by limiting recruitment to healthy workers.[19]

The pamphlet also presented testimony from persons who had imported indentured servants. A majority praised the Chinese as good workers whom they had employed in a variety of occupations but especially as plantation laborers. One important impact of the trade, Elías and Rodríguez claimed, was to lower the cost of labor in Lima. In the end, these arguments persuaded a majority of congressmen to allow the coolie trade to continue.[20]

Nevertheless, opponents of the trade remained vigilant, awaiting a more propitious time to renew the debate. That opportunity came with the change in political climate in the mid-1850s. President Ramón Castilla abolished slavery in 1854 and favored the abolition of the coolie trade. There was also increasing concern among the elite that the growing numbers of Chinese might inalterably degrade the racial composition of Peru. The Elías-Rodríguez monopoly expired in 1853, and it is doubtful that they argued as forcefully for the continuation of the coolie trade as they had earlier. Thus, after extended debate, in 1856 Congress reversed its earlier decision and prohibited further importation of Chinese to Peru.[21]

Ramón Castilla remained firmly opposed to the renewal of the coolie trade throughout his second term (1855–1862). However, planters and their allies in Congress continued to press for the trade and managed to secure official permission to import limited numbers of Chinese. It is also clear that planters smuggled some Chinese into the country.[22] As conditions for agricultural expansion remained good, proponents of the trade intensified their lobbying, and in 1861 they were able to put together enough votes to pass renewal of the trade over Castilla's veto. The coolie trade continued for another thirteen years, fueling the agricultural expansion of the coast.[23]

Although the balance of power in Peru had swung in favor of indentured servitude, the opposite was true in other parts of the world. Throughout the 1850s newspapers on the China coast had editorialized against it, and by 1860 they had been joined by the *New York Times* and the *Times of London*. The Chinese government also began to take a tougher stand by executing labor contractors and effectively blockading Macao. Great Britain incorporated the coolie trade into its campaign to halt the slave trade,[24] perhaps because its colonies did not depend on Chinese labor, as did some of its competitors on the world market. In 1870 Hong Kong was closed to the trade, and three years later British vessels seized two ships carrying coolies (the *Nouvelle Penelope* and the *María Luz*), incidents that were widely publicized and that helped to galvanize world opinion against this form of exploitation.[25] London also put intensive pressure on Lisbon to close Macao to the trade, and popular sentiment in the colony itself began to turn against the exportation of indentured servants.[26] Opponents of coolie labor in Peru, moreover, found articulate spokesmen in Pedro Paz Soldán y Unánue and Féliz Cipriano C. Zegarra, as well as the powerful daily *El Comercio*, which editorialized against indentured servitude and publicized atrocities commited against Chinese on coastal plantations.[27]

All of these pressures finally combined in 1874 to doom the coolie trade. The most destructive actions were the closing of Macao as a way station, which should be attributed to British pressure on Portugal, and the opposition of the Chinese government. An unhappy chapter in East-West relations, with many distinct parallels with the African slave trade, was now over.

The Chinese Worker at Cayaltí, 1875-1900

Peruvian planters, predictably, had an opposite view of events. In economic terms, the end to Chinese immigration aggravated the general decline of the sugar industry that the Depression of 1873 initiated and that the War of the Pacific prolonged. Growers attempted to combat the labor shortage by automating their estates,[28] but, always hoping that some form of servile labor could be found, were reluctant to convert to Peruvian wage labor. For the time being, they chose to make do with those Chinese already within the country and only gradually convert to wage labor.

Antero Aspíllaga Barrera viewed the end to the coolie trade with great alarm. He wrote that the Chinese were "everything to our agriculture and the best laborers we can obtain" and beseeched the Lord to allow immigration to continue.[29] Antero's concern proved justified, for within a few years the Aspíllagas were complaining of labor shortages and the rise in the price of indentured servants, which had jumped from 200 soles in 1864 to 500 soles in 1875, an increase of 150 percent.[30]

Until the outbreak of the War of the Pacific in 1879, however, the Aspíllagas avoided severe labor shortages by extending the contracts of several hundred of Cayaltí's indentured servants. Thus, in December 1875, Ramón Aspíllaga Barrera wrote to Antero, "I have contracted some Chinese, of those who had one-half year to go [on their indentureships], I have given them one year, those with one year [to go], one and one half years, those with one and one half [years to go], two years."[31] Over the next several months, the Aspíllagas continued this practice, always paying these workers the same wage, namely 40 to 50 soles per year.[32]

As the Aspíllagas began to contract nonresident Chinese workers, however, they found it necessary to offer them cash advances as an enticement for signing employment contracts. For example, during December of 1877 the Aspíllagas advanced 4,000 soles to 150 Chinese, for an average of 27 soles per worker.[33] Technically, these workers were not allowed to leave the estate until their debts had been repaid.[34]

In addition to contracted workers, the Aspíllagas also began to hire Chinese wage laborers (*chinos libres*). Because of the tight labor market, these workers could demand a significantly higher wage than contracted workers, which made the Aspíllagas reluctant to employ them in large numbers. For example, in 1876 *chinos libres* earned 70 centavos per day plus meals at Cayaltí, and 80 centavos to one sol per day with meals on neighboring rice farms, wages far higher than the meager sums earned by contracted workers.[35]

In 1877 and 1878 the Aspíllagas were encouraged by the possibility of importing Chinese from China and California. They were approached by H. Seymour Geary, a representative of Olyphant & Co. of the United States, who agreed to deliver 150 Chinese directly from China to Cayaltí.[36] The Aspíllagas placed a great deal of hope in this arrangement, writing that "the only salvation that is certain is that Oliphant [*sic*] has already sent the first shipment from China."[37] However, their hopes ended in bitter disappointment, as Olyphant only delivered one Chinese on the first voyage, and none at all on the second.[38]

Because new workers could not be imported, the work force at Cayaltí grew increasingly older, resulting in the expulsion of the most unproductive laborers. As the number of workers declined, the Aspíllagas became genuinely concerned over their ability to maintain production levels.[39] A short-term solution occurred, however, when the Chileans ransacked several estates during the War of the Pacific and temporarily displaced many Chinese workers who could then be contracted by surviving planters.

Although Cayaltí escaped serious damage during the war, the Chileans overran the Aspíllagas' small cotton plantation (Palto) located near Pisco as well as many other estates all along the coast. In many cases, Chinese workers welcomed the Chileans as liberators and helped them to burn and loot.[40] To prevent Palto's workers from running off, Ismael Aspíllaga Barrera boldly rushed south, transferring as many workers as possible to Cayaltí. He was also able to contract many Chinese from the Lima area because of the growing number of refugees. Contracted workers were offered advances of up to 50 soles, and *libres* a maximum of twice that amount. Beginning in February 1881, Ismael dispatched small groups of Chinese, ranging from ten to thirty, by steamship from Lima to Cayaltí. In this fashion, the Aspíllagas were able to maintain the size of their work force close to prewar levels.[41]

After the War of the Pacific, the system of wage labor changed significantly, as contracted Chinese (*chinos contratados de la hacienda*) were replaced by *chinos libres* and especially by a new type of worker, Chinese controlled by Chinese contractors (*chinos contratados de los contratistas*). The passing of Chinese workers contracted to the estate can be attributed to a number of causes. First, in practice this type of contract was simply an extension of indentured servitude, which entailed certain political risks for planters. Second, many contracted Chinese accumulated substantial debts, which they may have had trouble repaying as they grew older and less capable of working.[42] Third, by 1881 wages paid to free Chinese workers had fallen to 40 centavos a day with ration, a decrease of over 40 percent, which reflected their growing numbers and advancing age.[43] And, fourth, the Chinese themselves probably did whatever they could to change their status from contracted to free.

Although the number of *chinos libres* increased, their number was superseded by laborers controlled by Chinese contractors. This development was linked to the displacement of large numbers of Chinese during the war, and to the attraction of employment during a period of extreme economic and political chaos.

Contractors were an important new ingredient in the labor picture at Cayaltí and elsewhere. Their existence proves that not all Chinese in Peru were simple laborers, and also shows, as the following chapter makes clear, that the Chinese were willing to exploit each other. Chinese contractors were merchants who traded in both goods and men.[44] They almost undoubtedly had come to Peru as indentured servants and through guile, work, and resourcefulness, had managed to escape the bonds of the plantation and to accumulate small amounts of capital.

Judging from their altered names (Guillermo Pastor, Fructuoso Baca, Acon Bolivia),[45] they demonstrated a willingness to compromise culture for profit. The fact that they negotiated contracts with planters also shows that

Table 30
Composition of the Work Force at Cayaltí, 1877-1882

Date	Total No. Chinese	% Total Work Force	No. Contracted Chinese	% Total Chinese	No. *Libres*	% Total Chinese	No. Peruvians	% Total Work Force	Total No. Workers
Sept. 1877	424	95.3					21	4.7	445
Oct. 1879	413	91.6	375	90.8	38	9.2	38	8.4	451
Sept. 1881	438	98.4	375	85.6	63	14.4	7	1.6	445
June 1882	407	91.7	342	84.0	65	16.0	37	8.3	444

Sources: AH to AH, 11 September 1877, AFA; AH to AH, 14 October 1879, AFA; AH to AH, 27 September 1881, AFA; unsigned letter dated 8 June 1882, AFA.

they had acquired the linguistic skills necessary for their trade.

Chinese contractors first appeared at Cayaltí in October of 1884. At the time, the estate was suffering from a labor shortage that had delayed planting and development of a rice farm needed to help feed workers. Antero Aspíllaga Barrera had heard about the existence of Chinese contractors and he circulated a notice throughout the department offering them the right to operate stores on Cayaltí in exchange for supplying Chinese workers. Within a short period of time, several contractors accepted the offer.[46]

The Aspíllagas always signed agreements with contractors that stipulated the terms under which workers were to be brought to Cayaltí. In a standard contract signed in 1884, a contractor agreed to supply forty Chinese laborers as soon as possible and to increase this number to eighty over a longer period of time. He guaranteed that these workers would work where needed, complete a regular workday (in this case, 6:00 a.m. to 11:00 a.m., then 12:30 p.m. to 6:00 p.m.), and work at least five days a week. He also agreed that they would live in a separate neighborhood (*barrio*), and construct their own living quarters with materials provided by the estate. Moreover, the contractor consented to post a bond worth the value of all farm tools issued to his workers, to cover losses and damages, and to present personally to the Aspíllagas all workers' complaints about their jobs. As a final concession, he agreed not to contract any workers from among those already present at Cayaltí.

For their part, the Aspíllagas allowed the contractor to operate a store at Cayaltí to sell whatever products he wished, as long as this arrangement was satisfactory to his workers and he limited sales to them. The owners stipulated, however, that the contractor buy goods from them, unless they could be obtained more cheaply from a third party. The Aspíllagas also agreed to pay all workers' wages directly to the contractor. A daily wage of 60 centavos without ration was settled on. The Aspíllagas further consented to care for sick workers, to provide them with food and medicine, and to advance the contractor funds with which to contract more laborers, although all advances would be subtracted from the wages due his workers the following payday.[47]

Such arrangements gave the Aspíllagas more security in maintaining the size of their work force and transferred some of the responsibility for managing labor over to labor contractors. But by disbursing workers' wages through contractors, the Aspíllagas also increased agents' control over laborers and may have created opportunities for embezzlement.

During the second half of the 1880s, the numbers of Chinese contracted to contractors increased while the size of the free Chinese population was diminishing into insignificance. It was also during these years that the Aspíllagas and other planters began to recruit Peruvian workers from the coast and adjacent highlands (see table 31). This process was accelerated in

Table 31
Composition of the Work Force at Cayaltí, 1885–1890

Date	Free Chinese	% of Total	Chinese Contracted to Contractors	% of Total	Peruvians	% of Total	Total No. of Workers
Sept. 1885	178	31.6	202	35.8	184	32.6	564
March 1888	78	14.3	215	39.4	252	46.2	545
Nov. 1890	36	1.0	302	59.0	224	40.0	560

Sources: AH to AH, 25 September 1886, AFA; AH to AH, 23 March 1888, AFA; AH to AH, 12 November 1890, AFA.

the following decade, as Chinese workers became less productive and improving economic and political conditions justified increased expenditures on labor.[48]

As the Chinese grew older and weaker, they found it difficult to work more than a few days a week. For example, in June 1891 an Aspíllaga complained that only 300 of the 420 Chinese at Cayaltí actually worked, and that 50 percent of the work force was "already old and tired men."[49] Absenteeism became such a serious problem, especially on Mondays, that milling sometimes had to be stopped. In March of 1892, Baldomero Aspíllaga Barrera held an emergency meeting with the Chinese contractors to warn them that the estate was alarmed over high rates of absenteeism and to threaten to close down their stores if the problem continued. More *mayordomos* were assigned to monitor Chinese workers, but increased vigilance could not solve a problem created by exhaustion and aging.[50] As absenteeism continued, the Aspíllagas expressed their frustration and anger by ordering *mayordomos* to drive the Chinese out into the fields with clubs and whips.[51]

The inability of the Chinese to work at all jobs compounded the problem of absenteeism. Complaints mounted that they could do only light work, such as fertilizing, and by the end of the decade only the strongest could complete a meager one-half *tarea* in the field.[52] It was in this context that the Aspíllagas became increasingly critical of the Chinese and enthusiastic about Peruvian workers.[53]

By 1895 there were approximately five hundred Peruvian highlanders working at Cayaltí, and for the first time the Aspíllagas could complain about a labor surplus.[54] Under these circumstances, Chinese workers became expendable, and later that year the Aspíllagas antagonized Chinese contractors by restricting their rights to sell goods on the estate.[55]

By 1897 the Chinese population at Cayaltí had been reduced to 240, of whom only 50 percent worked at any one time.[56] Two years later the Aspíllagas notified all Chinese contractors that they would have to close down their stores by 6 February 1899,[57] thereby prompting all but one to leave Cayaltí with his workers in tow. The Aspíllagas commented that "only those Chinese of Fructuoso Baca and a few of the veteran *libres* [*los antiguos de la Hacienda*] who perform useful services, such as tractor operators, shall remain. We will pay what they owe in debts to their contractors, so that they might remain of their own free will."[58] The last mention of the Chinese at Cayaltí came in 1907 when, during a general reduction of the work force, thirty were expelled from the estate.[59]

Conclusion

Chinese wage laborers played a pivotal role in the development of Peruvian coastal agriculture during the second half of the nineteenth century. Indentured servants, recruited from a war-torn China, filled the vacuum created by the decline of the black slave population. The coolie trade flourished with the help of Chinese warlords and labor agents, Portuguese traders on Macao, and various European merchants who transported the Chinese across the ocean.

The end to the trade in 1874 caused tremendous concern among Peruvian planters, who did not have an alternative source of labor. Moreover, labor shortages were compounded by a general economic crisis caused by the Panic of 1873, the end of the guano boom, and the War of the Pacific.

Those planters who survived the crisis continued to rely on Chinese workers into the 1890s. At first, they simply extended the contracts of indentured servants and hired small numbers of wage laborers, the so-called *chinos libres*. However, during the Chilean invasion of 1880, large numbers of Chinese laborers were displaced from plantations. Many of these men came under the control of Chinese contractors, who sold their labor to planters.

The Chinese who made the journey across the Pacific brought with them a proud culture formed over centuries. They entered into a very difficult existence on Peruvian sugarcane plantations, working under patrons who, just a few years earlier, had relied almost exclusively on black slave labor. The struggle of the Chinese to maintain their culture in a hostile and alien environment, and the methods of social control they encountered, are topics essential to their experience and to the history of the Peruvian sugar industry.

6. Culture and Social Control, 1865-1905

The Aspíllagas viewed the economic contribution of Chinese laborers as fundamentally important to the survival and eventual success of Cayaltí. The success of Cayaltí, they firmly believed, would eventually make them rich and thus serve as a stepping-stone into the coastal oligarchy and positions of political power. Many of the sugar barons of their generation, all of whom benefited from Chinese labor, joined them in this rise to social, economic, and political prominence as the nineteenth century advanced.

The economic contribution of the Chinese is clear, but much less is known of their material and cultural experience at Cayaltí. No written testimony by the Chinese themselves has been found. However, the Aspíllagas did make regular observations about the behavior of the Chinese and the need to control and keep them. From these accounts it is possible to conclude that the Chinese attempted to maintain important aspects of their traditional culture while leading an uncertain existence, caused by the prevalence of serious diseases, largely inadequate services, and a harsh system of private justice.

The Aspíllagas were well aware of the difficult conditions under which their workers lived and worked, but concluded that "semislavery," as they described it, was necessary to maintain profits and to assure their eventual success. They also relied on their belief in the racial and ethnic inferiority of the Chinese as further justification for their labor regime, despite first-hand evidence of the intelligence and skill of the Chinese as workers and merchants.

Quality of Life

The Chinese lived in poorly constructed housing, which was frequently in need of repair, and low wages and the unavailability of goods in the estate store severely restricted what they could purchase. This situation stood in stark contrast with that of the Aspíllagas, who lived in a mansion, ate fruit from their private orchard, and drank wines imported from southern Peru and abroad.

Housing

In fulfillment of their contractual obligation, the Aspíllagas provided indentured servants with housing.[1] After indentureships had effectively expired by the mid-1870s, the Chinese continued to live in the same housing, as well as in some new units they themselves constructed.

The Chinese were segregated from Peruvians into neighborhoods, which the Aspíllagas gave exotic names, such as "Barrio Pekín." Within these districts, Chinese lived in large, flimsily constructed barracks called *galpones*, which were also commonly given names that evoked the Orient, such as "Galpón de los Cantones."[2]

Management typically crowded over two hundred Chinese into a single *galpón*. The only modicum of privacy some of them received came in a dormitory built in 1884 in which sections were partitioned off, with five persons occupying each area. This *galpón* was the best on the estate, and the Aspíllagas congratulated themselves for constructing it. It featured elevated bunks, a zinc roof, and a nearby canal where the inhabitants could relieve themselves.[3] Four years later, the owners did extensive repair work on another *galpón* and commented on the fine quality of the building materials, which consisted of clay, cane, branches from thorny bushes, and grass for the roof. In retrospect, these materials seem to have been quite ordinary, and one wonders what other dormitories were built of.[4]

Because of their crude construction, *galpones* were susceptible to rapid deterioration and, during inclement weather, to severe damage. In 1892, for example, the left side and part of the roof of the "Galpón de Pekín" collapsed during a rainstorm. Seven living quarters were completely destroyed and several persons were seriously injured. Moreover, the failure to repair the *galpón* properly resulted in a second collapse during a rainstorm in 1899.[5]

Material Possessions

There is little doubt that the Chinese had virtually nothing to put into their dilapidated homes. This was the result not only of low wages but also of the unavailability of goods. Moreover, as I shall show in the following section, the Chinese also spent money on opium and games of chance, which limited their ability to buy other things.

Because indebted Chinese were not allowed to leave the estate, their purchases were limited to what they could buy on Cayaltí itself. From the mid-1870s until the late 1890s there were four stores at Cayaltí, one run by the estate and three by Chinese contractors.[6] In addition, residents of Saña occasionally came to Cayaltí to sell goods, including cigarettes and opium, and residents of Cayaltí sometimes purchased goods on the estate and resold them for a profit.[7]

By the mid-1890s new stores were opening up and old ones were closing in response to the changing character and size of the estate.[8] The Aspíllagas viewed the exodus of the Chinese contractors as an opportunity to enlarge their own store and profit more from sales.[9] At the same time, however, they chose not to assume a monopoly, but allowed contractors from the highlands to open stores on Cayaltí and to sell goods that appealed to highlanders.[10] Management characterized these stores as small-scale operations with the dual purpose of making money and facilitating indebtedness.[11]

None of these stores had impressive stocks. By the late 1890s Chinese contractors were reduced to selling pork and opium on a small scale.[12] At the same time, the only articles available at the estate store were *aguardiente, pisco* (a domestic brandy), domestic wine, vinegar, and kerosene. The Aspíllagas stated that they hoped to increase the stock to include good liquor, pork, sardines, salmon, and paper lamps.[13] Even with the expanded list of goods, however, there remained only a few items available for purchase, and some of them might not have appealed to the Chinese, perhaps demonstrated by the fact that the Aspíllagas never made much money from their store. They continually wrote of expected profits that never accrued, despite standard markups of 20 percent to 25 percent. Slack sales and mismanagement would seem to have been the primary causes.[14]

Cultural Life

There is not a great deal of information available on the quality of life of the Chinese, but there is even less on their cultural life. The Aspíllagas were not curious or interested in Chinese culture, but generally viewed behavior patterns and appearances that deviated from what they were used to as abnormal. This did not lead to lengthy discussions in their correspondence; however, it is possible to piece together enough information to show that, when given the choice, Chinese attempted to retain their traditional culture. The result was a mixture of conformity, nonconformity, and deviant behavior.

Dress

Most Chinese had no choice but to dress like lower-class Peruvians. As indentured servants, they were sold clothing by the Aspíllagas, who were supposed to distribute it free, according to the contract of indentureship. The Aspíllagas purchased clothing in Lima, probably cotton, owing to the hot climate. Unfortunately, the value or quality of the clothing is unknown, although the Chinese did express a preference for durable clothes that would not tear easily while working. The Aspíllagas evidently generally honored this preference, although in January of 1865 they forced about one hundred Chinese to take inferior clothing.[15]

After indentured servitude had been phased out, preferences in dress do not seem to have changed. For example, photographs taken of Chinese on north coast sugar plantations around the turn of the century show them dressed in Peruvian-style clothing consisting of loose-fitting pants and shirts and broad straw hats.[16] Moreover, Ernst Middendorf observed that almost all Chinese dressed like Peruvians, except for a few wealthy ones and older indentured servants, who managed to retain their traditional dress.[17]

Diet

Adjustments in dress do not seem to have been a difficult change for the Chinese. They were, however, more hesitant to change their traditional diet. The main staples of China have been rice and pork. At Cayaltí and elsewhere the standard ration given to Chinese (and others) was one pound of beef and one and one-half pounds of rice for one day's work.[18] The Chinese, however, eschewed beef in favor of pork, and were able to cultivate, in the Chicama Valley at least, Chinese vegetables.[19]

At Cayaltí, pork could be purchased in the stores run by Chinese contractors. Contractors raised and slaughtered the hogs themselves, and the Aspíllagas commented that pork was the most popular product sold by the Chinese.[20] It is significant that the Chinese spent money for pork when they regularly received free beef. Diets were clearly more difficult to change than clothing.

Family

Diet and dress were two aspects of the cultural life of the Chinese that the Aspíllagas noted, because those aspects involved the selling and buying of goods. The Aspíllagas had much less to say about less obvious things, especially private ones. Nevertheless, the little that is known about family and religion, for example, is important, because of the obvious importance to the Chinese themselves.

Of the hundreds of thousands of Chinese who emigrated to the New World, only a handful were women. Of the 100,000 Chinese who came to Peru, for example, only 15 were women, and in Cuba, the census of 1872 lists only 32 Chinese women as compared to 58,368 Chinese men.[21] This must have put a terrible strain on the Chinese, because few married outside of their race. This unhappy circumstance seems to have been the result of lack of opportunity reinforced by a reluctance by both Chinese and Latin American cultures to accept notions of racial equality.[22] Nevertheless, some Chinese in Peru managed to deal with sexual tensions through homosexual behavior, and some others did marry or have extramarital relationships.

There are several references to homosexuality among the Chinese in Peru. The Aspíllagas called some Chinese at both Cayaltí and Palto homosexuals, and Middendorf commented on homosexuality among Chinese in Peru as a whole.[23] Still, others were able to marry or to have sexual relations with lower-class Peruvians, including blacks. For example, Alfredo

Sacchetti, writing in the *Boletín del Ministerio de Fomento* in 1905, ascribed the "progressive degeneration" of the Chinese to the fact that some had bred with blacks and Indians.[24] Then there is the sad case of the Chinese at Cayaltí who contracted syphilis, a sure sign of sexual contact.[25]

Of more significance, however, is the fact that mass marriages were arranged between Chinese and Indians at Casa Grande. The matchmaker was a Chinese contractor who, for a small advance, would travel to the highlands and return with the requisite number of highland women willing to wed Chinese. Middendorf then witnessed what followed:

When the recruits have arrived they are placed in a room with their faces toward the wall. Immediately thereafter the grooms enter the room and are lined up against the wall opposite the highland women, with their faces turned toward the wall, and each one directly opposite a woman. Then the contractor claps his hand, which is the signal for everyone to turn around, and those who face each other have to become man and wife. Luck's judgment permits no appeal.[26]

Religion

Formalized religion obviously did not enter into these marriages, or into many other aspects of the daily lives of the Chinese, as far as can be told. Most Chinese who came to Peru were Buddhists, and it is likely that they retained their faith, managing their own spiritual lives without the help of clergy. In China religion was a personal experience largely practiced within the home, where families maintained shrines.[27] There is no reason why they could not have done this in Peru. The only reference found to any type of formal worship, in fact, is Thomas Hutchinson's observation that there were temples (joss houses) in the Cañete Valley.[28]

Few Chinese at Cayaltí abandoned Buddhism for Catholicism, despite the efforts of missionaries and the Aspíllagas. For example, throughout the 1890s only nineteen Chinese converted out of a population of several hundred.[29] Baldomero Aspíllaga Barrera agreed to become the godfather of five who accepted Christianity in December 1900, even giving two of them the Aspíllaga name.[30]

Recreation and Drug Abuse

The same type of cultural resistance can be seen in other aspects of the Chinese experience. For example, the Chinese chose to celebrate Chinese New Year, as opposed to the traditional Christian holidays, which were important occasions for Peruvians at Cayaltí.[31] Moreover, the Chinese showed a preference for opium over alcohol and coca, which were plentiful and popular among Peruvians. The Chinese also exhibited a penchant for gambling, which was common in China, but evidently not among lower-class Peruvians, as the day of the lottery had not yet arrived.[32]

The Chinese played games of chance in *galpones* and in the stores run by

Chinese contractors.[33] The Aspíllagas, who owned race horses, characterized gambling among Chinese as a great vice, sarcastically calling it their main goal in life. For example, in 1882 an Aspíllaga wrote, "The *chinos libres*, with complete homage to their vices, burned out desire for work, and the only stimulus that they have to make money, which is gambling, are workers who each day are more repugnant and give less hope for the estates."[34] Five years later another Aspíllaga elaborated: "The Chinese is cheap and has only one notion of how to better himself—not through saving or by working but to search for happiness in the unforeseen disaster of gambling."[35]

The Aspíllagas considered gambling among Chinese to be a vice because it distracted them from their work. The owners of Cayaltí were not dedicated moralists but ambitious capitalists, clearly shown in their role as opium sellers on Cayaltí.

By the second half of the nineteenth century opium was being smoked on a huge scale in China, in both the countryside and the cities. The British supplied the drug and cultivated opium poppies on plantations in India.[36] It did not take long for British merchants, who already had strong commercial and financial ties in Peru, to discover that the opium market could be expanded to include Chinese on the other side of the Pacific (see table 32).

The Peruvian government controlled all opium sales through the licensing of retailers, who held monopoly rights over given areas.[37] For example, the Aspíllagas had the exclusive right to sell opium on Cayaltí.[38] For the owners of Cayaltí, selling opium was never a big money-making operation in itself; however, by encouraging its consumption, they forced many Chinese into debt, which helped bind labor to the estate during periods of labor shortage.[39]

The Aspíllagas apparently purchased most of their opium from H. R. Kendall & Sons of Liverpool, through whom they also sold most of their sugar.[40] However, in a pinch, the Aspíllagas did occasionally buy from locals, such as Wing On Ching & Cía. and Vigilio Dall'Orso of Piura, at higher prices.[41]

Despite their official monopoly and tight control over the events on the estate, the Aspíllagas initially had a problem with the sale of contraband opium. In July of 1875, however, Antero Aspíllaga Barrera effectively undercut the trade by instituting payment in script to indentured servants. The tactic was so successful that Antero called it "una magnífica medida" ("a magnificent measure").[42] The contraband trade never fully recovered even after script was no longer used, because of increased vigilance and frequent visits by government inspectors (*visitadores del estanco*).[43]

By virtue of their monopoly, the Aspíllagas earned a reasonable profit from selling opium. Until the 1890s, the Chinese consumed between 100 and 150 pounds of opium a month.[44] Standard markups brought the Aspíllagas between 2 and 4 soles profit per pound of opium sold, or between

Table 32
British Opium Sales to Peru

Year	Quantity (lbs.)
1853	744
1854	2,079
1855	2,793
1856	1,125
1857	3,152
1858	3,493
1859	6,224
1860	16,041
1861	7,704
1862	3,243
1863	?
1864	3,700
1865	4,535
1866	3,880
1867	10,136
1868	8,147
1869	3,876
1870	22,201
1871	52,422
1872	70,657
1873	59,473
1874	66,085
1875	65,833
1876	67,744
1877	63,130
1878	121,585
1879	97,399
Total	767,401

Source: Pablo Macera, *Las plantaciones azucareras en el Perú, 1821–1875* (Lima: Biblioteca Andina, 1974), p. cxviii.

200 and 400 soles a month.[45]

For the Chinese, opium represented a major expense. During the 1870s the standard price for an ounce of opium fluctuated between 70 and 80 centavos.[46] By the end of the decade, however, it had risen to between 1.20 sols and 1.70 sols; and it fluctuated between 91 centavos and 1.10 sols between 1891 and 1893.[47] Based on the amount of opium consumed, it is very probable that most Chinese smoked it. During the late 1870s and early 1880s there were, on the average, 410 Chinese at Cayaltí. During this period a minimum of 1,200 pounds of opium was consumed each year.

Therefore, per capita consumption would have amounted to about 2.9 pounds a year, which, using a value of one sol per ounce, would come to 46.4 soles. During this period, contracted Chinese represented, on the average, 86.8 percent of the Chinese population. Total yearly wages for these laborers was only 48.60 soles.[48]

Between 1885 and 1890 the average number of Chinese at Cayaltí declined to 337. The Aspíllagas continued to import the same amount of opium, however, so that per capita consumption would have increased to 3.6 pounds a year. Again using a value of one sol per ounce, 3.6 pounds would have cost 57.60 soles. By 1885 chinos libres and Chinese contracted to the estate had been replaced by Chinese controlled by contractors. Total yearly wages for these laborers were significantly higher than for their predecessors, but still only between 145 and 226 soles.[49]

For all of the Chinese, but especially for contracted Chinese, it would have been very difficult, if not impossible, to have purchased opium only with their wages. Although the estate provided them with many things, including housing, food, and some medical care, they still had to buy clothing and they preferred pork to beef, which was part of their wage. It should also be emphasized that total yearly wages given here represent a full year's employment, and, as I have shown, very few Chinese worked a full year.[50] As a result, it seems likely that almost all Chinese had to borrow money to smoke opium. Indebtedness, of course, bound them to the estate, and as long as they remained addicted to opium, their bondage would have been indefinite.

For the Aspíllagas, keeping the Chinese on Cayaltí during periods of labor shortage was a considerable bonus. It is, however, ironic that the Aspíllagas never discussed in their correspondence the correlation between the consumption of opium and decreasing work output, which was a major preoccupation.[51] If they did see the correlation, they must have concluded that it was better to have debilitated laborers securely bound to the estate than to risk their departure.

After 1890 opium consumption decreased along with the size of the Chinese population. Its sale had become so unimportant to the Aspíllagas that they even allowed Chinese contractors to sell it.[52] By then, because of increased contact with highlanders, some Chinese actually began to chew coca, which was undoubtedly extremely cheap, and to drink inexpensive alcohol.[53] It should be noted, however, that these examples of acculturation came when the Chinese population was considerably reduced and debilitated. Within a few years, there would be no more Chinese at Cayaltí.[54]

Health and Health Care

The use of opium undoubtedly contributed to the weakened condition of the Chinese, who were already subjected to a variety of serious diseases.

The Aspíllagas, however, expressed little concern over the health of their laborers, except to complain when they were unable to work.[55] They offered no personal or paternal sentiment, only a firm commitment to keeping the estate running. This attitude is reflected in the quality of health care at Cayaltí. There were inadequate shelter and sanitation, but the Aspíllagas did see the necessity for maintaining a physician and a modest medical facility, which they expanded over time.

The health problems that threatened to engulf Cayaltí were present throughout the country. This was especially the case in the hot coastal valleys, where virulent Old World diseases such as malaria, smallpox, and yellow fever were depressingly commonplace. Such malevolent pests persisted in large part because of the lack of vaccine and because of deplorable sanitary conditions that facilitated the spread of infection. Although the Spanish Crown began to distribute smallpox vaccine toward the end of the colonial period, that policy was discontinued by the Republic during the nineteenth century.

Moreover, sanitation problems were disgustingly apparent and posed health problems wherever people congregated, especially in cities. Sewage disposal was capricious, and drinking water was scarce and sometimes contaminated. The government did not have the money to make improvements, and during this politically turbulent period, sanitation and health care did not stand high on its list of priorities. Finally, toward the end of the nineteenth century, a reorganized Peru began the long process, still far from complete, of cleaning up Lima. Sewage disposal and water supply were improved, and innoculation against smallpox became mandatory. Although noteworthy, these improvements were isolated and never completely alleviated the threat of epidemic.[56]

The government was, of course, even less concerned with health conditions on isolated plantations. There, sanitation and health care were the sole responsibilities of planters. At Cayaltí there were several specific causes of illness among the Chinese. First, some of them were sick when they arrived at the estate from their trans-Pacific voyage. In August of 1864, for example, out of a shipment of twenty Chinese, seven were ill, one seriously enough to die shortly after arrival.[57] Once on the estate, the hot climate invited the outbreak of disease, especially during the summer.[58] Furthermore, unsanitary conditions in the *galpones* provided fertile breeding grounds for bacteria, as wastes did not properly drain away from living quarters.[59] Disease-carrying mosquitoes also found irrigation canals perfect places in which to breed, and food spoilage and unclean drinking water further contributed to the unhealthy environment.[60]

As a result of these conditions, there were several recurring diseases that took the lives of laborers, the most serious being typhus, dysentery, typhoid, malaria, and influenza.[61] For example, the influenza epidemic of April and

May 1890 affected about 50 percent of the Chinese community and kept several hundred men out of work for more than two weeks.[62] Two years later, another influenza epidemic took the lives of several Chinese, although not as many as died at the nearby estate of Tumán.[63] Sporadically through the years, other laborers died of syphilis, liver ailments, meningitis, tuberculosis, and one from an epileptic seizure. Other deaths, which could not be accurately diagnosed, were attributed to "suffocation," "seizures," and the like.[64]

It is impossible to know with absolute accuracy how many Chinese died during a given year. The best data available are for the period from September 1877 to October 1878, when fourteen Chinese died of various diseases in the estate medical facility, which the Aspíllagas called, with great exaggeration, a hospital. Many other deaths could have gone unreported.[65]

It is also difficult to judge how many Chinese were ill at one time. It is known that as much as 10 percent of the entire Chinese population was at times in the estate medical facility.[66] Nevertheless, this cannot be taken as an absolute figure, because many Chinese expressed a reluctance to enter the hospital, and those who were continually criticized by the Aspíllagas as being "exhausted" or "lazy" were in all probability sick.[67]

Faced with such a wide variety of disease and the need to keep the estate going year round, the Aspíllagas had to take some measures to treat the ill. Therefore, they provided a facility where the sick could receive rudimentary treatment from a physician. Although the presence of a doctor was unusual and commendable, Cayaltí's physicians were generally incompetent, a reflection of the state of the profession and of the undesirability of working on an isolated plantation.

The reign of inadequate doctors began very early. In April 1876 the physician was fired for incompetence and "vile habits."[68] His successor was no better, lasting for less than a month before being recognized as a "quack."[69] The Aspíllagas then hired a doctor from Saña who made periodic visits to the estate for two years, before he, too, after several strong reprimands, was dismissed for his mistakes.[70] His replacement seems to have lasted for over ten years, but only because management lost hope of finding someone better. When this man was fired in 1894, the Aspíllagas criticized him in the strongest terms, branding him incompetent, unrespected by his peers, and as a man who associated with the most "inferior" people on the estate.[71]

By the late 1880s the owners had come to the realization that they would have to invest more in medicine. In doing so, they were motivated primarily by the increased dangers of epidemic brought about by the growth of the estate population and by the outbreak of smallpox and cholera in the region.[72] The Aspíllagas first had their laborers innoculated against smallpox in 1894, and again in 1896.[73]

Although this was a major improvement, health conditions and medical care remained basically poor. During the summer, in particular, many people became ill and died. For example, during April and May of 1897 twenty-four persons died from an undiagnosed "fever."[74] One is led to conclude that the Aspíllagas stopped short of a full commitment to improved health care. They frequently stated that the main reasons for illness among the Chinese were their unhealthy habits and ignorance, and not unsanitary housing, harsh working conditions, drug use, and the like.[75]

Moreover, many of the improvements simply came too late to help the Chinese. By the late 1890s, most Chinese were already middle-aged or old and therefore more susceptible to disease, despite the improvements that had been made.[76]

Methods of Control

An equally important facet of the Chinese experience is the private system of justice that governed Cayaltí, and the lack of freedom associated with it. Primarily because of this system, the Chinese experience lies somewhere between that of the black slaves who preceded them and the Peruvian wage earners who followed. It is an experience that reflects a stage in the development of Peru characterized by little government control (and great disorganization), as well as by the lack of working-class consciousness. Moreover, at Cayaltí the added ingredient was the Aspíllagas' belief that the Chinese were racially and ethnically inferior, and therefore undeserving of better treatment. The contradictions in their argument are particularly instructive, because they accentuate the contradictions in the entire plantation economy.

Physical abuse of laborers usually resulted from mistakes in work, personal pique, or crime. For many years, the Aspíllagas attempted to monopolize the authorization of punishment, rarely turning over suspected criminals to the courts. In part, this attitude reflected the political chaos of the period, particularly during the Chilean occupation, when public authority periodically vanished and private citizens were compelled to act on their own. However, the Aspíllagas also believed that they had the right and responsibility to judge and punish to maintain authority on the estate.

To maintain their position as the sole source of punishment, the Aspíllagas attempted to prevent unauthorized beatings by *mayordomos*, which could lead to worker retaliation. Nevertheless, *mayordomos* could not always be prevented from acting on their own. The best example of this is an incident in September 1865, when two *mayordomos* arbitrarily administered one hundred lashes to a Chinese in the afternoon, for the simple reason that one of them did not like the victim, and then beat another

Chinese with a club the following morning for not answering roll call on time. Several Chinese responded by attacking the *mayordomos* with clubs and sticks, but were quickly beaten back by other employees. Ramón Aspíllaga Ferrebú was very upset over the entire episode.[77]

More typically, Chinese were punished on orders from the Aspíllagas for errors on the job, which resulted in losses for the estate, or for crimes that the owners judged them guilty of. For example, management once forced a laborer to work in irons as punishment for negligence that, the Aspíllagas believed, was partially responsible for the death of a co-worker. After an unstated period of time (probably a few days), his irons were removed, less because of his "numerous pleas, weeping and promises," than because he had been "well punished so that he might serve as an example."[78]

Similarly, twice during the period from 1878 to 1888, several other Chinese were punished for starting, or not preventing, fires that destroyed considerable cane acreage. For example, in 1878 management decided that fifteen Chinese should share the blame for a fire that blackened eleven *cuarteles* of cane. The Aspíllagas initially threw the fifteen into the estate jail, but then put them to work in the mill until such time that their debt had been repaid. It is interesting that the Aspíllagas felt so confident in their actions that, in a rare display of legalism, they notified the authorities in Saña of the initial arrest, although no interest was taken in the case.[79]

Ten years later, in a similar case, a Chinese watchman, who was responsible for watching over processed sugar, slept through a fire that destroyed 300 to 400 fanegas of sugar (one fanega equals 157 pounds). This time, the Aspíllagas simply threw the man into the estate jail, never mentioning for how long he would have to remain.[80]

The Aspíllagas' most arbitrary use of power came, however, when they ordered executions as punishment for murder. This occurred only a few times at Cayaltí, although there may be other cases for which there is no record, especially before 1870. The Aspíllagas always carried out a short investigation of the crime then pronounced sentence.

In most cases, murders of Chinese were committed by fellow Chinese. The motives involved were symptomatic of the injustices of the plantation system, in which both murderer and victim were bound. In all cases the Aspíllagas viewed the crime as an attack on society itself and felt that harsh and immediate punishment should be administered so as to provide an example. It is significant, however, that they felt most strongly about this when the victim was something more than a simple laborer. For the Aspíllagas, it was a more serious offense to murder outside of one's class.

In August 1876, a Chinese laborer struck his supervisor three times in the neck and head with a machete, killing him instantly. The motive for the murder was revenge for increasing the amount of weeding, which had been authorized by the estate. The Aspíllagas were particularly upset over the homicide, because the victim had been a "loyal and good servant" who had driven his men to complete their tasks. Just that morning, in fact, Antero had observed how well work was progressing in the victim's section.[81]

After the murder, the killer had fled into the wooded area of the estate. The Aspíllagas immediately ordered *mayordomos* to give chase and to execute the man on capture. They noted that "there is no other recourse so that he might serve as an example to these malicious laborers."[82] As the days passed without the murderer being captured, the Aspíllagas stated,

Much do we lament the death of this good and loyal servant and you can imagine the interest that we have in pursuing the author of the crime, who has disturbed the good progress and order of the estate. The crime, happily, is the work of only one Chinese, it is proven, and you can calm yourselves about the subordination of the rest of the laborers.[83]

After eighteen days of chase, a Chinese informer reported that a Chinese muleteer had given the fugitive refuge. The reaction was swift:

The assassin Aijin rests in peace in the same site where Aun is buried. Thanks to God that the malicious person did not escape, but almost in a providential manner, was apprehended. We are closely watching things and we have in custody the Chinese who gave shelter to the assassin, the muleteer Alan.[84]

No mention was made of the muleteer's fate.

A year later, a Chinese laborer killed a fellow worker, which evoked a different response from the Aspíllagas. Originally, animosity between the two had been aroused because of money one owed to the other. At one point, the debtor had been severely beaten by his creditor. Then, seeking revenge, the debtor plotted to kill the creditor while he rested during lunch. He waited carefully, then bludgeoned him to death. The murderer fled, but several *mayordomos* immediately gave chase on horseback and captured him within a short time. The Aspíllagas wrote Lima that, although they would ordinarily shoot the man, they felt that it might serve a better example if they gave him 150 lashes instead.[85] As they put it,

We have not brought the Chinese Aijin to justice [i.e., shot him] because you know that does not serve as an example to the rest of the Chinese that we have on this estate, which is what there is always need of having for the morality and correction of those who remain.[86]

When the supervisor was murdered, it was imperative to shoot the murderer on sight; however, when the victim was a simple laborer, 150 lashes sufficed.

There were other homicides at Cayaltí that brought interesting reactions from the Aspíllagas. For example, in July 1886, a Chinese merchant from Pucalá was robbed and murdered on Cayaltí. The Aspíllagas took an active role in the investigation, dispatching *mayordomos* into the countryside and mailing circulars informing local authorities of the crime. They felt that they had to do this "to show our Asiatics that we do not look with indifference on these crimes and that they can count on guarantees on this estate, which will justly attract laborers to us."[87]

Then in November 1875, a Chinese, desperate because of his debts, murdered a Peruvian. Ramón Aspíllaga Barrera said that the crime had "morally terrorized him" but that "we are tranquil because we can take sustenance in our good behavior and we ask for the protection of the Lord."[88]

By the end of the 1880s the Aspíllagas had switched tactics in their handling of homicides involving Chinese. For the first time, they began to put murderers at the mercy of the law. This happened first in 1888 and was repeated in 1892 and 1895.[89] Why the change? In all probability, it was in response to the improving political organization of Peru and to pressure from home and abroad to improve the plight of the Chinese.[90] The Aspíllagas did not want to take the risks that they had routinely taken in the past. They also had to consider the possibility of an incident's drawing national, and perhaps international, attention, which might damage the rising political career of Antero Aspíllaga Barrera. It may also be that the Aspíllagas finally recognized that presenting the Chinese with corpses did not prevent murder.

One of the main purposes of the Chinese Commission of 1887 was to investigate charges of the types of abuses described above. The commission, composed of both Chinese and Peruvian officials, found Cayaltí to be a model estate. Its report read, "The Chinese Commission remained completely satisfied of the good treatment that its compatriots receive" at Cayaltí.[91] This judgment was the result not only of a shoddy investigation but of a carefully arranged coverup.

The Aspíllagas were extremely sensitive about this inspection. As late as 1885 they felt that renewed Chinese immigration was not only possible but also crucial to the survival of coastal agriculture. They knew, moreover, that, if a commission uncovered numerous abuses, no new immigration would be possible.[92] Consequently, the Aspíllagas prepared well for the inspection, "covering up all complaints," and impressed the commissioners with their urbanity. The result was the favorable response mentioned above.[93]

Other estate owners were not as successful in hiding their abuses of the Chinese, even from the eyes of the myopic commissioners. Up and down the coast, the commission viewed abuses similar to those that it was unable to see at Cayaltí. On several plantations commissioners found Chinese working in chains or irons, and other laborers complained of having been whipped or imprisoned, and many more of having had their contracts illegally extended. For example, on the plantation Huayto, in the

Department of Lima, several Chinese had been put into chains by order of the owner, Don Octavio Canevaro. The commission ordered that the chains be removed and insisted that Chinese not be chained in the future. It was also at Huayto that the commission uncovered a case of mutilation. It seems that the estate doctor had sliced off the ear of a Chinese "for personal vengeance." The estate owner, however, had done nothing to discipline the doctor, who had fled shortly before the arrival of the officials. The commissioners left the case in the hands of the subprefect of the province.[94]

Despite all of this, the commission concluded that the Chinese were "prosperous" and "well treated" on the plantations. The head of the Peruvian delegation, Escobar y Bedoya, said in a letter to the director general del gobierno that all planters had respected his authority and that he had reached "conciliatory" solutions to the problems that he had encountered. He reserved his only criticism for the Chinese contractors, who, he complained, collected escaped Chinese and moved them from estate to estate so that they could not be captured by their "*patrones*." He also said that contractors were crueler to the Chinese than the most violent planters. He cited a case in La Libertad in which a contractor had shot three escapees, for which he received no punishment, "as if he were an *hacendado*." Escobar y Bedoya ended by recommending that Chinese contractors be outlawed.[95]

Such conclusions can only be ascribed to favoritism. The examples of mistreatment provided in the report itself clearly contradict the finding that the Chinese were "well treated." Moreover, Escobar y Bedoya encountered several problems that he was unable to solve, the most notable being at several major estates in the Chicama Valley, where the Chinese claimed that their contracts had been falsified. Even his criticism of Chinese contractors cannot be accepted at face value, for, although the contractors may have indeed been cruel to Chinese laborers, they would not have existed without the demand for labor created by the Peruvian plantation system.

Furthermore, other evidence from Cayaltí and elsewhere shows that the appearance of the Chinese Commission did not have a sobering effect on the treatment of Chinese by planters. For example, in 1893 the subprefect and the Chinese consul of Trujillo made an inspection tour of the Chicama Valley to determine the working and living conditions of the Chinese. The worst conditions were found on the estate La Viñita, owned and managed by Jesús García y García. The inspectors found that the Chinese had been working with unsigned contracts for a number of years, which, they reasoned, had reduced them to the status of slaves. Moreover, García y García was found to have physically abused five Chinese, who had been whipped, chained, and thrown into the estate jail. One Chinese had actually been incarcerated for fifteen years and three of the others for approximately nine years. The reaction of García y García to the formal charges brought against him was typical of the planter class: he said that as far as he was concerned, the contracts were legal and that was all that counted on his estate. As for the use of corporal punishment, he said that it was necessary to maintain order. There were no problems between him and his laborers; in fact, they all lived happily together side by side.[96] Unfortunately, the final outcome of the case is not known.

Alternatives

Not all Chinese labored on plantations. Some succeeded in becoming labor contractors and merchants, and others worked as wage earners in urban areas. Nonetheless, for plantation workers the alternatives to a life of labor were not really alternatives at all, but desperate reactions to a miserable situation. They were, in fact, some of the same responses that black slaves had to the plantation system: suicide, escape, murder, and rebellion.

When given the opportunity, the Chinese often sought revenge against the plantation system and the society it represented. This could take the form of either individual murders or massive rebellion. I have already mentioned two murders at Cayaltí, one involving a Chinese merchant and another a Peruvian, which fall into this category. In addition, I encountered two other cases, one much more significant than the other. The least important involved the murder of a *mayordomo* at Chiquitoy by several Chinese under his control in September 1887. According to a newspaper account, the *mayordomo* had ordered a field, which had just been completed, reworked, thereby sparking an outburst of anger by laborers, who hacked him to death with their hoes. An editorial in the Trujillo paper *El Tiempo* argued that the presence of the Chinese Commission had enticed the Chinese to commit the crime.[97]

Of greater significance, however, was the murder of the owner of Pucalá, an Izaga. George R. Fitz-Roy Cole described the incident:

The father of one of the writer's companions in this expedition [José María Izaga] was killed by his own Chinamen in an outburst of vindictive passion, when the coolies conspired together to revenge the harsh treatment they had received, and breaking into the house, beat their master to death with their farm tools. This was after long endurance; for one of the punishments this man had imposed on any coolie whom he had caught in the act of escaping was to hobble him with an iron chain, forcing him to work as usual with this heavy weight added, until he considered his punishment sufficient. For lighter offenses he used to beat them unmercifully, and curtail their rations to the starvation point. This went on till even the long-suffering Chinaman's patience was exhausted, and, rousing himself one morning, he avenged himself in the summary fashion already related.[98]

On rare occasions, the Chinese rebelled en masse. As far as can be ascertained, this occurred only twice, once in 1870 and again in the early years of the War of the Pacific. The earlier episode centered in Pativilca and Barranca. Ramón Aspíllaga Ferrebú described it as a "terrible uprising" (*formidable alzamiento*), which prompted him to take special precautions at Cayaltí, in the north, and to advise his son to do likewise at Palto, near Pisco. Unfortunately, I found no further details about the revolt.[99]

As noted earlier, when the Chilean army invaded Peru, many Chinese took up arms on the side of the invaders, helped sack Lima,[100] and put to the torch several plantations near Chimbote and in the Saña Valley.[101]

At Cayaltí, however, the Chinese did not rebel, and only a handful managed to escape as the result of the Chilean invasion.[102] This was indicative of the especially tight security and careful management that characterized the history of the estate during the last quarter of the nineteenth century, as laborers were closely supervised in their work, and *mayordomos* and management were the only ones with access to horses and firearms.

It is significant that all recorded escapes occurred between 1875 and 1882 (see table 33). First, this suggests that Chinese contracted to the estate, owing to lower wages and a harsher system of private justice, had more motive to run away than did Chinese contracted to contractors. Second, it is testimony to the economic and political chaos of the period.

Many runaways who fled Cayaltí sought refuge in the Chinese population in Chiclayo, the closest city.[103] Only once did someone go to Lima, and then only because "he had a woman there."[104] The escape of three Chinese to the Pisco area, and their eventual capture at Palto, was in all probability because they were originally from Palto and still had friends, and perhaps relatives, living there.[105]

On other occasions, the Aspíllagas strongly suspected that runaways had ended up working, either by choice or by coercion, on neighboring plantations. For example, in March 1879 they believed that ten runaways were at Pátapo, Vista Florida, Lurifico, and other plantations.[106] This was a serious problem, because planters rarely returned runaways to their original employers.[107]

Cayaltí always made a major effort to capture runaways and relied basically on two techniques: immediate and thorough searches of the estate and surrounding areas by *mayordomos* on horseback, and the use of informers. If an escape was quickly discovered, then the runaway had little chance to make it off of the estate.[108] However, if he did make it off of Cayaltí, his capture could be very difficult.

In pursuit of runaways, *mayordomos* were instructed to search neighboring villages and estates and were sometimes even told to journey into the sierra.[109] On one occasion, Ramón Aspíllaga Barrera himself took up the hunt for escaped Chinese.[110] Searches were generally accompanied by notices to neighbors that offered rewards for information leading to the

Table 33
Chinese Escapes from Cayaltí

Escapes, 1875–1879	No. Recaptured	% Recaptured	Escapes, 1879–1882	No. Recaptured	% Recaptured
24	8	33.3	21	6	28.6

Source: RAB to AAB, 21 September 1875, AFA; RAB to AAB, 5 October 1875, AFA; RAB to AAB, 8 October 1875, AFA; AH to AH, 8 May 1876, AFA; AH to AH, 21 May 1876, AFA; AAB to AH, 19 June 1876, AFA; AH to AH, 18 July 1876, AFA; AH to AH, 21 February 1877, AFA; AH to AH, 2 June 1877, AFA; AH to AH, 6 July 1877, AFA; AH to AH, 16 July 1878, AFA; AH to AH, 11 September 1877, AFA; AH to AH, 14 September 1877, AFA; AH to AH, 16 October 1880, AFA; AAB to IAB, 3 May 1881, AFA; unsigned letter dated 8 June 1882, AFA.

capture of a runaway.[111]

This paid off at least twice. Most notably, based on information received from the operators of the estate Palomino, the Aspíllagas caught four runaways in October 1875.[112] In another case, an escapee was captured on the outskirts of Chiclayo by a man who was paid a 50 sol reward.[113]

Whenever runaways were captured, they reaped the anger of the Aspíllagas. For example, once during a search in which Ramón Aspíllaga Barrera had participated, *mayordomos* killed a Chinese. Ramón showed no regret but instead rewarded those who had been responsible for the death. He then had the surviving runaways "severely punished" and thrown into the estate jail, where he interrogated them, asking them why they had fled. They answered, "as they always did," that they "were receiving insufficient wages for people." Ramón thought that was ridiculous. He then asked them if someone had paid or forced them to leave Cayaltí, which they felt was ridiculous. Ramón later commented to his brother Antero that, in addition to the punishment that he had given to them, he was certain that God would punish them even more.[114]

Faced with this type of existence, some Chinese at Cayaltí chose to take their own lives. Suicide also occurred among Chinese in Cuba as well as in other parts of Peru. According to Juan Pérez de la Riva, the frequency of suicide among the Chinese in Cuba gave the island the highest suicide rate in the world.[115] Peru must have rivaled Cuba for this dubious distinction, as many Chinese took their own lives on the guano islands, where they were forced to work, eat, and sleep on enormous mounds of bird manure.[116]

At Cayaltí, there were six recorded suicides among the Chinese, but there may have been additional ones for which we have no record. Five of these deaths came from taking massive overdoses of opium.[117] Details are lacking about the immediate causes of most suicides, although one was clearly precipitated by a whipping,[118] and the Aspíllagas thought that another had been brought on by a feeling of hopelessness over debts.[119] However, in other cases, it is arguable that the principal cause was extreme depression caused by a combination of overwork, illness, abuse, or inability to adjust to an alien environment.

Justification

It is important to understand how and why the Aspíllagas, and clearly other sugar planters as well, exercised such control over the lives of the Chinese, who were not chattel. Such an understanding is important, for it provides us with an insight into late nineteenth century Peruvian society, in terms of both labor relations and the character and world view of planters.

One of the most important characteristics shared by all Peruvian plantations was their autonomy. Sugar estates on the northern coast stretched for tens of thousands of acres over coastal valleys that they literally dominated. Moreover, they functioned as independent towns, providing their workers and staff with all necessary goods and services.[120] This function obviously enhanced planters' control over workers.

Moreover, planters' direct control over workers increased during periods of extreme political chaos, such as the years of the Chilean occupation. The disappearance of reliable public authority, for example, gave them the power to carry out executions without fear of prosecution.

The revival of public authority in the 1890s, however, did not significantly delimit their control over workers or their place in society. On the contrary, north coast growers oftentimes served as local officials or determined who would occupy local posts. Furthermore, following the war, several planters, including the Aspíllagas, emerged as major political figures on the national level.[121] The existence of a more stable government, in which planters shared power, assured them considerable support from the state in their business affairs. Laborers suspected of having committed crimes, to use the same example, could now be turned over to public authorities on the reasonable assumption that some form of justice would be done.

The Aspíllagas acknowledged the harshness of their regime of social control, but justified it on the grounds of economic, social, and political expediency. They frequently referred to the Chinese as "semi-men," "semislaves," and as laborers who worked as virtual slaves. They stated, however, that such exploitation was necessary to assure their success, not just the financial success of their estate, which was the first step, but their triumphal entry into the oligarchy and national politics.

The Aspíllagas were by no means the only planters to benefit from the exploitation of Chinese labor. Several sugar planters emerged from this period with their plantations intact and went on to become important politicians who would help to rule Peru, with a hiatus in the 1920s, until the military coup of 1968.

The Aspíllagas' sentiments toward labor were clearly expressed in this letter of May 1878:

It is not necessary to think of slavery, since it exists for but short periods of time; besides we are not the only ones, although they say that to follow the bad example of several is to take the advice of fools. But some need others, and this brings us forward as heroes who search for a sure death in order to live eternally in the pages of history.[122]

Nevertheless, the Aspíllagas did not justify their regime of social control in these terms alone. They also clearly believed that the Chinese were racially and ethnically inferior and therefore less deserving of humane treatment. By 1895 the owners of Cayaltí had already committed themselves to Peruvian labor and could easily have dismissed or pensioned off their remaining Chinese workers. However, there still remained a nagging problem:

As for the Chinese, we find them well, despite their old age, lending good services and they seem content despite their condition as semislaves. We will have to do a good deed some day and give them total liberty, but we encounter an insurmountable barrier—their own vices.[123]

That their own vices made them unworthy of "liberty," or even of more humane treatment was a conviction born of prejudice and one that made it easier for the Aspíllagas to exploit the Chinese. The owners of Cayaltí regularly referred to these men as perverse, lazy, racially degenerate, and dedicated to gambling and opium.[124]

It was particularly difficult for the Aspíllagas to accept suicide among the Chinese. This did not stem from religious conviction, but from a feeling of disgust and displeasure at losing workers.[125] This is how an Aspíllaga responded to one suicide:

One of the most capricious, haughty, and with poor character of the Chinese, only because he had received six lashes . . . poisoned himself. We have lost a laborer, but on the other hand maintained order of production.[126]

In 1893 the Aspíllagas made a general assessment of the Chinese that exemplifies the contradictions in their logic of social control based on racial inferiority:

The Chinese not only trouble us as racial degenerates, but because they can create with time very serious social problems, since they, be it because of their intelligence, or their habits, are absorbing all wholesale and retail businesses, even haciendas, without leaving any permanent benefit for the country, since they, although they could be over eighty years old, once they have money they take it to their country.[127]

Although his statement is clearly an exaggeration, apparently written in a state of mild panic, it provides us with a window into the mentality of the family. Of course, the obvious question is, If the Chinese were unworthy of better treatment because of their racial inferiority and "repugnant vices," then how does one explain their success as businessmen? Clearly, for a Chinese to emerge from indentured servitude to become a prosperous merchant or landowner during a period of crisis required the intelligence, tenacity, and cleverness worthy of a member of the coastal elite.

If pointed out to them, the owners of Cayaltí probably would not have been concerned about their lack of logic, however instructive it is for us in understanding them. The Aspíllaga Barreras were ambitious young men who strove for great success, even a sort of historical immortality, which could best be achieved through turning a profit during a period of great economic and political difficulty. The Chinese were the only readily available source of labor, and they had to be held onto at all costs.

Through the use of Chinese labor and technological innovation, the Aspíllagas succeeded in maintaining production and making money, despite the war and the crisis in the international sugar market. After the turn of the century, their success would be predicated on the recruitment of labor from local communities and the nearby highlands. This switch in labor supply systems would mark a significant transitional phase in the history of Cayaltí and north coast agriculture.

7. Labor Contracting, 1880–1933

As the last few Chinese grew old and weary and were relegated to jobs traditionally reserved for boys, the Aspíllagas were faced with the vexing problem of findng a new source of labor or going out of business. In discussing their future labor needs, they and other planters only gradually abandoned the hope of a labor regime based on servility. The Chinese had rendered good service for decades, and the desire was strong to renew the importation of foreigners. Despite the domestic and international barriers against this, Peruvian planters managed to import several thousand Japanese contract laborers between 1898 and 1923. Although these workers made a significant contribution to coastal agriculture in the central and south-central coastal valleys, the stream of immigration was too slow to satisfy the long-term needs of the plantations.

As a result, all along the coast planters also began to recruit labor from among the highland population of Peru, where the large peasant population constituted a viable labor pool. The process of labor contracting, begun fitfully and with trepidation by the Aspíllagas, eventually satisfied the labor requirements of Cayaltí and other north coast estates.

Labor contracting in Peru, and elsewhere in Latin America, has been referred to as *enganche*, from the verb *enganchar*, meaning "to hook or to entrap." As the pejorative nature of the term indicates, observers have viewed *enganche* negatively since its inception. Peruvian Indianist writers in the early twentieth century criticized *enganche* as semislavery, noting the prevalence of force, deception, and manipulation. A principal point of criticism concerned debt peonage, the process through which wage earners were bound by their debts to estates for long periods of time. More recently, Peter F. Klarén, Ernesto Yepes del Castillo, and others have also emphasized the importance of extraeconomic coercion in *enganche*.[1]

In fact, indebtedness was at the heart of the *enganche* system at Cayaltí and elsewhere in Peru. The fundamental equation involved payment with labor for debts incurred in a variety of ways. However, there is no compelling proof that the Aspíllagas, at least, utilized indebtedness as a master strategy to create a resident work force. Instead, they devised a variety of methods, ranging from physical detention to material incentives.

The recent literature on labor contracting in the Americas has shifted in emphasis to include analyses of the role of the state and the marketplace, although there is considerable disagreement over the relative importance of each.[2] The Peruvian government certainly condoned *enganche* and helped planters control workers, but it did not systematically assist planters in contracting peons. The marketplace, on the other hand, played an important part in *enganche*. At its most fundamental level, the development of labor contracting reflected the linkage of the expanding export sector on the coast with a labor pool in the sierra. Competition for labor among planters helped to determine wages and labor contractors' commissions, and the price of sugar on the world market and resulting profits and losses frequently determined the ability of the Aspíllagas, and presumably of other planters, to pay going rates.

The structure of the labor market was, however, far from perfect. In addition to the use of labor contractors and the prevalence of indebtedness, coercion and trickery were sometimes utilized in recruiting laborers. Moreover, it cannot be assumed that all highland peasants had equal knowledge of or access to employment opportunities on the coast.

Japanese Contract Laborers

Before planters all along the coast became firmly committed to *enganche*, they experimented with Japanese contract laborers, somehow hoping that the Chinese experience could be duplicated. The greatest enthusiasm for Japanese laborers occurred in the Cañete Valley, where the future president of the republic, Augusto B. Leguía, ordered several hundred Japanese for the plantation he was then managing.

The Aspíllagas had the impression that the Japanese were "without a doubt a superior and intelligent race, who will do much good for the industries of the country with their total effort."[3] Within a year, however, all Japanese would be expelled from Cayaltí, accused of being lazier and more inefficient workers than Peruvian peons.

The importation of Japanese to Peru coincided with a second wave of Asian emigration to the New World.[4] This time, however, emigration was not the result of internal disorder in the Orient but of carefully arranged agreements between Japanese emigration companies, chiefly the Morioka Emigration Company, and Peruvian planters. Most of the Japanese who came to Peru were poor farmers and laborers from Okinawa who, it was hoped, would adapt quickly to life on coastal sugarcane plantations. Work contracts stipulated that the Japanese be physically fit, of good character, and between twenty and forty-five years of age. Monthly wages ranged from

2.5 pounds sterling for men to 1.5 pounds sterling for women. Planters agreed to pay for the cost of the voyage to Peru, and emigration companies for the return trip. For each fifty workers delivered, emigration companies supplied a Japanese supervisor conversant in Spanish, who would be paid by the plantation. For their services, the companies received 2.5 pounds sterling for each contracted worker supplied. Workers, for their part, agreed to remain for a period of four years, or forfeit a bond posted in Japan with the emigration company.[5]

Between 1898 and 1923, 17,764 Japanese were imported into Peru, 14,829 by Morioka alone.[6] The majority went to estates on the central and south-central coast, where they worked alongside Peruvian peons. Relations between these workers were not always harmonious, and labor disputes arose over wages and working conditions. Although this was troublesome for planters, many continued to order new shipments of Japanese.

As time went by, however, mounting complaints by Japanese laborers over harsh working conditions and contract violations caused concern in Tokyo. By the 1920s, the flow of immigration to Peru had significantly subsided, and Peruvian wage laborers had come to constitute an overwhelming majority on most estates. Thus, in 1923 both the Peruvian and Japanese governments officially agreed to terminate the emigration of Japanese contract laborers to Peru. Of those Japanese who were still in Peru, some returned home, others migrated to Lima and became merchants and shopkeepers, and still others remained in agricultural regions and became tenant farmers.[7]

On the northern coast, the contribution of the Japanese was minimal. Estates in the Lambayeque Valley ordered from 50 to 75 workers, who, on the average, lasted only a few months. Chicama Valley plantations ordered more Japanese, but had equally disappointing results. For example, at Chiquitoy, of the 450 Japanese who arrived during November and December of 1898, only 47 remained by March 1909.[8]

Cayaltí duplicated this experience. Initially, the Aspíllagas were impressed with the fifty Japanese who arrived in late 1898, and praised their cleanliness and healthy physical appearance.[9] However, once the Japanese were put to work, complaints began to mount about their lack of productivity, as they had difficulty adjusting to the torrid climate and demanding work routine. Although they only completed half as much work as highlanders, they received higher wages, which compounded the problem.

The Aspíllagas complained to Morioka & Company, which agreed to shift the Japanese over to piecework. This, however, only led to further diminution in productivity, as the Japanese resented the increased work load. Outraged, the Aspíllagas resorted to threats and intimidation, which grew worse when they considered that the Japanese served as bad examples for highlanders, who increasingly looked like a superior solution to Cayaltí's labor problems.

After two long months, the Japanese were expelled from the estate. For them, it had also been a disappointing experience. After subtracting what they owed to the estate store for food and clothing, they only received from 4 to 9 soles in wages. If Morioka failed to relocate them in Peru, they also stood to lose their bond posted in Japan.[10] The Japanese experience at Cayaltí only served to disrupt the lives of men desperately in search of a livelihood.

Labor Supply Areas within Peru

The Aspíllagas could afford to be impatient with the Japanese because of the use of Peruvian peons from the highlands, who had been actively recruited to work on the estate since the 1880s. The use of nationals was not a completely new endeavor for north coast planters, who had occasionally hired Peruvians as far back as the seventeenth century. Moreover, during the nineteenth century, small numbers of highlanders would periodically wander down from the mountains looking for short-term employment in between planting and harvesting seasons back home.[11] Now, with all sources of foreign servile and contract labor either unavailable or unsatisfactory, planters had no choice but to exploit the large pool of peasant labor within their own borders.

Coast

Small farmers, tenants, and subtenants on the coast were certainly aware of the employment opportunities on the mammoth plantations that surrounded their farms. They could not avoid knowing something about the economics of plantation agriculture, having regularly fought with planters over land and water rights and watched as blacks, Chinese, and Japanese workers came and went from the big estates. They themselves had occasionally worked on estates, frequently on irrigation canals, where centuries of accumulated experience, passed on through generations, held them in good stead.[12]

As the nineteenth century entered its final decades, coastal planters hoped to employ large numbers of coastal peasants on their estates. As early as 1879, for example, the Aspíllagas had cast a covetous eye toward the inhabitants of the neighboring town of Saña:

The peons and *chinos libres* are behaving well and little by little their numbers will increase—[but] what we want is for all of the Sañeros to become our peons, since they are the most secure and best suited for us because they are the closest.[13]

There is little doubt that the process of land consolidation in the northern valleys created a larger labor pool by divesting peasants of their farms. The town of Saña lost land to Cayaltí, as small farmers in the Chicama Valley lost to Casa Grande. The plantation Laredo also expanded throughout the Moche Valley as the twentieth century advanced. Small farmers proved relatively more tenacious in the Lambayeque Valley, where a few Indian communities had survived the process of land consolidation during the colonial period. However, large estates occupied the best land and received the bulk of the irrigation water, which must have increased the difficulties of farming on a small scale.[14]

Despite this process of proletarianization, the coast did not yield a sufficient number of laborers to meet the needs of sugarcane plantations. In large part, this was a reflection of the relatively low population density (see table 34),[15] but it is also indicative of the inability of planters to turn inhabitants of the coast into peons. This was certainly the case at Cayaltí, and further research may show a similar pattern in adjoining valleys.[16]

According to the Aspíllagas, workers from the coast were unreliable as long-term employees because they refused to work for long periods of time. This clearly frustrated the owners of Cayaltí, who referred to them as zambos, a mildly pejorative terms for persons of mixed Indian and black ancestry. These views are clearly stated in a letter written in 1889:

Those from the coast, or zambos, are scarce. The Sañeros, if you could round up one hundred or so of them, could not be acclimatized in any manner whatsoever, because the majority of them are lazy men who go around looking for a new patrón every week, that is to say looking for where they can do less. At present, with the rice harvest, the work force on the large [sugar] estates always diminishes because of the attraction that this work has for them, but happily this is already passing.[17]

As far as can be determined, the largest number of Sañeros to work at Cayaltí was one hundred in 1923, or 4.6 percent of the work force. In general, it was only during floods or other calamitous times that relatively large numbers of persons from the coast could be found at Cayaltí.[18]

One can speculate that Sañeros were not eager to work for a plantation that had taken their land. But, more important, it is clear that Cayaltí, despite its huge size, did not monopolize the labor market in the Saña Valley. Rather, local peasants periodically sought work on sugarcane plantations in neighboring valleys, or on local rice farms during harvest time.

Largely frustrated at the local level, the Aspíllagas sought to recruit coastal workers from as far away as Piura and Lima, but with even more disappointing results. In March 1894, the Aspíllagas hired, through the services of a labor contractor, sixty-six Limeños to work at Cayaltí.[19] Those assigned to work in the fields had difficulty completing their assignments and were quickly reassigned to jobs in the factory or as assistants to artisans. Fifteen Limeños expressed their unhappiness by fleeing the estate, which made the Aspíllagas pessimistic about the future contribution of those who

Table 34
North Coast Valley Population, 1876

VALLEY/District	Urban Pop.	% of Total	Community Pop.	% of Total	Village Pop.	% of Total	Estate Pop.	% of Total	Total Pop. of District
LAMBAYEQUE/									
Chiclayo	11,826	90.70					1,214	9.30	13,040
Pocsi	513	20.40					2,007	79.60	2,520
Reque			1,209	79.30	316	20.70			1,525
Ferreñafe			7,054	96.20	105	1.40	178	2.40	7,337
Monsefú			7,311	94.80	398	5.20			7,709
Total	12,339	38.40	15,574	48.50	819	2.50	3,399	10.60	32,131
CHICAMA/									
Paiján			2,210	75.00	743	25.00			2,953
Santiago de Cao			1,360	61.30	82	3.70	776	35.00	2,218
Magdalena de Cao			409	44.70	159	17.40	346	37.90	914
Ascope	2,142	39.70					3,258	60.30	5,400
Chicama	345	17.70					1,608	82.30	1,953
Chocope	804	31.50			304	11.90	1,446	56.60	2,554
Total	3,291	20.60	3,979	24.90	1,288	8.00	7,434	46.50	15,992
SANA/									
Lagunas	498	56.10					389	43.90	887
Saña	283	11.80					2,119	88.20	2,402
Total	781	23.75					2,508	76.25	3,289
MOCHE/									
Trujillo	8,228	78.40	144	1.40	526	5.00	1,591	15.20	10,489
Moche	86	6.50	1,151	86.60	8	0.60	84	6.30	1,329
Total	8,314	70.35	1,295	10.95	534	4.50	1,675	14.20	11,818

Source: Census of 1876, the first national census.

remained. To compound these problems, local political opponents of the Aspíllagas viewed the presence of Limeños as evidence of the formation of a private army, and there were rumors that Cayaltí might be invaded in retaliation. The Aspíllagas considered this a serious risk and chose to expel all Limeños from the estate.[20]

Five years later, a labor contractor delivered forty peons to Cayaltí from the Department of Piura located to the north of the Department of Lambayeque. Some of these people were Indians, but the majority, like most coastal inhabitants, were racially mixed. The Aspíllagas branded them poor and unruly workers and quickly dismissed them from the estate. As the following quote from the *administrador del campo* shows, there was an undercurrent of prejudice against these people, which the failure to exploit them fully as laborers may have intensified:

The peons from Piura are of two types: Indians from Catacaos who are good enough workers, although not as good as highlanders, and *zambos*, *mestizos* or *encastados*. These are worthless and I would welcome with great pleasure their departure from the estate. They undermine work routine and more importantly the good order that there has always been here.[21]

Sierra

This critical view of Japanese and coastal workers was clearly formed in a comparative context with highlanders, who, by the 1890s, were being employed by the hundreds on Cayaltí and other north coast estates. In general, highlanders were praised for performing their jobs with skill and vigor and adapting well to managerial control.

The labor of highlanders fueled the development of plantation agriculture all along the coast, as planters reached out into contiguous areas of the highlands to hire peasants for their estates. Sugarcane plantations in the Department of Lambayeque contracted almost exclusively in the Department of Cajamarca, where they competed with one another for labor. They also faced competition from sugar estates in the Chicama and Moche valleys, although these plantations also tapped the labor pool in the highlands of La Libertad.

The large-scale migration of highlanders to the coast is attributable to a number of causes. By the late nineteenth century, the northern highlands was already a relatively populous area, and it underwent rapid demographic growth throughout the twentieth century. It is doubtful that the local economy could have absorbed this increase, since this was an area of primitive agriculture that was already experiencing severe land shortages in some provinces at the turn of the century. Moreover, economic and political instability in the area led to pervasive banditry, cattle rustling, and even civil conflict. It was under these conditions that many highlanders migrated to the coast to earn cash wages.

The northern sierra was significantly more populous than the northern coast. According to the census of 1876, the northern coast had a population of 62,000, compared with 213,000 for the Department of Cajamarca, and 119,000 for the highlands of La Libertad. The Province of Chota in Cajamarca, which became a center for labor contracting, had a population of 51,000. Moreover, the population of the highlands grew at a rapid rate during the twentieth century, despite a massive and continuous out-migration. Thus, the census of 1940 calculated the population of Cajamarca at 568,118, well over a 100 percent increase in less than seventy years. The Province of Chota, which had experienced perhaps the largest out-migration, registered a total of 94,984, nearly a 100 percent increase.[22]

The Department of Cajamarca's economy was predominantly agricultural and pastoral, except for some isolated coal mining in Hualgayoc. Residents of Cajamarca produced wheat, wool, sheep, mules, and minerals, which they sold in adjacent towns and villages as well as in the Amazon basin and on the coast. Revenues earned were primarily spent on the coast for cotton, sugar, salt, clothing, and mining equipment. In 1855 this exchange netted Cajamarca residents a surplus of 175,325 pesos.[23]

Nevertheless, the general pattern for the nineteenth century was one of economic decline. The ranching industry, in particular, suffered greatly. One study estimated, for example, that the number of sheep fell from 350,000 in the early 1880s to 225,000 by 1900.[24] Agricultural production also declined as both large- and small-scale producers continued to rely on primitive methods of cultivation, including wooden ploughs, little or no crop rotation, and poor seed choice.[25] Contemporary observers also complained about poor soils and bad roads in the province of Chota.[26]

Moreover, the pattern of land tenure in Chota, Bambamarca, and Hualgayoc, all principal areas of labor contracting, undermined prosperity. Already by the turn of the century, this was a region of pronounced *minifundia*, with the largest farms in some districts measuring only 10 to 12 hectares.[27] As the population grew, the pressure to migrate must have intensified. And, in fact, a number of persons from Chota interviewed in the 1970s indicated that they and their ancestors left home because of land scarcity.[28]

Conditions were not demonstrably better for tenants and subtenants on haciendas. For the right to farm a small piece of land and to graze a few head of livestock, tenants paid a nominal fee, typically one sol a year in the Province of Cajamarca in the 1930s. However, they were also required to work from two to five days a week for the landlord. This was a common arrangement in tenancy contracts as late as the mid-1940s. Tenants could, however, avoid this clause by leasing land to subtenants, who then acquired their labor obligation. Tenants sometimes even increased the labor

Source: Adapted from *Documental del Perú* (Cajamarca, 1970), in C. D. Scott, "Peasants, Proletarianisation and the Articulation of Modes of Production: The Case of Sugar-Cane Cutters in Northern Peru, 1940-69," *The Journal of Peasant Studies* 3, no. 3 (April 1976):342.

obligation of subtenants to add to their own income. This was particularly onerous for subtenants, because they were also invariably given the worst land to farm. That they were willing to accept these arrangements indicates land scarcity and the possible attraction of migrating to the coast.[29]

A recent student of *enganche* in northern Peru has stated that hacienda tenants and subtenants were not recruited to work on the coast.[30] However, after the turn of the century, many *hacendados* became labor contractors and insisted that tenants and subtenants pay their labor obligations by working on coastal sugarcane plantations. Moreover, when the World War I boom increased the demand for labor, some sugar planters purchased or leased sierra haciendas for the purpose of tapping resident peasant populations as well as raising cattle and growing foodstuffs for their plantations. As late as the 1940s, one of the largest monthly expenditures of the Hacienda Chusgón—then owned by the sugarcane plantation Laredo— was for loans to peons going to work for the mother corporation.[31]

The attractiveness of migration to the coast increased after the turn of the century. In response to the growing demand for foodstuffs on the coast, *hacendados* in Cajamarca began to rationalize production on their estates. Not only did they acquire more land, better livestock and grains, but they increased the labor obligations of tenants. Although wages rose during this period, they seldom equalled the sums paid on sugarcane plantations.[32]

Moreover, this process intensified as the century progressed. For example, in the 1940s the Gildemeisters and the Nestlé Corporation of Switzerland chose to develop their highland estates into efficient dairy farms. The resulting changes necessitated the expulsion of many tenants and subtenants, who subsequently migrated to the coast. Another change came in the 1950s, when some haciendas in the area were dissolved and their land made available for purchase by tenants. Ironically, sugar plantations also benefited from this development, because the fastest way for tenants to obtain cash was through signing an *enganche* contract. Interestingly, one of the dissolved estates, Llaucán, had been purchased in the 1920s by Víctor Larco as a means of forcing tenants and subtenants to work on his Chicama Valley sugar plantation.[33]

Civil disorder and lawlessness exacerbated the difficult economic conditions peasants frequently faced in the early twentieth century. The proliferation of banditry in some areas brought special pleas from local officials for help from the central and regional governments. For example, in 1902 the subprefect of Huamachuco, a recruitment area for estates in the Chicama and Moche valleys, complained to the prefect that armed bands roamed the countryside committing the worst possible crimes. He lamented that in the Districts of Marcabal and Sarin, towns were filled with "thieves and assassins" who carried firearms in public, and he pleaded with his superior to create two new rural police stations.[34] In a similar vein, several citizens from Cutervo, a recruitment area for Cayaltí and plantations in the Lambayeque Valley, asked for the central government in 1904 to create a new province for the sole purpose of controlling banditry. They claimed that the area was overrun by private armies that included bandits from as far away as Ecuador, Piura, and Amazonas.[35] Moreover, in the 1920s, the Province of Chota was torn apart by civil disorders that were quelled, with considerable force, by the central government.[36] These disruptive conditions affected the livelihoods of peasants and, in some cases, provided further impetus to migrate. As recently interviewed Chotanos explained, losses incurred to cattle rustlers were sometimes recouped through selling their labor on the coast.[37]

Even under normal conditions, highland peasants periodically needed cash, and one way to obtain it was through working on sugar estates. For example, a contemporary noted that, because of the competition for land, peasants were frequently involved in law suits either with each other or with *hacendados*, and that even the most basic legal advice cost money. Moreover, the same observer wrote that peasants were deeply committed to a regular pattern of religious celebration, common in preindustrial Catholic societies, that cost money for food and drink, and sometimes (for them) fairly sizable sums when custom dictated gestures of largesse within the community.[38]

Eric Wolf has written that, under the economic and social conditions just described, peasants tend to sell their labor, sometimes even becoming full-time wage earners.[39] Moreover, Lewis Taylor, in his recent study of Cajamarca, argues that the combination of the capitalization of small-scale farming and land scarcity made the earning of wages by peasants "indispensable." He concludes that "extra-economic coercion in order to force the sale of labour-power to capital became unnecessary."[40]

The flow of migration from Cajamarca to the coast was massive over a period of several decades. Nevertheless, this was less of a spasmodic outpouring of the masses than a controlled movement of humanity, directed by labor contractors (*enganchadores*) and sugar planters.

In the literature on *enganche* in northern Peru, labor contractors are probably the most-neglected and least-understood element. This is a serious omission, because they were, in many ways, the linchpin of the system. On their own, sugar planters would have had a difficult time contacting and hiring the thousands of highlanders needed to work their estates. Contractors served as the essential middlemen, delivering the requisite number of peons at the appointed time. *Enganchadores* were, basically, merchants who dealt in people. Many of them owned stores in sierra towns and had traded on the coast for years. It is only logical that they would have been generally aware of the growing labor shortages on the plantations and willing to add peons to the list of goods traded on the coast. In addition, planters permitted the most important contractors to operate estate stores stocked with their own merchandise. This was an added enticement. Some contractors were also highland *hacendados*, who had the advantage of a ready labor pool in the form of tenants and subtenants who owed their patron substantial labor obligations.

Position and wealth facilitated labor recruitment. An important merchant, like José Santos Medina Cedrón of Bambamarca, sold goods on credit to local peasants, who agreed to discount their debt by working at Cayaltí. In this fashion, Medina Cedrón not only made a profit on sales but also earned a commission from the Aspíllagas, based on the amount of work done by peons under his contract.[41]

Planters generally recognized that highland *hacendados* could also supply large numbers of peons, and sometimes lent them money to acquire additional estates. In 1897 the Aspíllagas went so far as to write that "the peons from Chota can only be contracted by *gamonales* [*hacendados*] from the area [as] they know and understand its complexities."[42] Years earlier, they had helped Medina Cedrón secure the lease to the Hacienda del Colegio in Chota, which they hoped would yield an additional 100 peons for Cayaltí. Moreover, the largest contractor for the estate Pomalca, Eduardo Tiravante, owned at least two haciendas in the Province of Chota, Churucancha and Mollebamba. His contracts specified that he supply from 200 to 250 peons from these properties. It is also significant that an *enganchador* found to recruit exclusively on the coast, Miguel Arbulu Gonzales, rented small to medium-sized estates in Lambayeque.[43]

Some contractors combined economic leverage with political power. Considering the web of indebtedness that characterized *enganche* and the various contracts involved, political position and influence undoubtedly helped to smooth over or to avoid potentially costly and annoying legal conflicts. Certainly, when the prominent merchant-*hacendado* Daniel Orrego chose to enter the *enganche* business, he did not suffer from being a governor in the Province of Santa Cruz. Nor did the *enganche* business of Catalino Coronado in Chota decline after he was appointed subprefect of the province.[44] Even sugar planters got into the act, as when Baldomero Aspíllaga Barrera was elected senator for Jaén, a province he had only visited once, but from which Cayaltí drew laborers.[45]

Labor contracting could be a family business, passed on from father to son,[46] and even from husband to wife. For example, Matilde Martín Vda. de Pinillos, a leading contractor for Laredo, tapped the large peasant population (almost three thousand in 1913) on the estate she leased from the Dominican Order in the highlands of La Libertad.[47] In this case at least, a woman conducted the trade in men.

There were some minor labor contractors who supplied plantations with handfuls of men. But planters preferred to deal with the bigger agents, the merchants and *hacendados*, because they could guarantee large numbers of workers and they were less of a financial risk. For example, big contractors could use their stores and haciendas as collateral to guarantee loans received from planters. Needless to say, haciendas and stores represented substantial collateral.[48]

In return for a guarantee to supply a large number of peons (e.g., 250), planters frequently granted *enganchadores* monopoly recruitment rights in a given district. For example, Pomalca gave this right to Melchor Montoya Espino for the District of Bambamarca in 1900, and to the Tiravante brothers for the District of Chota several times between 1900 and 1930. Likewise, Cayaltí extended this privilege to Medina Cedrón for the District of Bambamarca during the late nineteenth century.[49]

The practice of granting monopolies reduced the competition for peons, although it was never eliminated, because more than one estate always contracted in any district. In November 1919, for example, there were twelve contractors recruiting in the District of Bambamarca (Cayaltí's principal recruitment area), with a total outlay of 50,000 soles for making cash advances to peons.[50]

Clearly, *hacendados* and merchants required debtors, or tenants with labor obligations, to work on the coast.[51] However, peons unencumbered with debts or other contractual obligations also signed on. This frequently occurred at Sunday markets, where thousands of peasants gathered to sell their goods and to drink and celebrate. Contractors set up tables on the square and offered peasants cash advances in return for working on the coast. In an atmosphere conducive to borrowing, *enganchadores* had many takers. Similarly, contractors would appear at local festivals with large quantities of alcohol that they would sell or give away to peasants. Once the celebrants were sufficiently inebriated, contractors would extol the advantages of working on the coast, frequently exaggerating wages and the quality of living and working conditions. Reduced to a semicoherent state, peasants took the bait and signed on.[52]

Such trickery was not, however, always necessary to induce peasants into signing contracts. Many highlanders sold their labor without accepting a drink.[53] Moreover, we cannot assume that all peasants who accepted the contractors' liquor had been duped. The fact that contractors continued the practice of mixing alcohol with business for decades suggests that some peons, at least, had a notion of what they were getting into. With their minds already set on going to the coast, they may simply have taken advantage of the free alcohol. This is only speculation, but it underscores the complexity of *enganche* and cautions against generalizing about the prevalence of extraeconomic coercion.

The signing of a contract also gave legal form to the process of recruitment. Peons received a cash advance from contractors, generally from 10 to 50 soles, which they agreed to repay with their labor on the coast. Peons might also agree to work off previous debts or rent. To assure repayment, the peon and a cosigner put up as collateral their possessions and labor and surrendered all rights to contest the contract in court. Peons also agreed to work a minimum number of days, typically ninety, in case they repaid their loans very quickly. Although it was unstated in the contract, peons discounted their debts involuntarily. Thus, each payday either the contractor or the planter, depending on the source of the loan, received the peon's wage (except for a small amount, generally 10 centavos) until the loan was repaid. Peons did not starve, because they received a daily ration.[54]

Planters attempted to control labor supply, in part, through contracts with *enganchadores*. These agreements obligated contractors to supply a number of peons within a certain period of time (usually one or two months) to work at whatever job the estate desired. Planters generally advanced contractors enough money (usually by check) to cover the cost of loans to peons. To assure repayment, contractors sometimes put up as collateral property in the sierra, usually an estate or a business. Finally, *enganchadores* were granted a percentage of the total amount of wages earned by their peons as a commission. A commission of 20 percent was common, although it fluctuated.[55]

Demand for Labor

As planters entered into agreements with contractors, they had to balance the need for workers with their ability to pay competitive wages and commissions. Until the outbreak of World War I, planters were faced with a falling demand for their product and a real crisis in the industry. Prices and therefore profits remained low. However, planters were able to secure loans from foreign and domestic creditors during these years that allowed them to buy new equipment for their estates,[56] and to offset dwindling income. Despite the availability of credit, however, the Aspíllagas always linked income with expenditures. Since their principal expense was labor, their ability to pay current wages and commissions was generally measured against projected revenues, as calculated by the price of sugar. With prices hovering around the break-even point, even the slightest fluctuation downward led them to seek a reduction in their labor bill.

The beginning of hostilities in Europe dramatically changed this situation by forcing European sugar beet producers out of the world market and driving prices and profits skyhigh. This gave the Aspíllagas and other growers a freer hand in meeting labor bills, although it did not always result in higher real wages for peons. By the end of the war, planters had accumulated substantial profits and had improved their ability to deal with losses in income as the price of sugar fell with the return to the market of European producers. However, the onset of the Great Depression created a new crisis in the industry and forced planters once again to cut their labor bills.[57]

During and following the First World War another important change occurred in *enganche*. This was the growing number of "free " workers, or *peones libres*. These were noncontracted workers who sold their labor directly to the estate. Their existence is evidence of a growing duality in the labor market and the formation of a more permanent work force.

Cayaltí

The Aspíllagas' first serious encounter with *enganche* occurred in September 1878, when, faced with a severe labor shortage, they arranged for a contractor to deliver fifty highlanders to Cayaltí and advanced him, along with another agent, 1,700 soles to recruit additional peons. Within a few weeks, however, most of the highlanders had repaid their loans and returned to the sierra, and no one else had arrived to take their place. Understandably frustrated, over the next several years the Aspíllagas shied away from *enganche*, only occasionally advancing small sums of money to contractors.[58]

Their breakthrough came in 1886 when they signed a contract with José Santos Medina Cedrón of Bambamarca. Medina Cedrón did not insist on cash advances from the Aspíllagas. As a prosperous merchant, he not only had money of his own, but also was owed money by a large number of peasants. This gave him the leverage to force his debtors to repay their debts by working at Cayaltí. In this fashion, by March 1888, he had supplied 120 persons from Bambamarca to Cayaltí.[59]

This successful encounter with *enganche* encouraged the Aspíllagas to liberalize their policy on cash advances and to tap labor pools in other parts of the sierra. Thus, in a new contract with Medina Cedrón, the Aspíllagas agreed to pay 25 percent of all loans to peons and to help him gain the lease to the Hacienda del Colegio in Chota. In return, he agreed to supply the Aspíllagas with two hundred peons.[60]

Not only Medina Cedrón but *enganchadores* from Bambamarca, Santa Cruz, and Sorochuco began to supply Cayaltí with highlanders. This reflected increased demand for labor as well as the growing awareness of the financial benefits of *enganche*, particularly for contractors. In addition, general economic and political conditions in the sierra grew more conducive to migration, as the fighting stopped in Chota, and the mining industry in Bambamarca, which had taken labor away from the coast, began to decline. Thus the highland population at Cayaltí steadily increased from 230 in May 1890 to 900 by the turn of the century.[61]

During the 1880s, however, the Aspíllagas complained of a pronounced seasonality of labor supply, revolving around climate and planting seasons in the highlands. Thus, highlanders tended to return home by September or October to plant crops before the first rains. Some of them would return to the plantations as early as November, but they would leave again by February or March, which were the hottest months on the coast and coincided with a second planting season in the sierra.[62]

Although the problem of seasonality was never completely alleviated, there was a trend away from violent fluctuations in labor flow in the 1890s. This partial stabilization of the work force resulted from highlanders accepting new loans and being recontracted on the estate itself.[63] More will be said about the implications of this development later in this chapter.

As all north coast sugarcane plantations converted to highland labor, *enganche* became a competitive business that pushed wages and contractors' commissions upward (see table 35). This was a serious problem for planters, because the price of sugar throughout the 1890s was dangerously low (table 2). The Aspillagas, for one, were trapped between falling revenues and contractors' growing demands to raise wages and commissions. The situation developed into a minor crisis in 1897, when the price of

Table 35
Daily Cash Wage and Contractors' Commissions at Cayalti

Year	Daily Cash Wage* (soles)	Value in Cents	Contractors' Commissions (% of daily cash wage)
1897	0.40	.1940	20
1899	0.50	.2425	25+
1902	0.40	.1940	25
1905	0.50	.2425	25
1907	0.50	.2425	25
1914	0.60	.2832	25
1919	1.12	.5510	25
1923	1.30	.5265	25
1929	1.30	.5200	10-15
1932	1.30	.4589	10

Sources: *For 1897-1914*: AH to AH, 7 July 1897, AFA; AH to AH, 29 April 1899, AFA; AH to Los Contratistas, 1 May 1899, AFA; AH to AH, 9 May 1899, AFA; N. Salcedo to AH, 4 March 1902, AFA; BAB to AH, 4 February 1903, AFA; VAT to AH, 3 September 1907, AFA; VAT to AH, 28 August 1907, AFA; VAT to AH, 30 August 1907, AFA; VAT to AH, 8 May 1912, AFA; letter dated 19 July 1919, AFA.
For 1919-1930: Unsigned letter dated 19 July 1919, AFA; IAA to RAB, 16 November 1923, AFA; LAA to RAB, 2 February 1929, AFA; Unsigned letter dated 13 June 1932, AFA.
*Wages were determined by piecework, and included a daily ration of beef, rice, and salt.
+In 1899, commissions were calculated on the basis of a 40-centavo cash wage. Nevertheless, there was still a 5 percent increase in commission.

sugar plummeted, and *enganchadores* began withdrawing peons to other estates that were offering higher wages and commissions. For the moment, the Aspíllagas permitted the work force to diminish, knowing that this also reduced expenditures during a time of rapidly shrinking profits. They realized, however, that such reductions in the work force would eventually result in a significant decline in production. Therefore, when the price of sugar rose modestly two years later, they increased wages and commissions, and there quickly followed an increase in the number of workers (table 36).

Table 36
Work Force at Cayaltí

Year	No. of Workers	Year	No. of Workers
1897	700	1914	950
1899	900	1919	1,600
1902	750	1924	1,850
1905	1,250	1929	1,900
1907	744	1930	1,750

Sources: *For 1897–1914*: AH to AH, 2 July 1897, AFA; AH to AH, 24 January 1899, AFA; AH to Los Contratistas, 20 March 1899, AFA; Francisco Pérez Céspedes to AH, 5 April 1902, AFA; Francisco Pérez Céspedes to RAB, 18 August 1905, AFA; VAT to AH, 28 August 1907, AFA; AH to AH, 11 September 1914, AFA.
For 1919–1930: Unsigned letter dated 19 June 1919, AFA; LAA to RAA, 17 October 1924(b), AFA; RAA to Señores Aspíllaga Anderson Hnos., S.A., 12 November 1929, AFA; RAA to Señores Aspillaga Anderson Hnos., S.A., 10 March 1930, AFA.

From the turn of the century until 1915, when the effects of the World War I shortage began to be felt, the price of sugar remained low. The Aspíllagas and other planters went into debt during this period, borrowing heavily from foreign creditors. Most of this money was used to make technological improvements aimed at increasing production and labor productivity.[64] Still, long-term indebtedness was not attractive, and the Aspíllagas had to hold down expenditures until the price of sugar rose. Since their largest expense was the labor bill (primarily wages), they continued to cut wages and the size of the work force whenever the price of sugar fell to a new low, or when several particularly bad years ran together. As before, they could not hold down wages for long, however, as contractors would gradually move workers to estates where wages and commissions were higher.

During this period, there were two major reductions in the work force, in 1902, when the price of sugar fell to its lowest level since the Aspíllagas had been in business, and in 1907, after two years of particularly low prices and a drought. In 1902 the reduction followed a 20 percent cut in wages (and a de facto 20 percent reduction in contractors' commissions). On the other hand, in 1907 wages and contractors' commissions remained unchanged, as the Aspíllagas simply dismissed four hundred workers by asking contractors to eliminate their least-productive peons. After both reductions, wages and commissions were eventually increased, and the size of the work force grew.

The outbreak of World War I sent a shock wave through the world sugar economy. As the sugar beet fields of Europe became its battlefields, the supply of sugar fell precipitously, forcing prices to all-time highs. Although the disruption of shipping and problems with international finance caused some initial difficulties for producers, the long-term impact was a dramatic increase in their profits. In Peru, this meant, among many other things, that the Aspíllagas no longer had to balance their labor bill against declining revenues. Now they had surplus income and could hire as many workers as they required.

Under these market conditions, the Aspíllagas and other north coast producers chose to increase production through expanding acreage in cane and making technological improvements, including modifications that permitted mills to operate twenty-four hours a day.[65] These developments necessitated larger work forces, and for this reason sugarcane plantations in the Chicama and Moche valleys began to devise new methods of labor contracting. Thus, they started to use employees as contractors and to lease and purchase haciendas in the northern sierra to facilitate labor recruitment.[66] As a result, by 1915, Laredo, Cartavio, and Sausal each had about fifteen hundred laborers, and two years later Casa Grande, the largest producer, had a work force of five thousand. At Cayaltí, the Aspíllagas also increased the size of their work force by expanding the scope and intensity of labor recruitment and raising wages and commissions.[67]

However, the process of labor contracting was complicated by the inflation of the war years, which caused real wages to fluctuate. Planters were in part to blame as they replaced hundreds of acres of staples with sugarcane, thereby causing a scarcity of foodstuffs and spiraling prices for basic commodities. This hurt peons and other lower-income groups the most.[68]

Nevertheless, despite fluctuating real wages, highlanders still migrated to Cayaltí and other north coast plantations in ever-increasng numbers. The general scope of the problem may explain this apparent paradox, as many plantations did not offer higher wages than Cayaltí. Also, by causing poor harvests and great suffering, the devastating drought that struck the northern sierra in 1916 significantly increased the number of highlanders seeking work on the coast. At one point, the outpouring of humanity was so great that the Aspíllagas instructed contractors to turn peons away. This still did not stop them from migrating to Cayaltí on their own, however, where they discovered firsthand that their services were not needed.[69]

During the war the work force at Cayaltí grew from 950 to 1,600 (see table 36).[70] The estate also emerged from the period a larger producer, with more acres in cane and increased mechanization (see table 20). If production levels were to be maintained or increased, then the size of the work force could not diminish, unless the estate made expensive technological improvements. As we have seen, Cayaltí did not continue to modernize in the 1920s.[71]

Although the price of sugar declined during the 1920s, it remained significantly higher than in the prewar period, especially during the first half of the decade. The Aspíllagas increased the size of their work force during this period, as production levels inched upward. Nevertheless, these were modest increases, indicative of the relative sluggishness of the market. Thus, from 1919 to 1929 the number of workers at Cayaltí increased by only three hundred.[72]

The collapse of the world capitalist economy in 1929 caused the price of sugar to fall to record lows. At Cayaltí, the Aspíllagas reduced expenditures by cutting *libres'* and staff wages, by reducing contractors' commissions, and by releasing approximately 150 ill and less-efficient workers. They feared taking more drastic measures, however, because sugar workers had grown more militant, and the possibility of a strike could not be discounted.[73] Fortunately for planters, the Depression had ushered into the presidency of Peru a politically inexperienced army colonel, Luis M. Sánchez-Cerro, who looked to the Aspíllagas and other conservative political leaders for advice. They managed to convince him to devalue the sol in 1932, which served as a de facto decrease in real wages and saved them, temporarily at least, from dismissing more workers or drastically cutting wages.[74]

The period during and immediately following the war also witnessed a growing dualism in the labor force at Cayaltí, as the number of noncontracted workers (*peones libres*) increased. The fundamental distinction between contracted and noncontracted workers rested in the nature of their indebtedness. Contracted workers, by definition, were indebted to a contractor or to a planter. *Libres*, on the other hand, were not indebted to contractors, although they might receive loans from planters. *Libres*, in effect, had severed their ties to contractors and probably had sold their land in the sierra. They were no longer seasonal workers, but full-time wage earners. Planters characterized *libres* as independent workers who sold their labor to the highest bidder. According to the Aspíllagas, they also tended to establish themselves and their families on the coast, only returning to the sierra infrequently. However, there is no mention of their occupying an elite status among workers, or of their serving in more skilled positions.[75]

By 1924 *libres* outnumbered *contratados*, as the data in table 37 show. Most of these "free" workers had come to Cayaltí as *contratados* but, with the support of the Aspíllagas, had changed their status. Contractors sometimes insisted that peons repay their debts before they became *libres*, although at other times the debt was repaid after the transformation had already occurred.[76]

Table 37
Contracted and Noncontracted Workers at Cayaltí

Date	No. Contracted	% of Total	No. Noncontracted	% of Total	Total No. Workers
1905	1,100	88.0	150	12.0	1,250
1919	1,080	67.5	520	32.5	1,600
1924	810	43.8	1,040	56.2	1,850
1927	?		1,000		1,850 (est.)

Sources: Francisco Pérez Céspedes to RAB, 18 August 1905, AFA; unsigned letter dated 19 June 1919, AFA; LAA to RAA, 16 October 1924 (b), AFA; LAA to RAA, 21 July 1927, AFA.
Notes: *Libres* also existed in large numbers on neighboring estates. For example, in January 1941, San Jacinto had 810 *peones libres* and 67 *contratados*. Four years later, *libres* constituted 63 percent of the work force: see Informe sobre Mano de Obra, 26 May 1945, AFA. *Libres* are discussed at Pomalca and Pátapo in *Contratos de la Hacienda Pomalca*, AFA; contract between Jesús Arnoco and Hacienda Pomalca, 29 May 1911, AFA; J. Orrego to Catalino Coronado, 29 September 1911, AFA.

Both highlanders and management benefited from this change. *Libres* received higher pay than contracted workers, and more money was a powerful inducement during a period of rising prices. The Aspíllagas and other planters benefited by reducing their dependence on contractors and gaining greater control over workers. Finally, management also saved money, despite having to pay higher wages, by curtailing advances and commissions to contractors and undercutting their economic power on the estate, where their stores competed with the plantation store.[77]

Indebtedness, Permanency, and Bondage

The increase in the number of *libres* at Cayaltí and elsewhere indicates the development of relatively more permanent work forces on north coast sugarcane plantations. Indeed, years earlier the Aspíllagas had observed that even contracted workers were remaining on the estate for longer periods. Longer periods of residency involved the recontracting of workers on the plantation itself, a practice so common by the turn of the century that a community of highlanders, mostly from Bambamarca, was beginning to form on Cayaltí:

The contractor Negrete, who has the most peons [400 in 1905], only occasionally receives a peon from his associate Zárate in the sierra. All of his peons, one can say, are contracted here, so that they have a constant body of workers [*una peonada constante*].[78]

We now have peons from Celedin with the advantage that they have a temperament very similar to coastal dwellers and they become acclimatized more easily than others, although it is true that those from Bambamarca could not have become better acclimatized. We have here a true community from Bambamarca, people who have become accustomed [to Cayaltí] in such a way that they do not move from here. [Moreover] . . . all come with their families.[79]

The Aspíllagas were naturally enthusiastic about these developments, as a core of several hundred workers was desirable at all times to maintain production schedules.

Traditionally, the formation of more stable work forces has been linked to the prevalence of debt peonage. Indebtedness was, in fact, a permanent feature of wage labor regimes at Cayaltí and other Peruvian sugar estates. All contracted laborers received an initial advance and could also receive additional loans from contractors and the estate. In some cases, interest was charged on these advances. Receipts for all loans were kept by contractors' agents and the estate, and each payday peons discounted their debts, receiving only a nominal cash sum. In some cases, but not at Cayaltí, peons received only I.O.U.s from the estate (*libretas*), which could be cashed in at a later date, or credits (*fichas*), which could be spent at stores. *Libres* could also receive loans from the estate.[80]

In addition to acquiring loans on their own, peons could inherit the debts of family members. There are many examples of this in the correspondence of Catalino Coronado, who contracted for all of the major sugar plantations in the Lambayeque Valley. Typically, a peon would agree (in writing) to repay with his labor loans his parents received from Coronado. In one case, there was a standing agreement whereby the parents could receive from 8 to 10 soles (worth about one week's work) without a note from their son. If a highlander died with an outstanding debt, Coronado could still collect from the family. This sometimes led parents to send another son to the coast, or to the confiscation of property secured as collateral.[81]

In a situation in which loans were readily available from more than one source, peons sometimes accumulated large debts. At Cayaltí, it was not unusual for peons to owe the estate over 100 soles.[82] Moreover, in 1923, the vast majority of peons contracted to Coronado owed plantations money, some as much as 300 soles. This was in addition to loans acquired directly from Coronado, which also amounted to large sums of money (tables 38 and 39).

In addition to receiving cash loans, contracted workers could acquire debts through buying goods on credit from contractors. The correspondence of Catalino Coronado shows that he did a lively business on Lambayeque Valley estates, selling a variety of foodstuffs and soft goods imported from the highlands. The Aspíllagas also commented frequently on the high

Table 38
Money Owed Tumán and Pátapo by Laborers Contracted to
Catalino Coronado, Available Months, 1923

Month	No. of Peons	No. Indebted	% of Total	Range of Debts (soles)	Total Owed (soles)
Jan.	267	229	85.8	.55-322.40	16,125.37
March	436	379	86.9	.50-313.35	18,259.22
June	245	186	75.9	.80-279.92	11,283.92
Sept.	212	175	82.5	.10-308.35	10,029.27
Dec.	244	197	80.7	.50-231.30	15,149.07

Source: Planilla de peones del Señor Catalino Coronado, 1923, AFA.

Table 39
Money Owed Catalino Coronado by Laborers under His Contract

Year	Total Owed (soles)
1912	5,247.52
1913	5,691.79
1914	5,083.21

Source: Resumen de la cuenta del Hermigrando Fonseca con Catalino Coronado, February 1912 to September 1914, AFA.

volume of business of the stores run by the larger contractors at Cayaltí, especially José Negrete. Unfortunately, we have no information on prices or credit practices, except that peons could buy on credit.[83]

Nevertheless, contractors did not have a monopoly on sales, as a variety of stores existed on estates, and peons could travel to nearby towns to make purchases. At Cayaltí, a small army of itinerant vendors and operators of temporary corner stalls were also permitted onto the estate. These petty merchants sold bread, liquor, cloth, and additional items that were also available in larger stores.

Moreover, the store operated by the Aspíllagas at Cayaltí strongly contradicts the "company store" model, which portrays planters as selling goods at inflated prices to force workers into indebtedness. Not only did the plantation store have to compete with other retailers, but it did not even sell goods on credit until the 1930s, and only then as a relief measure. The Aspíllagas were careful not to be undersold by merchants in Chiclayo, the departmental capital, or by stores on neighboring estates. They even occasionally took steps to regulate prices in contractors' stores and to police vendors. It should also be remembered that workers did not have to depend on stores for many of their basic staples, because they received a daily ration of beef, rice, and salt as part of their wage. Of course, additional food was desirable and other items had to be purchased, especially for workers with families.[84]

Despite the policy of the plantation store, the prevalence of indebtedness through loans is undeniable. Peons always signed a note guaranteeing repayment of loans with their labor, and planters and contractors were reluctant to permit indebted peons to return home until their debts had been canceled. Many historians have seen this type of policy as an important vehicle for the formation of permanent work forces on large Latin American estates. Peons are sometimes even seen as being forced to remain on haciendas for a lifetime, as on henequen plantations in late nineteenth-century Yucatán.[85]

In northern Peru, debt peonage did not take on this extreme form, although it was practiced in other ways. For example, contractors routinely practiced versions of debt peonage by compelling tenants, subtenants, and simple debtors to repay their obligations by working on the coast, or by moving peons from one estate to another without their consent. Sometimes planters forced contractors into these wholesale transfers of workers, as when the Aspíllagas made sharp reductions in the work force at Cayaltí in 1902, but other times *enganchadores* simply took their workers to estates that were paying higher wages and commissions.[86]

More traditional forms of debt peonage also occurred, as seen in these statements by the Aspíllagas from the late nineteenth and early twentieth centuries:

You cannot imagine what we have to do to obtain people, to the extreme of deceiving the bastard peons who each day become more demoralized.[87]

We have only allowed those to go who have repaid their loans and, in spite of everything, there are more than two hundred highlanders.[88]

Yesterday Mr. Sebastián Tello told me that the Negretes [contractors] were going to have to take two hundred men to Tumán and that they were about to pay what they owed to the estate. That I cannot believe, and if such a thing is attempted, I will tell them that while they do not pay in labor what they owe they cannot move those people from the estate. We will see how things develop. I will try to manage them with the utmost calm and sagacity.[89]

As these examples indicate, the Aspíllagas clearly benefited from debt peonage. This was especially true during periods of labor shortages at

Cayaltí, as in March 1891. Then, the cleaning of the main irrigation canal and the resumption of milling after a temporary shutdown created extraordinary labor demands. As the Aspíllagas later explained, they succeeded in accomplishing both jobs because "we have only let go those who have paid their loan."[90]

It would be easy to assume that the Aspíllagas made money easily available to peons as a ruse to entrap them in a web of debt peonage. Clearly, they *were* aware of the benefits of indebtedness. However, they also complained about the large sums of money that they had to sink into advances to contractors and loans to peons to acquire a work force. It was, in fact, a rather sloppy way of doing business. In their correspondence they never discussed debt peonage as a master strategy for creating a permanent work force, and they appeared most concerned with getting their money back, preferably in the form of labor, as stated in the *enganche* contracts. If they did compel indebted workers to remain behind, they also sought to entice them to stay by improving housing and offering them daily rations of beef and rice. They also recognized that it was impractical to have peons remain at Cayaltí for decades and work until a ripe old age. Worker productivity declined fairly quickly in a setting where malaria was endemic, temperatures soared to over 100 degrees, and the work was taxing. Moreover, many indebted peons refused to submit to a regime of bondage, oftentimes running away while owing large debts.

It was difficult for the Aspíllagas to make Cayaltí attractive, or even comfortable. Highlanders must have thought that they were entering Hades as they came down from the cool, temperate sierra into the coastal desert and its irrigated valleys. The presence of a wide variety of communicable diseases not generally found in the highlands reinforced this impression. Fresh recruits were particularly susceptible to illness, and it required several trips to the coast or long periods of residence to build up immunities.[91] If they retained their health, highlanders next had to adjust to a regimented work routine requiring long hours of labor under the sizzling sun or in steamy mills or distilleries, which differed markedly from their traditional tasks of cultivating cereals and tubers and tending sheep.[92]

The Aspíllagas attempted to make life at Cayaltí more palatable. For highlanders in need of cash, wages and loans served as an initial inducement to remain on the estate. But the owners realized that additional measures were needed. For example, they considered the offering of a pound of beef and a pound of rice for each day's work an attraction, for highlanders would not have been able to buy these relatively expensive items on a regular basis back home. Equally compelling, they believed, were their efforts to improve housing, especially the construction of single-unit houses for highlanders with families. As the Aspíllagas saw it, "It is necessary to make them [highlanders] houses in such a way that they can establish themselves with their families, because this is the bond [*lazo*] that makes them more permanent."[93] Beginning in 1907, management also encouraged permanency by awarding yearly cash bonuses to the coastal worker and the highlander who had resided on the plantation the longest.[94]

These measures are clear evidence that the Aspíllagas did not seek to increase permanency through the use of debt peonage alone. Equally important is the realization that living and working conditions and seasonality affected permanency. Throughout the period under consideration, many highlanders routinely repaid their loans and returned to the sierra, and there was nothing that the Aspíllagas could do about it. Such migrations were generally tied to planting and harvesting seasons back home, and they continued throughout the region well into the 1960s.[95]

Nevertheless, many highlanders chose to sever their ties with the sierra and to settle on the coast. These more permanent workers offered years of service to the sugarcane plantations. However, we must be careful not to exaggerate length of employment. After several years of labor, some peons either fell ill or became exhausted from the arduous work routines. Serious problems resulted from absenteeism and worker output, which sometimes fluctuated wildly and disrupted production schedules. For example, over a two-week period in 1908, the amount of work completed in the field at Cayaltí varied by as much as 50 percent, without a significant change in the size of the work force.[96] The Aspíllagas blamed the general problem on highlanders who had become debilitated through hard work and illness. For this reason, in 1907 and 1908, they carried out a general replenishment of the work force.[97] Although this was an extreme case, complaints about absenteeism and illness among workers regularly appeared in the Aspíllagas' correspondence. Under the circumstances, a policy of universal debt peonage, which would have forced all workers to remain on the estate indefinitely, would have been illogical and counterproductive.

As it was, even the partial use of debt peonage caused management some fairly serious problems. As stated earlier, this was not the most cost-effective way of maintaining a wage-labor force, as significant sums of money had to be expended for advances to contractors and loans to peons. This became a serious problem during the periods of crisis in the industry, especially the early twentieth century and the 1930s, when many estates were operating at a loss.

Moreover, management was regularly faced with the problem of what to do with ill or injured peons who were indebted but could not work. These workers occupied valuable housing, received free medical treatment, and sought additional loans. Twice during the early twentieth century the Aspíllagas expelled seriously ill workers from the estate on the assumption that they would never be able to repay their debts. However, this was an extreme measure, and, generally speaking, debilitated workers remained on the estate.[98]

Regimes of debt peonage are generally portrayed in the literature as being maintained through violence and intimidation, sometimes with the collusion of the state. The elements for such oppression certainly existed at Cayaltí and on other north coast sugar estates, where the experiences with the Chinese were still fresh in planters' minds. However, Peruvian peons proved to be resourceful at avoiding bondage, although not without a price.

Complete control over highlanders was difficult to achieve for a variety of reasons. In the first place, they were considerably mobile, traveling long distances from the highlands to the coast and, unlike the Chinese, they blended into the general population and had friends and relatives within the region. Moreover, there was considerable competition for their labor among contractors and planters, which tended to break down cooperation among employers and create opportunities for avoiding bondage. Finally, they were intelligent and resourceful. As they became aware of the various nuances of *enganche*, they succeeded in beating the system often enough to contribute significantly to the breakdown of total control.

Financial entanglements were the key to binding peons to estates. But the easy availability of loans also afforded workers the opportunity to swindle contractors and planters. These swindles generally took the form of peons accepting advances, sometimes using fictitious names, from different contractors on separate estates. If contractors became aware of the situation, solutions were not easily found. Rarely could agreements be reached that would allow peons to work off both debts simultaneously. More commonly, the contractor who currently controlled the peon in question refused to cooperate with his competitor. Planters, who did not want to risk losing the labor of an able-bodied peon, even temporarily, almost always supported this recalcitrance.[99]

Perhaps the champion swindler-peon of all time was an extraordinary man who, using two different names, compiled some 4,000 soles in loans from three separate contractors. These *enganchadores* were among the most important and experienced in the region, but they were unable to apprehend this wily con artist. His case is certainly an exceptional one, but it shows that peons could work the system to their advantage, and that there was considerable inefficiency and waste in *enganche*.[100]

Students of debt peonage have generally assumed that permanency offered no benefits to peons. This certainly was the case on the henequen plantations in Yucatán, and wherever other such vile working and living conditions existed. Where better conditions prevailed, as in some areas of northern and central Mexico, permanent workers formed an elite among peons.[101] On the northern coast of Peru, however, permanency did not necessarily confer special status. Long-term employment could be desirable during periods of crisis, though, when the supply of labor outstripped the demand. It is difficult to pinpoint when such conditions existed, but in 1901 Cayaltí's chief engineer accused mill workers of purposely running up their debts to ensure themselves permanent employment.[102] Mill workers were, of course, more skilled than field hands, and it cannot be assumed that their behavior was indicative of a general pattern. However, neither can it be assumed that this strategy was discounted by other workers, especially during the drought of 1916 and the Great Depression.

Under normal conditions, permanency was less desirable for highlanders who retained ties to the sierra. For these peons, indebtedness did not necessarily present an insurmountable barrier to returning home. On occasion, they received permission from their contractors and planters to visit the sierra, with the proviso that they return to repay their debts. Some indebted highlanders, however, sought to sever their ties with plantations and took the extreme step of running away. The correspondence of north coast planters and the contractor Catalino Coronado indicates that large numbers of indebted peons regularly ran away from estates. On occasion, escapees explained their reasons for fleeing to their contractors. In most cases, they cited inordinately long hours and excessive work loads as their principal reasons for fleeing. This suggests difficulty in adjusting to a regimented work routine and the pressures of plantation life. In one notable case in 1903, runaway peons from Laredo complained to their contractors that they had been required to work from 4:00 a.m. to 8:00 p.m. By the end of the day, they were sometimes too exhausted to prepare a meal. The peons said that they had complained to the administration, asserting that "they were not slaves," but when the long hours continued they simply ran away.[103]

Escapes were not a new development on Peruvian sugarcane plantations or, for that matter, on Latin American plantations in general. Since the sixteenth century, large numbers of African slaves had run away, sometimes forming colonies in the interior. The incidence of escapes was naturally much greater in areas dominated by slave economies, such as Brazil and the Caribbean, but runaways were also commonplace in coastal Peru.[104]

Following the emancipation of blacks in Peru, Chinese laborers were imported to take their place. The Chinese sometimes fled from coastal sugar estates, particularly during periods of general calamity, such as the Chilean invasion of 1880 (see table 33).[105] With the passing of the Chinese population and the commitment of *enganche*, the opportunities for escape increased significantly. Now planters did not have a "captive" labor force, but one that fluctuated in size and personnel. The number of workers also rose dramatically, which made supervision more difficult. Moreover, once highlanders had fled, they blended into the general population and could not be singled out by race, like blacks and Chinese.

At Cayaltí, the Aspíllagas attempted to prevent escapes by having foremen (*caporales*) supervise peons while they worked. Supervision was difficult, however, because foremen were responsible for fifty to one hundred men, who might be spread out over a considerable area. Peons who were determined to run away could hide in groves of mature cane (which grew far above their heads), or in deeply cut irrigation canals, and then take advantage of the lack of electric lighting to escape into the night. More devious tactics could also be employed, as when highlanders asked for permission to visit home or neighboring villages, but never returned.[106]

Once indebted peons had fled from estates, foremen and contractors gave chase. Some runaways simply went to neighboring estates, where they accepted a loan from another contractor and began work. As previously mentioned, this created a difficult situation, because rival contractors were reluctant to return escaped peons once they had advanced them money. If runaways were quickly captured, they were thrown into plantation jails and sometimes severely beaten.[107] But if they made it to the highlands, capture became more difficult. By the 1950s the Lambayeque Valley estates had organized posses that patrolled the sierra for escapees, returning those they retrieved to the coast in large trucks.[108]

For the most difficult cases, contractors and planters could generally count on the assistance of public officials, some of whom doubled as labor contractors.[109] There are several recorded cases in which county judges jailed runaways in the sierra until they could be prosecuted or forcibly returned to the plantations. Nevertheless, contractors and planters sometimes had to encourage officials to act by paying them a gratuity. For example, in 1908 contractors in the Chicama Valley paid the local governor one sol for every runaway he captured, and the Aspíllagas were contemplating a similar reward system in the same year.[110] Thus, although local officials were not always honest or efficient, they did aid in the recapture of escaped peons.[111]

If a runaway could not be caught, contractors could still recover their money through the courts. When peons accepted their initial advance, they put up their property and the labor of a cosigner as collateral.[112] If peons defaulted on their loans, the courts could force cosigners to go to the coast, or award property to contractors. In the Sorochuco area, two contractors for Cayaltí accumulated several plots of land in this manner, as did Catalino Coronado in Chota.[113] Once again, local government acted to protect the interests of contractors.

The safeguards that contractors and planters enjoyed, however, still did' not offer them complete protection from defaults on loans. Some highlanders simply had no property to confiscate, and cosigners could not always be located or forced to work. For example, Catalino Coronado's agents at Pátapo threw several cosigners into the plantation jail for failure to work.[114] Moreover, by signing on one another's peons, contractors made it difficult for themselves to recover outstanding debts. Competition for labor also created an atmosphere of easy money that made it possible for peons to accumulate large debts. Sums that reached 300 soles or more might not be retrievable by confiscating a small plot of land, or by forcing a cosigner to work. Thus, it should not be surprising that both contractors and planters regularly suffered some financial loss as a result of escapes. For example, in February 1921, one of Cayaltí's contractors claimed that runaways owed him 2,000 soles, and in 1926 the Aspíllagas were trying to track down 170 escapees. Moreover, in January 1946, 79 runaways owed the plantation Laredo 1,763.37 soles.[115]

The prevalence of runaways clearly contradicts any theory of permanency that relies exclusively on debt peonage. Certainly, peonage and other forms of coercion and brutality existed in abundance, but they were not always successful in controlling and intimidating peons, nor in leading to the formation of stable work forces.

Summary and Conclusions

The traditional interpretation of *enganche* stresses the importance of coercion in the recruitment of highland labor and the effectiveness of debt peonage in the formation of permanent work forces. The preceding analysis shows, however, that both coercion and the marketplace played important roles in labor recruitment, and that debt peonage was only one of several causes of worker permanency.

Over the course of several decades, many highlanders responded to wage incentives by migrating hundreds of miles from their unprosperous villages to sell their labor on the coast and by moving from one estate to another in search of higher incomes. Planters could largely control the supply of labor to their estates through the allocation of advance money to labor contractors and the signing of formal *enganche* contracts. The amount of money that they could invest in labor generally depended on income, and the price of sugar on the world market largely determined income. During the periods of crisis the size of the work force, at Cayaltí at least, tended to ebb and flow with the projected ability to pay. Beginning with the boom years of the First World War, however, producers could afford to maintain larger, more stable work forces.

It was also during the war years that the number of "free workers" (*peones libres*) grew. *Libres* had severed all contacts with contractors and freely sold their labor on the coast. Their presence represented a growing duality in the work force, although there is no evidence that they enjoyed a special status among peons or worked at different jobs.

Enganche did not, however, evolve within a completely free labor market, and the existence of debt peonage cannot be denied. Labor contractors sometimes compelled highlanders to work on plantations to repay outstanding debts or labor obligations. Peons also occasionally signed *enganche* contracts while drunk, or acquired the labor obligations of tenants, friends, or relatives.

Coercion and bondage, however, were not primarily responsible for the formation of more stable work forces. Permanency was the result of a variety of forces, including improved housing, food rations, and bonuses, as well as debt peonage. Seasonality, worker exhaustion and illness, and runaways, moreover, undermined long-term permanency.

Enganche successfully fulfilled the labor needs of the Aspíllagas and neighboring planters, who had been faced with a labor crisis with the passing of the Chinese. Labor contracting was an efficient system in that it responded to cash incentives and afforded planters a means of replenishing the work force. However, it was also an inefficient way of doing business, as large sums of money had to be sunk into advances to contractors and loans to peons, and some of this money could not be retrieved.

Labor contracting, finally, altered the plantation community. Work forces now consisted almost entirely of transplanted highlanders, many of whom had come with their families. The Aspíllagas, and other planters, were faced with serious problems in accomodating and controlling thousands of peons who labored in a new environment.

8. The Plantation Community, 1890-1933

The success of *enganche* changed the character, composition, and size of plantation communities and presented the Aspíllagas and other planters with new problems in controlling the work force. In demographic terms alone the transformation was significant, as the number of workers at Cayaltí grew from 900 in 1896 to nearly 1,421 in 1932. Moreover, because most highlanders acquired female companions and had children, Cayaltí was transformed from a work camp into a community of households larger than most towns in the department.

The Aspíllagas' objective at Cayaltí was the efficient and profitable production of sugar. This required maintaining workers and their families in a manner that would not place the estate at a disadvantage with its competitors in labor recruitment. Services provided to workers—such as housing, medical care, recreation, and goods at fair prices—resulted from economic necessity rather than from humanitarian concerns.

The provision of a wider range of services also reflects the Aspíllagas' changing philosophy of controlling workers. After the turn of the century, they generally preferred worker accommodation and manipulation over violence as the safest way of maintaining order and production on the estate. This policy developed in response to the growing size and complexity of the plantation population as well as to the development of a working-class movement in the region.

Under these circumstances, the Aspíllagas recognized that the frequent application of whippings, jailings, and executions could result in massive retaliatory actions by workers. Although they never abandoned the use or threat of such tactics, the owners of Cayaltí de-emphasized them in favor of improving services and keeping workers and their families occupied and entertained when they were not working. The Aspíllagas' goal was to have contented workers who would be complacent, dutiful, and productive. They did not create a paternal regime at Cayaltí, but they did fashion a paternalistic veneer in labor relations that helped to defuse conflicts between management and labor and retard the growth of a working-class movement.

The Demographic Growth of Cayaltí, 1896-1932

Many managerial problems that the Aspíllagas faced were the result of the growing size of the plantation community. This was especially true in the areas of housing, health care, and control. The most significant feature of the estate's demographic growth was the formation of households. Although the composition of the work force was constantly changing, there were still large numbers of highlanders who remained on the estate for months or even years at a time. This increased the desirability of migrating with families, as some were already doing by the turn of the century, or of acquiring female companions while on the coast. The latter practice was particularly popular and remained commonplace into the 1960s.[1]

Around the turn of the century, management began to take careful note of the size of the plantation population. Estimates of the total number of inhabitants—workers, women, and children— were made in 1896 and again in 1912. Then in 1923 and in 1932, the Aspíllagas ordered censuses taken of the plantation population. These data show that women and children constituted around 50 percent of the plantation community from the turn of the century until 1932. In 1923 approximately 50 percent of all workers lived with women, and they had an average of 1.3 children. Interestingly, only 4.9 percent of these couples were married. By 1932 the number of workers maintaining households had increased to 65 percent; however, the census did not record the incidence of marriage or the number of children.

Housing

These population statistics demonstrate that Cayaltí was emerging as a more complex community during this period. It no longer resembled a labor camp populated with degraded Chinese coolies and itinerant peasants from the highlands, but, rather, a small town inhabited by a mixture of transients and workers with households. The Aspíllagas had encouraged worker permanency, for obvious economic reasons, by improving living conditions. An important element in their program was the construction of new housing.[2]

Traditionally, workers had been housed in dilapidated dormitories called *galpones*. These poorly constructed barracks afforded workers little or no privacy, a condition that was likely to discourage rather than encourage permanency. Therefore, the owners began to construct new, detached houses and to refurbish *glapones* into separate apartments. The pattern of construction always segregated workers from administrative personnel and artisans, who lived in larger homes on different parts of the estate.[3]

The Aspíllagas attempted to build new houses as the need arose, but supply always lagged somewhat behind demand, which forced them to

Table 40
Population of Cayaltí

Year	No. of Workers	% of Total Population	Nonworkers (Women and Children)	% of Total Population	Total Population	% Growth
1896	900	45.0	1,100	55.0	2,000	
1907	1,078	51.1	1,033	48.9	2,111	5.6
1912	980	40.8	1,420	59.2	2,400	13.7
1923	1,315	43.0	1,743	57.0	3,058	27.4
1932	1,421	51.2	1,352	48.8	2,773	−9.3

Sources: AH to AH, 28 January 1896, AFA; VAT to AH, 1 May 1907, AFA; VAT to AH, 12 January 1912, AFA; VAT to AH, 22 August 1912, AFA; Censo de 1923, AFA; Censo de 1932, AFA. In 1923, there were 742 women and 1,001 children.
Note: Population figures for workers, their partners, and children. Not included are the families of staff, artisans, and owners.

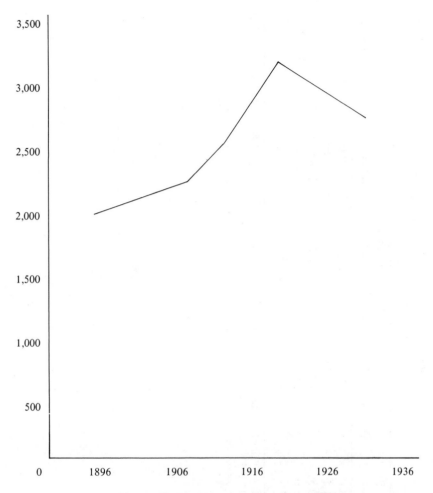

Fig. 1. Population of Cayaltí, 1896-1932

construct eighty to one hundred units at a time. Large blocks of new housing went up in 1890, 1894, 1900, 1906, 1915, and 1917. Most of these homes were simple adobe structures, well-suited to the dry climate but small and crudely constructed.[4]

There were, however, some exceptions to this pattern. For example, in 1894 new houses were constructed of wood and adobe with zinc roofs, imported at some expense from Europe. The interiors consisted of a living room, kitchen (with hearth), and a patio area where domestic animals could be kept.[5] Houses built in a similar fashion went up in 1915, with the welcome addition of cement floors, which significantly improved sanitary conditions.[6]

Nevertheless, not all workers were housed in new, detached units. In general, the Aspíllagas placed workers with families in the better homes and crowded single peons into *galpones*. Management did, however, remodel these ancient dormitories to provide workers with some privacy. For example, in 1900 the Galpón de Pekín was completely rebuilt into eight apartments, and two peons were assigned to each unit.[7]

After 1917 the Aspíllagas avoided constructing new housing in favor of patching up older buildings. This reflects their general unwillingness to invest in the plantation, as they also began to lag behind their competitors in technology at this time.[8] Some of the *galpones*, in particular, were allowed to deteriorate to the point where they were described as "very ugly" in 1923. Ismael Aspíllaga Anderson agreed to repair them, but only "little by little and in the most economical way."[9] Similarly, houses damaged in the flood of 1925 were given only cosmetic repairs and allowed to deteriorate within a few years.[10] Extensive overcrowding compounded this problem, as more than one family was put into single houses or apartments, and some buildings contained twenty-five to forty-five persons.[11]

The general condition of housing at Cayaltí seems to have been duplicated on neighboring estates. A report written on Chicama Valley estates in 1912 said that most workers lived in separate units of varying quality, "according to what the planter believes are the needs of the worker and the amount of money he is willing to invest." The best homes were at Chiclín. In fact, the author of the report, who was a member of the elite, believed that they were too good for workers ("superiores á la cultura del bracero"). Larger than any workers' homes at Cayaltí, Chiclín's houses consisted of two rooms in addition to a kitchen and a patio. Construction materials consisted of adobe, wood, and cane.[12]

A second description of housing in the valley, written in 1921, indicates a somewhat different picture. By then, some plantations were experiencing overcrowding, and it was not uncommon for three to ten persons to be living in one- or two-room homes with dirt floors.[13]

In the neighboring Lambayeque Valley, surviving building contracts show that some homes built at Pomalca were superior to anything available at

Cayaltí. In 1904 and 1915 houses consisting of two rooms, kitchen, and corral were constructed. In the latter year, building materials included adobe, cement, brick, and rock, and individual rooms measured 4.5 meters by 4.5 meters.[14]

Provision of Goods

Housing was only one service that planters provided for workers and their families. As the population grew, larger quantities of food and other commodities also were made available. The Aspíllagas had operated their own store for decades, with an eye toward earning modest yearly profits. They had never sought to maintain a monopoly over sales on the estate, instead permitting contractors to operate stores, vendors to peddle goods on the estate, and peons to travel to neighboring towns to make purchases. Competition among the various retailers tended to keep prices at reasonable levels.

Around the turn of the century, the Aspíllagas viewed the closing of Chinese markets as an opportunity to expand the size of the plantation store and increase profits on sales.[15] They ordered tens of thousands of soles' worth of merchandise from Chiclayo and Lima, including ham, sardines, salmon, flour, coffee, garbanzos, beans, rice, corn, kerosene, cigarettes, starch, candles, matches, cotton cloth, and toys.[16] All products were marked up 20 to 30 percent to match current prices in Chiclayo.[17]

The estate store, however, never turned much of a profit. One reason concerned the nature of the competition. Contractors' stores were popular because they sold goods imported from the sierra and allowed customers to buy on credit. Many peons, especially recent migrants, clung to traditional tastes and did not have the money, or perhaps the patience, always to pay with cash. This apparently outweighed the risk of going further into debt and remaining on the estate for longer periods of time.[18] Itinerant vendors and operators of small corner stalls also enjoyed some popularity among peons, the latter in part because they sold on credit. And workers were willing to travel a few miles to neighboring communities to save a few soles, as in September of 1912, when nearby merchants were selling rice and flour at bargain prices.[19]

The plantation store also suffered from mismanagement and embezzlement for several decades. Until 1908 the Aspíllagas entrusted the store to a manager and rarely bothered to check the books. In September of 1908, however, it came to their attention that no profit had been realized that year, despite sales totaling $20,855 at a 30 percent markup.[20] The following year, the Aspíllagas investigated store management more thoroughly. They discovered that the store had suffered a loss of $1,205, with $24,250 in sales, and concluded that the store manager and his assistant had embezzled considerable sums. Although the Aspíllagas did not press charges, as the store manager lay gravely ill, they subsequently took a greater interest in the running of the store.[21] Profits, which rose from $429 in 1911 to $2,862 in 1913, reflected this greater interest.[22]

The Aspíllagas' interest in the store, moreover, increased with the outbreak of World War I. The conflict ushered in a period of rising prices, particularly for staples, which threatened to cause labor unrest on plantations. Like other planters, the Aspíllagas were reluctant to grant workers large wage increases to offset rising prices, arguing that profits would fall with the termination of hostilities. The one concession that they made was to sell some key staples at cost and to keep the prices of other goods at parity with prices elsewhere. These tactics succeeded in keeping the rise in the cost of living to a minimum until 1919, when the index rose by an alarming 73 percent (table 41). There can be little doubt that this was a cause for labor unrest that year on the estate.[23]

The situation was exacerbated that year as Augusto B. Leguía, whose principal opponent in the presidential campaign was Antero Aspíllaga Barrera, successfully exploited the inflation issue, and particularly its adverse impact on workers. Once in office, Leguía continued to press for lower prices, even establishing a special commission to oversee merchandising. Not surprisingly, particular attention was given to Cayaltí and other plantations owned by prominent political opponents of the regime. Succumbing to this pressure and to growing concern over potential worker violence, the Aspíllagas sold some staples at a loss and granted laborers a modest wage increase. As a result, the cost of living fell by 46 percent between 1919 and 1920 and did not rise again for two years.[24]

With the passing of the inflationary crisis, merchandising policy ceased to be a political issue. Leguía, whose concern for the working classes emanated from political expediency, could no longer use inflation as a weapon to punish his adversaries. The Aspíllagas now took less interest in the plantation store, delegating daily management to an employee. The policy of the store was to sell staples for a minimal profit (usually 8 percent above cost), and to earn more on luxuries, such as liquor and quality cloth, which sold for 15 to 25 percent above cost. The owners never expected to earn large profits from the store, but were disappointed at yearly earnings of less than $2,055 for 1923. This they blamed on mismanagement and petty theft by customers. Under new management the store earned $5,600 in 1925.[25] Sales subsequently increased as the owners began to discourage itinerant vendors from coming onto the estate and to regulate prices in contractors' stores. The latter decision undoubtedly angered contractors, but should be seen within the context of the declining importance of contracted workers and the growing numbers of free laborers.[26]

The Great Depression forced the Aspíllagas to make further merchandising reforms. As the price of sugar plummeted, they reduced wages and

Table 41
Price and Wage Index in the Saña Valley
(1913=100)

1913	1914	1915	1916	1917	1918	1919	1920	1921	1922
100	100	118	109	100	109	182	136	136	136

Source: Bill Albert, *An Essay on the Peruvian Sugar Industry, 1880–1920 and the Letters of Ronald Gordon, Administrator of the British Sugar Company in Cañete, 1914–1920* (Norwich: School of Social Studies, University of East Anglia, 1976), table 50, p. 171a, adapted.
Note: Wages are for male field workers and do not include rations (except 1916 and 1920).

laid off over one hundred workers. Management tempered these actions, which could have provoked labor unrest, by lowering the prices of staples, permitting *peones libres* and staff to receive $4.00 in credit each week, and ordering the store to remain open seven nights a week.[27]

Clearly, through these reforms the Aspíllagas also gained greater control over merchandising on Cayaltí. None of these decisions were made, however, with the objective of developing a traditional company store. The extension of credit was strictly limited, and the plantation store still did not have a monopoly over sales. Throughout this period, the owners viewed their store as a means of making a modest profit and of pacifying workers by lowering prices on key staples.

Health Care

The emerging managerial philosophy of the Aspíllagas, which favored accommodation and manipulation to repression, can also be seen in the provision of health services. Rather than simply expel ill workers from the estate, the owners provided them and their families with free medical care from a physician. This was an extension of services provided the Chinese, with the difference that now more and better services were offered to a larger number of people. The Aspíllagas recognized the necessity of preventing the outbreak of an epidemic that could paralyze production, and this was their primary motivation in providing health care. They rarely expressed any genuine concern for the welfare of their workers and their families.

Health conditions throughout Peru were in a deplorable state,[28] and this situation was mirrored at Cayaltí and on other north coast estates and communities. The population of the region had increased significantly since the advent of *enganche*, and highlanders were particularly susceptible to coastal diseases, against which they had no immunity. As migrants acquired families, problems with overcrowding and clean water supply exacerbated an already-dangerous ambience. Deteriorating sanitary conditions invited the outbreak of an epidemic that potentially could shut down Cayaltí. The estate physician, in a 1909 letter to the Aspíllagas, provided a graphic description of the filth that peons and their families lived in:

I want now to take up a point that is, perhaps, the most important because it refers to the hygiene of this hacienda. Residents here, principally in the districts where the peons live, and in the center [of the estate] have deeply rooted the antihygienic custom of throwing onto the ground dirty water and excrement, or, in the majority of cases, satisfying their necessities right next to their homes. It will not escape your attention, although you are not doctors, that certain infectious-contagious diseases, such as typhoid fever and dysentery, which I put as examples because both exist here, especially the latter, are highly dangerous, because the micro-organisms that produce the disease live for some time in the feces of the sick and convalescent. The flies and various insects that come into contact with these wastes are transmitting agents, since they contaminate objects, food, etc., of healthy individuals. The wind itself, which here raises dense clouds of dust, is an agent of the same sort, especially if there exist sources of drinking water in its path.[29]

Such conditions as the doctor noted served as fertile breeding grounds for infectious diseases. In addition to intestinal disorders, maladies commonly found in the region read like a list of the greatest killers of all time: bubonic plague, smallpox, measles, influenza, cholera, malaria, pneumonia, yellow fever, typhoid, typhus, and tuberculosis. Periodic outbreaks of these diseases occurred into the 1930s, although some were more lethal than others. Malaria was endemic to the region, but rarely did it reach epidemic proportions. Rather, it caused prolonged illness in large numbers of people and periodically took some lives.[30] Among those who contracted the disease were Ismael and Rafael Aspíllaga Anderson.[31]

Intestinal disorders, particularly among children, were also endemic and regularly took dozens of victims, including the son of Ismael Aspíllaga Anderson in 1930.[32] The other diseases struck periodically, sometimes reaching epidemic levels and carrying away over one hundred persons. Influenza, tuberculosis, and measles (in children) proved to be the most difficult to combat.

Beginning in the late nineteenth century, the Aspíllagas had taken an active role in combatting illness at Cayaltí. It would be inaccurate, however, to conclude that primarily humanitarian concerns motivated the Aspíllagas to provide medical care. They were in the business of producing sugar, and for that they needed healthy workers. They were not generally concerned with peons and their families as individuals. The Aspíllagas balanced concern over health with concern over medical expenditures, sometimes admonishing doctors for "extravagant" orders. The nature of their relationship with workers also tempered the owners' concern for health care. Laborers were considered "servants," not children, wards, or clients. There was only so much that should be done for them. Moreover, it was difficult to develop long-lasting personal ties with workers, given the periodic turnover in the work force. These attitudes and circumstances influenced the Aspíllagas' commitment to health services and helped to define their philosophy of control:

Here there are many people, many women and children. The number of people of very marginal utility is something that will come to concern us in the question of houses and other circumstances. The teenagers are unbearably ill-bred, harmful, and lazy. I have them under watch or in the school or at work. I believe that what happens at Cayaltí does not occur on other haciendas where there is more work and much less or no philanthropy.

The ill, although one fights with ignorance, are attended. There are, happily, no plagues, as occurs in Chiclayo and other locales. I have warned the doctor to abstain from ordering specialties that are costly and only serve to produce long periods of recovery.[33]

Antero was upset because Cayaltí was spending increasing sums on health care. The need for such expenditures was graphically demonstrated in 1888, when the entire highland population was either killed or driven off the estate by an outbreak of typhus.[34] Subsequently, peons were supplied with fresher food and cleaner water and admonished to clean their houses thoroughly. In 1894 workers and their families were also innoculated against smallpox and given quinine and disinfectants as preventives against malaria and dysentery.[35]

The effect of these measures was mixed. Only a few persons subsequently died of smallpox, either through failure to be vaccinated or because of an ineffectual batch of vaccine.[36] The distribution of quinine also helped to combat malaria. However, that disease remained endemic as disease-carrying mosquitoes flourished in the myriad irrigation canals that crisscrossed the estate. Eventually, the pervasiveness of malaria would compel the Aspíllagas to characterize it as an occupational hazard,[37] much like black lung disease in coal mining. Moreover, the distribution of disinfectants alone never could have prevented dysentery, given remaining problems with sanitation, food spoilage, contaminated water, and personal cleanliness. Physicians also complained that mothers did not always exercise proper care in the cleaning and feeding of their children. As a result, dysentery and other intestinal disorders, especially during the summer, remained commonplace and the principal cause of death among young people.[38]

In the early twentieth century, Cayaltí was more successful in combatting bubonic plague. Generally only associated with the Middle Ages, the plague was still a major threat to Peruvians in the twentieth century. Because the disease was spread by the fleas of guinea pigs, efforts to combat it were hindered by traditional culinary tastes (guinea pig is a popular food among highlanders). Once contracted, the plague always proved fatal. It struck the north coast several times in the 1900–1910 decade, taking a terrible toll in the native communities of Monsefú and Reque in the Lambayeque Valley.[39] Nevertheless, Cayaltí's doctors effectively prevented it from reaching epidemic proportions on the estate by immediately expelling all stricken workers, slaughtering and burning all guinea pigs, fumigating houses, and forbidding outsiders from entering the estate.[40]

Physicians were less successful in treating measles, influenza, and tuberculosis, as each disease reached epidemic proportions at least once during the early twentieth century. Serious outbreaks of influenza, each resulting in over 100 deaths, occurred in 1900, 1906, and 1907.[41] Tuberculosis took several lives in 1905 and again in 1907, and many other stricken workers were simply expelled from the estate, condemned to die elsewhere.[42] Measles also reached epidemic levels in 1908, killing 103 persons, mostly children.[43]

The number of serious diseases put a tremendous burden on Cayaltí's physicians. In stark contrast to their predecessors on the estate, these men appeared truly dedicated to their profession, and some credit should be given to the Aspíllagas for hiring them. An epidemic was a particularly trying time for the doctor, but a normal workday was also difficult. A report filed in 1912 detailed the magnitude of daily responsibilities: during a five-month period from April to 21 August, the doctor treated 7,566 cases, or an average of 1,513 per month. This meant that anywhere from 56 percent (July) to 76 percent (May) of the estate population was treated for some illness during these months.[44] Although these figures appear alarmingly high, they were in fact not abnormal. There was no epidemic during this period; these months did not fall within the summer, which was always the most insalubrious time of year; and some women and children characteristically did not go to the doctor when ill. This report presents a clear picture of an unhealthy community.

The same report also presented some mortality information. It showed that, under normal conditions, life was most precarious for children, for thirty-seven of the fifty-two recorded deaths were youngsters. Tragically, twenty-three of the children died without receiving medical attention, thereby underlining the fragility of life during the early years and the reluctance of mothers to submit their offspring to medical treatment.[45]

That he wrote this report was indicative of the doctor's concern with improving health care. He began to suggest new ways of decreasing the incidence of common diseases and treating the sick. The Aspíllagas were generally receptive, although they took careful note of expenditures and cautioned against prolonging convalescence.

Efforts to prevent disease focused on improving living and sanitary conditions, expanding innoculation programs, and examining new workers for signs of serious illness. According to the doctor, disease was facilitated primarily by overcrowding in houses, poor construction, unnourishing diets, and poor sanitary conditions. Both the physician and the Aspíllagas also believed that highlanders had an inherited lifestyle and fatalistic view of life that impeded them from taking proper care of themselves. This sentiment was clearly expressed by Cayaltí's doctor in 1912:

Another point directly related to the morbidity of adults, which happily is not of equal proportion with the number of deaths, is the lifestyle of the peon. Notwithstanding finding himself in an environment of course superior to that in which he has been born, he cannot avoid the influence and customs that he has acquired in the place of his birth. His characteristic traits are the complete lack of hygiene, the frequence with which he surrenders to the abuse of drink, bad diet . . . and in many cases his indifference to life itself, which impresses on his character the fatalistic stamp of the Oriental races.[46]

Like other racial stereotypes, the last point can be dismissed as a convenient and simplistic explanation of a complex problem.

Overcrowding, as noted, was another cause of serious health problems at Cayaltí. The doctor noted that it was not unusual for eight to ten persons to be living in houses designed to accomodate three to four. He also lamented that most households compounded health problems by raising guinea pigs and hogs for food, cooking indoors over an open flame without proper ventilation, and sleeping on the ground, which facilitated contact with insects and helped to cause rheumatism.[47] Although the Aspíllagas did improve housing, construction generally lagged behind demand.

Illness was also linked to poor sanitary conditions. Here management did succeed in making significant improvements. Trash cans were placed around the estate, signs were posted encouraging people to dispose of their garbage properly, and a corps of street cleaners was created. In addition, beginning in November 1922, at least once a month sanitation workers would clean all houses, kill all guinea pigs, and remove other domestic animals that might be present. The last-mentioned measures were important in preventing any serious outbreak of bubonic plague.[48]

Additional improvements included periodic inspection of workers' homes to locate those who were sick but unwilling to seek medical assistance; examination of newly arrived workers, turning away those who already showed signs of serious illness;[49] enlargement of the estate hospital;[50] and the offer of free food to sick workers and, if they had a family, one-half pay.[51]

These improvements made Cayaltí a more attractive and healthier place to live. The Aspíllagas tempered these measures, however, with a concern over excessive expenditures on medical care. Most of the improvements that they authorized were labor-intensive, particularly the creation of sanitation crews and the giving of more responsibilities to doctors. Beyond vaccine for workers and their families, they were reluctant to fulfill doctors' orders for medicines. They complained that treatment did nothing but prolong illness and dismissed some medicines as "exotic," although they had no medical expertise themselves. They also refused to build outhouses, because "the people would not use them." They based this assumption on their evaluation of workers as bumpkins and servants, an attitude that undermined the provision of improved services.[52]

Control

Keeping workers housed, fed, and well enough to work were among the most important managerial concerns of the Aspíllagas. As the size and complexity of the plantation community grew, they were also faced with serious problems in keeping the peace. For highlanders, the transition from highland peasant to sugarcane worker was not an easy one. The character and pace of work as well as living arrangements changed almost entirely, resulting in some social and psychological disorientation. The principal manifestations of these difficulties were alcoholism and absenteeism, both of which threatened to undermine production schedules and tranquility.

In addition, during the First World War sugar workers began to strike with greater frequency and to form mutual aid societies and primitive trade unions. This presented an even greater threat to the Aspíllagas, who sought to prevent these activities at Cayaltí. They devised more sophisticated methods of social control that relied less on violence in favor of manipulation and accomodation of the work force. This scheme was calculated to prevent retaliatory violence by workers that might cause extensive physical damage to the plantation and increase worker solidarity. The Aspíllagas expressed this philosophy of control several times:

Our opinion is that in this hacienda all violence and force be forsaken, that it should not be authorized to anyone, because it is a grave error and counterproductive.[53]

Everything with calm, since more flies are killed with honey than sticks. And so I say to Ventura, enthusiasm for his orders and systems of work is fine, but not with violence.[54]

We desire likewise that in the mill the same discipline established over years to be conserved, but without violence. . . . [We prefer] good judgment and sagacity, in order to keep the workers respectful and at the same time grateful and respectful to the hacienda and its representatives.[55]

Management recognized that some workers were more disruptive than others, with the basic distinction being between workers with families, who were better-behaved, and single peons, who tended to be the troublemakers. Clearly, this was an important reason why management had encouraged highlanders to migrate with their families. However, the owners also complained that the children of highlanders were often rowdy, rude, and instigators of violence and crime.[56] They were reaping the results of children reared in a crowded, unhealthy environment without the stabilizing influence of religion or, in many cases, of normal family life.

At the heart of many of these problems, the Aspíllagas believed, was the excessive consumption of alcohol. Highlanders were known to consume large amounts of *chicha* during holidays and celebrations, but at Cayaltí excessive drinking became an everyday occurrence and contributed to outbreaks of violence and crime.

There is clear evidence that highlanders did consume large amounts of alcohol on the estate. Beer and wine were sold on Cayaltí, but the most popular alcoholic beverage was cane alcohol (*cañazo*), a by-product of sugar processing available in large quantities at cheap prices. For example, in 1912 a gallon of *cañazo* sold for 15 cents.[57] In the same year the estate administrator estimated that an average of 1,600 gallons were sold on the plantation each month, for a per capita consumption of 2.9 gallons a month, or almost a pint a day.[58]

Management complained, sarcastically, that highlanders worked primarily to buy alcohol, which resulted in several days of drinking and long periods of absence from work. The owners tended to ascribe such behavior to lack of character and racial deficiencies, a clearly facile explanation. In the following letter, they also criticized the newly formed Sociedad Pro-Indígena, a pressure group created to improve the plight of the Peruvian Indian, for not focusing on the problem of alcoholism:

While they [peons] have money they do not work, and only two or three days [a week will] they show up for their ration of food and a new allotment of money for their next payday, which goes for a new allotment of alcohol. As these men earn more, they lose more workdays. . . . To attempt to improve the condition of the worker, in this sense, is a grave thing. The "Sociedad Pro-Indígena," which calls itself defender of the rights of the Indian, should begin by finding the way to defend them from their most pernicious enemy, alcohol, which all who manage people, pro-Indian or not, know is the reason that the Peruvian peon is not what he should be. An individual who drinks remains at the margin of his rights, defended today by a society that has the role of a "Society Protecting Animals," created as that, arising from a romantic sentiment, from altruism, true or false. And as there is no interest in doing real work, but only simulation, its results are completely null, and everything continues as before.[59]

The Aspíllagas believed that alcoholism was one of the principal causes of violence among workers.[60] Violence most commonly took the form of knife fights and wife beatings.[61] However, clashes also occurred between large numbers of peons who had migrated to Cayaltí from different parts of Peru. For example, in 1894 a fight broke out between peons from two different parts of the sierra (Bambamarca and Sorochuco) that resulted in one death and several injuries. Twenty-five workers, along with their wives, were subsequently incarcerated in the estate jail, and the authorities were notified. Another clash occurred in 1899 between Piuranos and highlanders that resulted in several injuries but no deaths. The Aspíllagas blamed the disturbances on the Piuranos, whom they characterized as "insolent and disorderly." Management expelled these workers from the plantation and made no further efforts to recruit peons from this region.[62]

A riot that took place in 1915 was more serious. The actions of a visiting highland merchant who was jailed for being drunk and disorderly precipitated the violence. After his incarceration, an angry mob of peons formed and demanded his immediate release. Instead, the plantation police broke up the mob with extreme force, severely beating several workers and threatening to kill others. More workers soon appeared, however, forcing the police to seek refuge in the *casa hacienda*. The disturbance turned into a riot as laborers proceeded to loot the homes of the police, steal liquor from local stores, and run wildly throughout the compound, all the while receiving encouragement from the teenagers of Cayaltí. The riot was quelled only when a contingent of armed employees joined forces with police from the town of Saña to force peons back into their homes. The evening of rioting resulted in one death and several serious injuries. Afterwards, a "tomblike" silence fell over the estate.[63]

The riot demonstrated the potential for widespread violence at Cayaltí as well as the repressed anger that some workers harbored toward the plantation police. The incident caused great concern among the Aspíllagas, who feared that a dangerous precedent may have been set. The riot made them focus their attention even more closely on plantation security.

In addition to violence, the owners were also extremely concerned with absenteeism. This had been a chronic problem among the Chinese as they grew older and less capable of working six days a week. Highlanders, despite their youth, also demonstrated a reluctance to work as hard as the Aspíllagas demanded. This attitude forced management to hire surplus labor and to provide additional services, all at considerable expense. Absenteeism was especially high on Saturday, payday, and on Monday, the first workday of the new week.[64] Although illness must be considered a serious cause of worker absence, its prevalence on Saturdays and Mondays suggests that workers did not want to work a full week. The Aspíllagas, with good reason, blamed alcoholism and the lack of a working-class ethic. The problem of adjusting from peasant labor to wage labor, especially hard, methodical, gang labor, was a serious one. Management complained that higher wages did not automatically decrease absenteeism rates nor increase worker output: "Our laborers or peons are such that a raise in wages does not . . . increase the number of workers or work output. They have such little initiative; if they earn more they work less."[65]

Absenteeism, alcoholism, and violence forced the Aspíllagas to re-evaluate security on Cayaltí. During the late nineteenth century they had relied on force to control the Chinese, with *mayordomos* and contractors acting as police, and themselves as judges and executioners. Gradually, as the state became better organized, peons suspected of crimes were turned over to public officials. However, local police could not deal effectively with everyday problems on the estate, especially as the population grew into the thousands. Moreover, the Aspíllagas did not want to delegate full responsibility for policing workers to public officials, as they wanted to maintain as much control as possible over affairs on Cayaltí.

The owners continued to rely on *mayordomos* and foremen to supervise peons in the field and in the mill. But problems of control also occurred in the compound after work or on weekends and holidays. To deal with them, in February of 1894 the Aspíllagas created their own police force.[66] Cayaltí's police force was always small, never numbering more than six men plus a *comisario*. Officers were paid $12.15 per month, about as much as the highest-paid *mayordomo*, and the *comisario* $19.40.[67] The police were given a number of responsibilities relating primarily to maintaining order and cleanliness. They regularly patrolled the streets to break up fights, admonish workers for uncleanliness and idleness, enforce prohibitions against the sale of *cañazo*, and guard the *casa hacienda* and other estate property. They had the power to put anyone who even looked suspicious in jail.[68]

The impact of the hacienda police, however, was more cosmetic than repressive. Most of their responsibilities were mundane, and it was impossible for five men to police thousands. The Aspíllagas were soon complaining about the ineffectiveness of the police, perhaps unreasonably. By the late 1890s they were described as "inept" and "counterproductive," as alcoholism, absenteeism, and rowdiness all remained everyday problems. For the Aspíllagas, the laziness of the police was a contributing cause, and by the turn of the century three officers and the *comisario* had been fired.[69]

The riot of 1915 caused management to seriously evaluate internal security. Ramón Aspíllaga Barrera believed that the officers had actually provoked the riot and were completely ineffective in suppressing it. He replaced the *comisario* with the governor of Saña, a petty politician whom the Aspíllagas controlled, and added an extra policeman to the staff. Ramón hoped that the governor would control the workers of Cayaltí as well as he did the people of Saña.[70] To help assure this, management banned the sale of *cañazo* on the estate and confiscated all firearms, except those belonging to the staff.[71]

Within a year, however, Ramón was once again lamenting the ineffectiveness of the plantation police. The ban on *cañazo* had proved useless, as vendors smuggled large quantities of it onto the estate. The prohibition was eventually lifted and *cañazo* began to be sold at higher prices, which, temporarily at least, reduced consumption.[72] However, sobriety was most apparent among *libres* and workers with families, both of which groups had made a better adjustment to plantation life.[73]

The plantation police presented the Aspíllagas with a difficult problem: they wanted order on the estate, but not at the risk of confrontation with workers. Unnecessary violence was to be avoided at all costs, and a larger, more repressive police force might initiate counterproductive clashes with workers. In the end, the Aspíllagas chose to live with a certain amount of untidiness rather than promote strict discipline that could lead to reprisals, perhaps as serious as walkouts and strikes.

Other managerial decisions also demonstrated this philosophy of control.

For example, even after a decade of labor unrest on the north coast, the Aspíllagas were reluctant to allow the stationing of the national police, the Guardia Civil, on the estate. In the words of Ismael Aspíllaga Anderson, the "certain" result would be "many problems and surprises, since they [the Guardia] are very abusive."[74]

Moreover, the Aspíllagas always cautioned *mayordomos* against the unnecessary physical abuse of workers and quickly reprimanded staff who went against their wishes. The best illustration of this point is an incident involving the illegitimate son of Antero Aspíllaga Barrera, Guillermo Aspíllaga Taboada. Guillermo and his brother Víctor had been given important managerial positions on Cayaltí, and because of their blood relationship to the head of the family, one might assume that they enjoyed more privileges than other employees. Guillermo learned, however, that serious mistakes were severely punished. In 1908 he was head supervisor in the mill, with general responsibilities over production. One morning he discovered a worker stealing a bit of lime to mix with his coca. Enraged, Guillermo attacked the peon with a club and inflicted serious head and shoulder injuries. What followed was completely unexpected. Urged on by his fellow workers, the injured peon first complained to the governor of Saña and then to the subprefect of Chiclayo. He demanded that the Aspíllagas pay him $97 in compensation for his injuries, or he would take them to court. Although they were able to settle out of court for $76.15, the Aspíllagas were upset: they had been forced to explain the incident to local political authorities, and mill workers had supported their comrade. Both were dangerous precedents. Guillermo Aspíllaga Taboada, the son of the co-owner of Cayaltí, was dismissed. His father lamented that his son had no immediate job prospects and a large family to support.[75]

Controlling workers without relying primarily on violence required more sophisticated managerial planning and execution. The Aspíllagas, however, were willing to invest the time and money. Cayaltí was a family business, their primary source of income, and a symbol of their status and pride. They also had confidence in their ability, frequently reminding one another that they only needed to exercise tact, intelligence, and restraint to dominate peons. In the long haul, the benefits were worth the effort, as a more contented work force was less likely to riot, strike, or join labor unions and dangerous political movements.

Early on, management recognized that highlanders needed diversions to release accumulated tensions and frustrations that might otherwise result in drunkenness and violence. The owners, therefore, provided them with recreational facilities, including sports equipment and silent films, which were shown twice a week and on holidays. Workers were frequently reminded that these facilities had been provided by their patrons.[76]

In a similar vein, the Aspíllagas also permitted workers to attend local festivals three times a year: Carnaval in February, a holiday in Monsefú in September, and Guadalupe in December. These holidays were immensely popular with peons, and management calculated that more good could be gained by allowing them to go than by forcing them to work. This was not an easy decision for managers deeply concerned with absenteeism, especially since it was usually their best workers who attended.[77] On one occasion, the Aspíllagas provided five hundred Cayaltí residents with free train transportation to the estate following a festival in Monsefú. According to Ismael Aspíllaga Anderson, returning celebrants deeply appreciated this paternalistic gesture:

As I told you in my preceding letter, I gave free passage to those who will be returning from Monsefú Friday and Saturday. I have now the satisfaction of telling you that all of our workers who went to that fiesta returned with their families, five hundred in number, without an accident. I received them at the train station and the three trains loaded with people in clusters . . . entered [the estate] giving *vivas* to the hacienda and to their patrons . . . like a true fiesta. In the evening when we went out to the cinema the people received us with triumphal exclamations and palms, and appeared, from the most important to the most modest, most affectionate, respectful, and courteous. I listen to everyone, but in one hand [I have] bread and assistance, and in the other authority. I have the premonition, the certainty, that that which you have told us, that we can become the idol of our servants and workers, will very soon become a reality. [Thus will come the] satisfaction and pride that we want and we should give you, and that we also want and desire for ourselves as well as God's blessing. My sick ones have told me this morning that my visits are a remedy and they receive me so contented that I never cease to see them. All this is forming for us an environment that we should have, in which they love us and respect us, and so the security of our Cayaltí, of its valuable capital assets, of ourselves, of all the inhabitants of Cayaltí, will be guaranteed.[78]

The type of paternalistic bond that Ismael sought to create was explicitly calculated to create an ambience favorable to the security of the estate. It was a policy based on the great social, economic, and political gap that separated the Aspíllagas from their workers. It was assumed that peons would be so grateful to their patrons for services and expressions of personal concern that the Aspíllagas would become their "idols." Taken literally, this was an idealistic position, but their policy did succeed in creating a paternalistic veneer in labor relations that provided a more secure environment for their capital.

The Aspíllagas' philosophy of control was perhaps given its fullest expression in the annual New Year's party. What began as a simple three-day rest period in 1877 developed into a fairly elaborate celebration exploited by management to create paternalistic ties and to facilitate the formation of a work ethic. Recreational activities included soccer matches, bullfights, cockfights, dances, acrobatics, plays, fireworks, and a banquet. But, from the viewpoint of management, the most important events were the granting of bonuses, pensions, gifts, and special awards for meritorious work.

Beginning in 1907, yearly bonuses became a standard feature of the party. Workers received from $1.50 to $2.43, staff from $5.00 to two weeks' wages, and children in the plantation school, a few cents. Special bonuses and pensions were also regularly awarded for commendable service to the estate. For example, in 1900 the Aspíllagas promoted a mechanic to a staff position for his fine work and for learning to read. They noted that this action would serve as an inducement for the rest of the workers to improve themselves. That same year management also pensioned a staff member in a long ceremony that reduced the poor man to tears. Clearly pleased with themselves, they described that year's party as "solemn and significant."[79] In 1906, $2.40 was awarded to "about ten workers who had most distinguished themselves in their conduct and work," including the coastal worker and highlander who had been on the estate the longest. Similarly, in 1910, bonuses were given to the twenty-five workers with the best attendance records, and in 1927, to the ten who had been working on the plantation the longest. Luis Aspíllaga Anderson had identified around twelve who had been on Cayaltí for thirty-five to forty years.[80]

The New Year's holiday was an important rest period for workers, and an opportunity for the Aspíllagas to implement their policy of control. A family member presided over each activity to remind workers that their enjoyment emanated from their *patrón's* generosity. By granting bonuses for good work, outstanding attendance, and long periods of residence, management was also encouraging peons to behave like efficient wage earners. For the Aspíllagas, the ultimate objective was to create a work force that was both industrious and respectful.

Management had the same objective for the children of Cayaltí, although in a somewhat different context. Children were potential workers, and it was important to instill in them proper attitudes about work and authority. Management attempted to achieve this goal in the plantation school. It was established in 1887 "to form in this manner true citizens, and inculcate in them the idea of progress and give them aspirations to improve their condition."[81] Management also hoped that the school would have a "moralizing" influence and result in "disciplined" behavior.[82]

The school was structured to fulfill these objectives. Ideally, all children were to attend class until the age of twelve and then assume jobs in the field.[83] The Aspíllagas did not expect instruction to result in "intellectual development," but, rather, in social adjustment.[84] Although reading was taught, emphasis was placed on exercising, marching, and learning to play in a band.[85]

The school was not, however, a complete success. The principal problem was poor attendance, as enrollment fluctuated between 100 and 130, far below the total number of school-age children.[86] The Aspíllagas blamed this on parents' lack of interest, but a contributing factor was management's insistence that parents pay for most of the cost of running the school. This came to around $120 a year, and basically represented the salaries of the teacher and band leader as well as the cost of supplies. It would probably have been easier for the Aspíllagas to pay the entire sum than for a typical peon to pay a few soles.[87]

What impact the school had on those children who did attend, moreover, is difficult to judge. For example, during the 1915 riot the Aspíllagas singled out teenagers for special criticism. It seems that the influence of a rough, crowded, and unhealthy environment had had a more telling effect than a few years of primary education.

Paternalism

The foundation of a plantation school is but one example of the evolving managerial philosophy of the Aspíllagas, which sought to control workers more through manipulation than through violence. Their strategy of control involved fewer risks in a plantation society that was growing more complex and less responsive to more primitive methods of domination. Since the turn of the century, Cayaltí had acquired a larger work force, laborers had established households on the estate, and all along the coast there were rumblings of a working-class movement.

The reliance on relatively less-violent methods of control also reflected the need to help first-generation plantation workers adjust to an alien and harsh environment. The Aspíllagas strove to minimize adjustment problems, which undermined efficient production, by providing inducements in the form of recreational facilities, nonmonetary income (housing and food rations), as well as fines and bonuses. Significantly, within a broader historical context, similar problems of adjustment were experienced among first-generation industrial workers in Great Britain and the United States, and early industrialists in those countries sought similar solutions.[88]

It may seem curious that the Aspíllagas never tried to use religion as a mechanism of control. The owners of Cayaltí sometimes asked for the Lord's assistance in overcoming business problems, but they never hired priests to say mass on the estate or to instruct peons in the faith. The use of religion as a tool to control the minds and behavior of rural laborers is, however, most closely associated with less technologically advanced estates, like cattle and wheat ranches, and with the smaller plantations of the antebellum southern United States. Its relative effectiveness probably declined on large sugar estates, such as Cayaltí, where the organization of labor more closely resembled a factory model and where there was a periodic turnover in the work force.

The strategies of control the Aspíllagas, and other early industrialists devised, might easily be described as paternalistic, but the question remains as to whether they constituted paternal regimes. Paternalism is generally found in early industrial societies, where it represents an adaptation of personal patronage relations commonplace in peasant communities. Warm human feelings dominate relations between employer and employee, as opposed to the impersonal workings of the marketplace. Considerations of kinship, caste, or hereditary "estate," influence employment rather than simply on-the-job performance. Work is also arranged on the basis of duty or loyalty, rather than on cash in exchange for labor.[89]

Cayaltí represents an interesting case. It combined elements of early industrial relations within an agricultural enterprise, and after 1890 it drew the bulk of its work force from traditional peasant communities. Nevertheless, it would be difficult to conclude that paternalism dominated labor relations at Cayaltí.

In the first place, contracted workers served two masters: *enganchador* and planter. Contractors were sometimes members of the elite from peons' home towns, and as such, persons in a strongly superordinate position. Peons frequently requested favors and loans from their *enganchadores*, and on such occasions subordinated themselves in a manner that suggests a paternalistic relationship. Following are two examples of peons addressing the contractor Catalino Coronado: "I know that my patron is at once more than my father"; and "You are father to all your peons, as there is no one else of whom to ask a favor but you."[90] If we assume that these letters are truthful expressions, it must have been difficult for peons to serve both contractors and planters with an equal emotional commitment.

At Cayaltí, warm human feelings did not dominate relations between the Aspíllagas and their workers. In the provision of services, the owners were not motivated by common humanity or Christian sensibility, but by economic self-interest. The offering of loans and health care did not hinge on worker loyalty or employer gratitude, but were institutionalized services available to all employees, regardless of length of employment or job performance. Such services were considered essential to the recruitment and maintenance of a stable work force.

Moreover, the development of warm human feelings was inhibited by the shifting labor force and the Aspíllagas' view of highlanders as racially and socially inferior. Although the existence of racism does not eliminate the possibility of paternalism, at Cayaltí it made it more difficult to achieve. The Aspíllagas took a critical view of the social habits of highlanders and attributed those habits to the supposed racial deficiences of Indians, despite the fact that most of their peons were Spanish-speaking mestizos. It must be harder to fashion true feelings of affection for people whose character, habits, and background one dislikes.

It is also important to remember that certain services, notably the sale of staples at a loss during the inflation of the First World War, were reactions to outside political pressures and a substitute for increasing wages. In general, the provision of services should be viewed as an additional market relation with peons in which the Aspíllagas utilized their superior bargaining position to, in Alfred Marshall's words, get back "by underhand ways part of the wages which they nominally paid away."[91]

Additional elements of the paternalism paradigm do not fit Cayaltí. Hiring practices were not influenced by considerations of kinship[92] nor by expressions of worker loyalty toward the Aspíllagas, but on contractual arrangements with *enganchadores* or peons themselves. Moreover, the fundamental basis for the relationship between owners and workers was not exchange of patronage for loyalty, but of cash for labor. In fact, in the field the relationship was based on piecework, which, according to Marx, was the system best suited to capitalism.[93]

Still, having said this, there were paternalistic elements of some importance in labor relations at Cayaltí. The Aspíllagas clearly sought personal identification with the provision of services and the paying of wages, and these activities were associated with the family and not with an abstract corporation. The personal touch could also be exploited to full advantage on special occasions. For example, when Ismael Aspíllaga Anderson provided workers with free train transportation from the fiesta in Monsefú, he knew that they would be grateful to him and to the estate. This may have been only a gesture, but it still called forth expressions of sincere gratitude from workers.

Workers and their families also benefited from improved health care, housing, and other services, regardless of the Aspíllagas' motives. In fact, the nonmonetary portion of their income covered many traditional expenses and left them with more cash to spend on other items. For example, in Lima in 1900 the poorest workers, who earned less than sugar workers, spent all of their income on rent and food.[94] Moreover, cost-of-living surveys of low-income families in the United States in 1874–1875, 1888–1889, 1901, and 1917–1918 show that food and rent constituted around two-thirds of expenses.[95] In the final analysis, nonmonetary income (as well as recreational facilities and other paternalistic gestures) made life a bit more bearable for these people and did not leave them completely at the mercy of the cash nexus of the labor market.

Finally, by choosing to manipulate and accommodate workers, instead of repressing them as vigorously as they had in the late nineteenth century, the Aspíllagas also improved their chances of avoiding serious labor conflicts.

This was an important consideration in view of the rising tensions between labor and management on neighboring sugarcane plantations. If they could prevent the outbreak of serious strikes at Cayaltí, they might also avoid unionization and politicization of their workers. These were important considerations for all sugar planters, and certainly no less so for such a politically sensitive family as the Aspíllagas. Their style of labor management, although it did not constitute paternalism, left them more maneuverability in controlling workers in the face of confrontation.

9. Confrontation

In December of 1927 Antero Aspíllaga Anderson wrote to his father,

> Unfortunately, the truth is that we have not found here the old days in which the people were otherwise and good and with whom one did not fight. Those were other times; they were times in which one could take trust. Now we are in another epoch in which everything is completely different. On the estate much has been reformed and much progress has occurred, and with all of this [has come] more work, more vigilance, more complications, more worries, more of everything, all of which is inherent to progress.[1]

In rather emotional terms, young Antero described an atmosphere of confrontation at Cayaltí, which he accurately attributed to conflicts "inherent" to the economic development of the plantation and, more obliquely, to the growing militancy of sugarcane workers. Since 1912, workers had periodically struck the plantations in the region and voiced a variety of demands headed by a desire for higher wages. Although Cayaltí was not immune to labor conflicts during this period, it avoided major confrontations and suffered only minor strikes until the 1940s. The center of strike acivity was, instead, the Chicama Valley, site of the largest, technologically most-advanced estates. There, the plantations Casa Grande and Roma were the foci of confrontation between labor and capital, with contiguous estates frequently becoming engulfed in the disturbances.

How and why did Cayaltí escape the violence? The answer lies both in structural differences between the major producers and in the actions of individual estate managers. Cayaltí had undergone fewer technological and organizational changes than most major producers, which led to greater continuity in labor relations. Whereas Casa Grande was constantly modernizing—building a new mill, buying the latest tractors, hiring efficiency experts—Cayaltí muddled along with archaic equipment and a trusted crew of employees who had been with the family for decades. The end result was significantly lower production, but also relatively less tension between labor and capital.

These differences, however, do not fully explain the lack of violence at Cayaltí. Considerable credit must also be given to the Aspíllagas for effectively defusing many potentially dangerous situations and, in general, for taking personal control over the daily management of the estate. Although they were not the most successful businessmen of their generations, the Aspíllagas took great pains to protect Cayaltí from labor unrest. Their actions can be contrasted with those of other planters, who sometimes ignited explosive situations through managerial blunders.

Political Background

The rise of a working-class movement on the northern coast made the government a more important actor in social control, particularly in the suppression of strikes and labor unions. This caused planters considerable concern, because the Civilistas' domination of national politics began to unravel during the First World War. The Civilistas' problems actually began in 1912, when the party's candidate for the presidency, none other than Antero Aspíllaga Barrera himself, was defeated by a political upstart, Guillermo Billinghurst, with the support of the urban working classes. Billinghurst was subsequently overthrown in 1914 by a coalition of Civilistas, Augusto Durand of the Liberal party, and the military. General Oscar Benavides, the coup leader, served as interim president until the Civilista candidate, José Pardo, was elected the following year.[2]

Billinghurst's election demonstrated—rather painfully to Antero personally—the potential political strength of the working class. The Aspíllagas did not believe that the Pardo administration effectively represented the interests of capitalists during the turbulent World War I period, a view that indicated the growing split in the Civilista leadership and that foreshadowed the emergence of Augusto B. Leguía in 1919. The concern of the Aspíllagas, who represented the older, more conservative branch of the party, is clearly expressed in this letter from Ramón Aspíllaga Barrera to his brothers in 1917:

The truth is that the capitalists of Peru, especially those in agriculture, are alarmed by the jealousy, envy, exaggeration . . . that excites the majority of our countrymen, with or without official representation. They consider us swimming in gold and obligate us to share with everyone that which today we have worked to gain. They forget the bad times that we have gone through, only living more or less well and the necessity that we now have to form a reserve for the normal or bad times that have to return. These jealousies and emulations have made the majority of capitalists despondent and even resolved to liquidate their businesses and pass them on to foreigners, in fear of the chaos that may come. Frankly, that is the borderline of courage for us and a very unpromising future for our heirs.

These doctrines and situations cannot continue. And as capitalists and men of good we will then have to take over the control of the state and throw out the phony politicians, not only from the opposition, but even among those who are part of the government, who waste their time with political or personal questions in place of the very simple and plain [task] of honorably administering the country. . . . [Administering] a land such as Peru only requires that government leaders leave us to go our own way, and so it was effectively proven in the administrations of Piérola, and Romaña, [when] they [workers] neither attempted to have strikes nor were the ambitions of the people awakened who should accept their position.[3]

Clearly, a great deal had changed since the turn of the century, including the workers' commitment to organize and strike to improve their position in society. This was something that could not be obliterated by presidential decree or by legislation. It had become an important goal for workers, and a threat to capitalists' profit margins and political dominance. In the years to follow, the working-class movement continued to gain momentum, and in 1919 a series of massive strikes in Lima forced President Pardo to grant workers an eight-hour day.[4]

For the Aspíllagas, the decree was another disappointment, although more for political than for financial reasons. On sugarcane plantations, the decree only affected mill workers and tractor drivers, as field hands worked by piecework. Thus, at Cayaltí the labor bill only rose by 5 to 10 percent.[5] However, the winning of the eight-hour day represented a significant political victory for workers and a major defeat for the Civilistas and the interests they served.

Further disappointment would come to the Aspíllagas in 1919. In that year Antero would once again lose the presidential election, this time to Leguía, who would remain in power for eleven years. Leguía proved a tenacious adversary, initially courting the political support of the working classes and eventually exiling Antero and other Civilista leaders. However, he did little or nothing to undermine the economic domination of the coastal oligarchy, from whose ranks he came, and sided with planters in the 1921 Chicama Valley strike. Still, the Aspíllagas and other planters viewed Leguía as an enemy and felt threatened during his regime.[6]

Colonel Luis M. Sánchez-Cerro overthrew the dictator in 1930 and established the National Revolutionary Junta to govern until new presidential elections could be arranged. Although the Civilista party had been severely crippled during Leguía's term, the Aspíllagas and other party members now worked closely with Sánchez-Cerro and the junta. They all shared a hatred of Leguía, and the politically inexperienced army colonel looked to these former government leaders for advice in running the country and planning for the election.[7]

Strike Activity in the Chicama, Moche, and Lambayeque Valleys

These political developments were understandably of great importance to north coast planters, especially during a period of labor unrest, when they might require the assistance of the army and the Guardia Civil. Strikes occurred throughout the region during these years, with the largest ones erupting outside of the Saña Valley.

An analysis of labor confrontation on regional plantations provides a useful comparative framework for studying labor relations at Cayaltí. Such a perspective illustrates the reasons for the success or failure of the Aspíllagas in avoiding strikes and provides a view of the wider arena of labor strife within which the owners of Cayaltí operated.

The history of labor conflicts in the Chicama Valley has already been examined in some detail and there is no need to present a lengthy analysis here.[8] Since the late nineteenth century, a handful of major producers, led by Casa Grande, Cartavio, and Roma, had dominated the valley. A series of strikes rocked these plantations in 1912, 1917, 1921, and 1931. Each had its own distinctive features linked to grievances on individual estates, mismanagement, changes in the structure of the regional and national economies, and political developments. The violent history of the valley proved a fertile breeding ground for the formation of the Alianza Popular Revolucionaria Americana (APRA) party,[9] Peru's most successful leftist organization and the dominant force in the politicization and unionization of sugarcane workers in the region.

The strike that erupted at Casa Grande in 1912 was the largest in the history of the nation. The plantation was in the process of rapid transformation by means of technological improvements, extensive land consolidation in the valley, managerial reorganization, and the partial phasing out of *enganche* in favor of noncontract labor (*libres*).[10] By disrupting normal social relations and work patterns, these changes sowed considerable discontent among both workers and managerial personnel. Particularly controversial were the replacement of several Peruvian employees with Germans, who were characterized as "imperious" by the Aspíllagas,[11] and uncompensated increases in work loads.

In the early stages of the strike, disgruntled contractors and former employees incited workers to violence. Strikers commenced an orgy of destruction, burning cane fields, sacking stores, and breaking machinery. Amid rumors that the death of all German employees had been called for, troops were dispatched from Lima to quell the disturbances. In the meantime, however, the strike had spread to the neighboring plantations of Cartavio and Chiquitoy, and to Laredo in the Moche Valley. All of these estates suffered significant damage before the army, with local police and militia, brought a temporary peace to the region. In all, as many as 150 workers lost their lives.[12]

Peter Klarén and Bill Albert have emphasized the violent, disorganized nature of the strike and the failure of workers to win permanent gains.[13]

Workers were indeed violent and disorganized throughout most of the strike; however, they eventually formed a strike committee, hired two attorneys, and formally negotiated with management.[14] In the settlement that followed, the Gildemeisters made several significant concessions, including a general wage increase, the construction of a larger hospital and new housing, the firing of a German employee, and the payment of back pay to several staff. For their part, strikers agreed to return to work within a few days.[15]

In addition to its obvious local importance, the 1912 strike signaled to all planters in the region the potential for conflict on their own estates. Most plantations were undergoing the same transformation as Casa Grande, although at a slower pace, and the tensions that had exploded there might someday surface closer to home. However, planters were also aware that the Gildemeisters had blundered by hiring employees fresh off of the boat from Germany. Although these men were well-qualified technicians, they displayed little knowledge of the local culture and few of the subtle managerial skills necessary to control workers in an environment with a high potential for violence.

The 1912 strike was but a prelude to a more intense period of conflict that began after the outbreak of World War I.[16] The war sent a shock wave through the Peruvian export economy, dramatically increasing the value of sugar (and other exports) while causing significant inflation. The upshot of these developments was to raise the cost of living for workers at the same time that planters' profits soared. Planters exacerbated their workers' plight by refusing to grant them large wage hikes (real wages fell during this period) and by further increasing the cost of foodstuffs by replacing staples grown on their estates with cane. The contradictions inherent in the increasing poverty of workers and the growing wealth of planters helped to fuel violent confrontation on plantations. Moreover, sometimes urban workers who urged sugar workers to organize and strike influenced these struggles.

Although there was considerable agitation by sugar workers all along the northern coast, the center of strike activity was once again Casa Grande. The most significant conflict occurred in 1917, when field-workers learned that their counterparts at Cartavio were earning nearly twice as much as they. The strikers' cry for increased pay and lower food prices soon spread to Cartavio and Chiclín, and planters were faced with the prospect of paralyzed production at a time of record prices for their product. Unlike in 1912, this strike was surprisingly nonviolent, with only a few cane fields being put to the torch. Strikers eventually formed strike committees and negotiated with planters, but their lack of cohesion and the reluctance of growers to grant concessions resulted in a stalemate. Rather than continue negotiations and risk further losses in production, planters chose to crush workers with the full force at their disposal. The army was called in, and strikers were forced back to work without having won any significant gains.[17]

In the same year, a similar strike occurred on the plantation Pomalca, one of the largest producers in the Lambayeque Valley. Workers struck for higher wages to compensate for rapid inflation.[18] Management was willing to offer workers temporary relief in the form of cash bonuses and free food, but would not negotiate with them on wages. Rather than risk a stalemate that would shut down production during a period of record profits, planters called in the army to force strikers back to work. In the process of crushing the strike, troops killed several workers and injured many others. Writing from nearby Cayaltí, Ramón Aspíllaga Barrera predicted that the bloodshed would deter future strikes in the valley, but conveniently forgot to mention one of his maxims of labor management, namely, that repression leads to retaliation.[19]

Although these strikes failed, workers had learned a valuable lesson in class relations. By choosing massive repression over conciliation, planters made it clear, at least to some workers, that they would have to organize to secure advances. Thus, the following year workers at Cartavio succeeded in forming a primitive labor union (the Sociedad Obrera de Auxilios Mútuos y Caja de Ahorros de Cartavio, the Workers' Mutual Aid and Savings Society of Cartavio) that won an eight-hour day for the plantation's factory and workshop workers.[20]

The end of the First World War did not immediately alter the course of the Peruvian sugar economy. The war-torn European economy recovered slowly, and it was two years before beet producers could resume full production and re-enter the world market. In the interlude, the demand for sugar increased and prices reached record highs, resulting in unprecedented profits for Peruvian producers.[21] The inflation of the war years also continued, eroding workers' wages and setting the stage for further conflicts with planters.[22]

During the period from 1919 to 1921 workers on most north coast estates clamored for increased wages and improved living conditions. This time, however, planters adopted a more conciliatory position and granted many demands. There were several causes for this change in policy. In the first place, planters distrusted Leguía, who had now seized the presidency. They did not know if he would be willing to authorize the use of troops to crush strikes, as had José Pardo and other Civilista presidents. Moreover, planters also had to consider the growing militancy of sugar workers, the unattractiveness of shutdowns at a time of record profits, and the increased demand for labor as estates expanded their production capacities.

By 1921 the world sugar economy was finally returning to its prewar equilibrium. Demand no longer outstripped supply, and prices plummeted. In Peru, planters' profits abated and so did the inflationary spiral.[23] Labor relations on plantations, however, would never return to prewar conditions. The conflicts of the war years established an adversary relationship between labor and capital on strike-torn estates, and set the stage for more intense conflicts in the postwar period.

Responding to workers' demands for higher wages, in 1920 Víctor Larco Herrera, owner of the plantation Roma in the Chicama Valley, granted a 33 percent increase. Within a year, however, the sugar market had collapsed, and Larco rescinded the increase, explaining that it had only been a temporary bonus. This was a serious miscalculation on his part, as workers not only demanded full reinstatement of their wages but an additional increase. They also added a long list of demands, including the abolition of *enganche*, extension of medical care, suppression of the plantation police, and formal recognition of the newly formed Sociedad Obrera de Auxilios Mútuos y Caja de Ahorros de Roma. When Larco rejected every demand, the entire work force went out on strike.[24]

The 1921 strike was particularly significant because of the solidarity displayed by workers and the role of the Leguía government. This was the first plantationwide strike in the region formally led by a union, and it served as an important organizing force and vehicle for gaining the support of other workers. Strikers were quickly joined by workers on neighboring plantations and railway workers and longshoremen in Salaverry, actions that linked the sugar workers' movement with the urban proletariat. The union also established a strike fund that proved vital when Larco denied strikers food and water.[25]

Local authorities responded to the strike by arresting union leaders and attempting to force laborers at Roma back to work. This tactic failed, however, when the union organized a mass exodus of workers to the outskirts of neighboring towns, where they were sustained by the contributions of fellow strikers. It was at this juncture that President Leguía became involved, dispatching from Lima Agustín Haya de la Torre as a representative of the Sección de Trabajo del Ministerio de Fomento (Labor Branch of the Ministry of Development).[26] Haya ordered the release of union officials and established an arbitration board composed of union leaders, local government officials, and management from Roma. The negotiations that followed resulted in an agreement incorporating most of the workers' demands.[27]

Víctor Larco Herrera, however, soon negated the settlement by shutting down the mill at Roma in favor of milling his cane at Casa Grande. This action necessitated the firing of dozens of men, including several union leaders, and was interpreted by workers as an attempt to break their union. The result was another strike backed by workers from neighboring estates and urban areas. To bolster their negotiating position, this time workers also formed the Sindicato Regional de Trabajo (Regional Labor Union), the first regional agricultural labor organization in Peru.[28]

Once again, local and national officials intervened and urged planters to adopt a conciliatory position. However, planters stubbornly refused to negotiate and had union leaders arrested. This brought strikers additional backing from local unions and compelled Leguía to send the minister of development, Lauro Curletti, as the new government arbitrator. Although Curletti was generally critical of living and working conditions on Chicama Valley plantations, he refused to recommend wage increases or to sanction unions without government approval. His report signaled a hardening of the central government's position toward labor, a position that a presidential decree designed to end the strike further articulated. In his pronouncement, Leguía granted workers several concessions, including an eight-hour day and the end to *enganche* by independent contractors, but he backed Curletti on the crucial issues of wages and union recognition.[29]

Unfortunately, the decree satisfied neither workers nor planters, and the strike continued.[30] Leguía was now in a difficult position. The strike was hurting the already-sagging sugar industry, and the president had to worry about falling export taxes and unfavorable balance of trade figures. His own prestige had suffered as a result of the government's failure to reach an accord. Historians have also mentioned that his early support for the working class was insincere, designed only to help secure his regime and unnerve his political adversaries. Leguía's own background, moreover, linked him more to the interests of capital than labor. At one point, for example, he had managed a large sugarcane plantation in the Cañete Valley. All of these factors influenced his decision to crush the sugar workers' unions and force strikers back to work at gunpoint. The process took some three months, from January to 21 March 1922, and resulted in scores of deaths among workers. Troops remained garrisoned in the valley to prevent future agitation.[31]

The 1921 strike clearly accelerated the struggle between labor and capital in the Chicama Valley. The formation of unions marked an important watershed in local history, and their brutal suppression by troops demonstrated the intransigence of planters and the central government. This strike also showed, once again, that managers could exacerbate explosive situations through imprudent decisions. Víctor Larco Herrera made decisive errors in rescinding the wage increase and then choosing to grind his cane at Casa Grande. Ironically, despite the ultimate crushing of the strike, Larco also lost. He never recovered from the financial losses suffered as a result of the shutdown, and following a disastrous flood in 1925, he sold out to Casa Grande.[32]

Labor relations in the Chicama Valley remained tense throughout the remainder of the decade, although the presence of troops prevented the outbreak of serious strikes. The Great Depression, however, unhinged the export economy and brought Augusto B. Leguía tumbling from power. Planters were now confronted with an economic crisis and an uncertain political future. They hoped to avoid financial ruin by laying off workers and reducing wages, and they pegged their political fortunes on the presidential candidacy of Colonel Luis M. Sánchez-Cerro, the military *caudillo* who had ousted the dictator Leguía.

The concerns of workers, of course, were dramatically different. Wage reductions and layoffs had sparked strikes in the past, and workers' political fortunes had never really been represented, that is, until now. The 1931 political campaign witnessed the emergence of the APRA party, and the presidential candidacy of its founder and leader Víctor Raúl Haya de la Torre. As Klarén has noted, Haya was from Trujillo and therefore sensitive to local social and economic issues. The party platform, calling for the right to strike and organize unions, a minimum wage, the abolition of *enganche*, and improved health care, was clearly designed to gain the support of sugar workers. According to Klarén, party cells sprang up at Cartavio, Laredo, Chiclín, and Casa Grande. APRA also won the support of local merchants and small farmers who had been hurt by the expansion of Casa Grande.[33]

The 1931 election was closely contested. Haya received nine out of ten votes in the Province of Trujillo, and a clear majority in the northern departments. However, this was insufficient to offset the support that Sánchez-Cerro received from the oligarchy and the urban working classes. Sugar planters welcomed the victory of the mestizo army colonel, but the Aprista hierarchy, which later conspired to tap the support of sugar workers to bring about the downfall of the new president, rejected the election as fraudulent.[34]

APRA organized a massive labor strike in the valley, followed by a political revolution. Support was garnered from a handful of disaffected military officers, but the bulk of the rebel forces consisted of sugar workers. The party succeeded in paralyzing sugar production in the valley and capturing the departmental capital of Trujillo. Nevertheles, troops were quickly dispatched from Lima and Piura and the air force bombed rebel positions. The Aprista leadership fled across the border into Ecuador, leaving sugar workers to answer for the execution of thirty-four army and Civil Guard officers killed during the occupation of Trujillo. When the city was retaken and the bodies discovered, the army shot perhaps as many as fifteen hundred suspected rebels. With the revolution crushed, an uneasy peace gradually returned to the valley's sugarcane plantations.[35]

The 1931 Aprista rebellion brought to a close a cycle of conflict between labor and capital in the Chicama Valley that had culminated in the participation of sugar workers in a leftist political revolution. Along the way, unions had been formed and forcibly dissolved, and the lives of many sugar workers had been lost. With the crushing of the 1931 rebellion, APRA was forced underground and unions were outlawed on sugarcane plantations. Nevertheless, the events of the previous decades had left an indelible impression on local workers, who remained loyal to the party in the decades ahead.

In the same year as the Trujillo revolution, a major strike occurred in the

Lambayeque Valley. The strike does not seem to have been inspired by APRA, but to have grown out of economic problems caused by the Great Depression. It began at Pátapo, a major producer located in the eastern end of the valley. Pátapo's workers had secretly formed a union, the Sindicato de Obreros de Pátapo (Workers' Union of Pátapo), in affiliation with the Sindicato General de Chiclayo (General Union of Chiclayo). The union presented the administrator of the estate, Juan Pardo y Miguel, with a long list of demands, including formal recognition of the union and the right to strike, an increase in wages, an eight-hour day and overtime, and improved living conditions.[36]

The existence of the union and the strike caught Pardo y Miguel by complete surprise. The Aspíllagas believed that he had actually provoked the strike by beating workers and, more recently, by forcing them to work on May Day.[37] Overwhelmed and outmaneuvered, Pardo y Miguel called a general meeting of local sugar growers, including Ismael Aspíllaga Anderson. Ismael emerged from the meeting concerned over Pardo y Miguel's apparent willingness to meet most of the strikers' demands, except an increase in wages. He believed that recognition of the union would encourage sugar workers on other estates to organize. He noted that the strike had already spread to Pucalá, a plantation contiguous to Pátapo and that Pucalá's administrator also seemed willing to compromise with strikers.[38]

Because of these concerns, the Aspíllagas used their considerable influence with the National Revolutionary Junta, which had been formed pending the 1931 elections, to suppress the strike. Working with the prefect of Lambayeque, the Aspíllagas arranged to have several persons arrested and expelled from the department. The list of deportees included the editors of the proworker newspaper *El Trabajador*, a union organizer from Pátapo, and three union leaders from Chiclayo.[39] In addition, the Aspíllagas convinced the junta to issue a decree forbidding planters to grant pay increases or to decrease the size of the work load.[40]

These actions, however, failed to influence the course of events significantly. Pardo y Miguel proceeded to make a settlement with workers at Pátapo that incorporated most of their demands, including recognition of the Sindicato de Obreros de Pátapo.[41] The agreement shocked other planters, who conspired to break the union and arranged for the arrest and deportation of two strike leaders on Pátapo. This action seriously underestimated the unity and tenacity of workers, however, as almost immediately a general strike was declared in the department. Those adhering to the walkout included workers from Pátapo, Pucalá, Pomalca, field-workers from Tumán, and longshoremen from Pimental.[42]

The local government and planters responded by mobilizing a campaign of terror and repression. Several hundred strikers heading for a general meeting in Chiclayo were detained by troops and then dispersed with gunfire. This resulted in as many as eleven deaths.[43] Police then arrested dozens of union leaders, union lawyers, and prolabor journalists. The proworker newspaper *El Trabajador* was closed down, and planters conspired to launch an antiworker campaign in the conservative paper *La Hora*. On the plantations, union organizers were arrested and expelled from the department, and planters arranged to have air force planes buzz their estates in a show of force. Within a few weeks, Ismael Aspíllaga Anderson could write to his brothers that an enforced peace had been brought to the area.[44]

Although the 1931 strike in the Lambayeque Valley was not linked to APRA, it signaled profound political changes in the region. The most important developments were the creation of a union at Pátapo, the solidarity demonstrated between rural and urban workers, and the existence of a proworker press. These changes frightened the Aspíllagas and other planters because they foreshadowed an era of increased confrontation with workers.

For the moment, however, planters had the political power to crush unions and all threats from the Left. The problem was, as the Aspíllagas recognized, that planters' reliance on violent repression bred anger, frustration, and hatred among workers. Although the Aspíllagas recommended the use of troops to crush the Pátapo union, they avoided unnecessary force in the daily management of workers and strove to avoid conflicts that could lead to unionization at Cayaltí. They were extremely critical of estate managers like Pardo y Miguel, whose brutal methods of control helped to cause the strike at Pátapo, an event that created problems for all planters in the department.

Cayaltí

Cayaltí was the only major producer in the area to escape the 1931 strike virtually unharmed. This was not unusual. The Aspíllagas had not experienced a serious labor conflict, one that caused a lengthy shutdown or significant damage to estate property, since strikes had become commonplace in the region. One of the reasons for this was structural. By choosing to invest less in technological expansion after 1911, Cayaltí fell behind Casa Grande and other estates in production capacity; however, by retaining a more archaic system of production, the Aspíllagas also retained more maneuverability in controlling workers by means of paternalistic devices whose origins lay in preindustrial social relations. The owners of Cayaltí also kept close contact with workers by actively participating in the daily management of the estate.

The Aspíllagas were acutely aware that Cayaltí could become engulfed in a storm of worker violence that might lead to unionization and politicization.

This was their great fear, and they dedicated considerable time and effort to preventing it. They were not opposed to the use of repression, but they used it judiciously. They blamed a great deal of the strike activity on the north coast on outside agitators, especially urban trade unionists and proworker journalists. They also noted that strikers sometimes traveled to other estates, and that mill workers tended to be more militant. These observations led them to screen new hirings, particularly in the mill, and to tighten security on the estate whenever a strike broke out in the region. The Aspíllagas also periodically expelled troublemakers from the plantation and used their political influence to suppress leftist political activities in the region.

When strikes did occur at Cayaltí, the Aspíllagas tried to convince workers of the unreasonableness of their demands. If strikers remained steadfast, however, the owners were generally willing to grant modest wage increases and improvements in living conditions, rather than risk a violent and prolonged conflict that could poison labor relations for years. As a matter of prudence, the use of troops was seen as a last resort.

The first noteworthy labor conflict at Cayaltí occurred in 1912. The Aspíllagas had taken certain precautions in the wake of the violence at Casa Grande, such as arming the staff. They also turned away workers who had come from the south, after giving them a few soles to travel to the next plantation.[45] These measures, however, did not prevent a large number of cane cutters from demanding higher wages and smaller work loads. Antero Aspíllaga Barrera, who was then running the plantation, handled the situation with great caution. Noting that cane cutters had complained to him in the past about low wages, and that neighboring estates were paying 15 to 20 centavos an hour more than Cayaltí, he decreased work loads and increased wages by 10 centavos per hour. The settlement pleased workers, and Cayaltí continued to pay less than its competitors. Antero explained to his brothers that "it was not possible to continue as before without at the least losing workers and having conflicts, which prudence and our own understood interests counsel us to avoid." To resist the workers' demands, he concluded, would result in "constant and disagreeable complaints."[46]

The outbreak of the First World War dramatically intensified labor conflict on the northern coast, as we have seen. Cayaltí was subject to the same kinds of pressures as other estates—rising cost of living for workers coupled with record profits for planters—but it managed to avoid serious disturbances. This was largely the result of management's success at placating workers and improving plantation security.

After the riot on the estate in 1915 and strikes the following year in the Moche Valley, the plantation police force was enlarged and instructed to guard against outside agitators, who the Aspíllagas believed were responsible for disrupting normal labor relations:

It is proven that there are agitators who enter the estates and disturb the tranquility of the workers and the relations between them and the *patrones*. [It is also proven] that dangerous elements come from the mills, so that, as I know we have already told you, you should make sure that not a single new worker or family enters the estate.[47]

At the same time, management also limited visits by families and friends of workers to twenty-four hours, and asked the governor of Chiclayo to suppress anarchist activity in the department capital and in Saña.[48]

In 1917 one of the principal causes of strikes in the Chicama and Lambayeque valleys was the rising cost of living.[49] The Aspíllagas responded by holding down the cost of staples at Cayaltí, arguing that it would be "stupid and dangerous" to do otherwise.[50]

They also believed that the rise in the cost of living was being unfairly exploited by political agitators as a weapon to attack planters and their interests. This was part of their growing concern that the economic and political dominance that the oligarchy had enjoyed in partnership with foreign interests was now fading. They were concerned by not only the growth of a working-class movement, and the anticapitalist propaganda that it generated, but also by weak leadership within the Civilista party.

Their concerns culminated in the defeat of Antero Aspíllaga Barrera in the presidential election of 1919. That same year also witnessed the outbreak of a series of minor labor disputes at Cayaltí. The basic cause of the disturbances was the skyrocketing cost of living, which rose by 73 percent during the course of the year (table 41). On four separate occasions, beginning in March and lasting through November, workers demanded wage increases to offset rising prices. Once the Aspíllagas uncharacteristically requested the presence of soldiers as an deterrent to worker violence. But the situation remained calm, and each time they consented to workers' demands and increased wages.[51]

The first years of the new decade were relatively peaceful at Cayaltí, as the cost of living fell by 46 percent in 1920 and remained stable for the next two years (see table 41). There were some minor disputes in the years to follow, but the Aspíllagas managed to defuse them before they escalated into strikes. For example, in 1923 Ismael Aspíllaga Anderson interrupted a shutdown in the mill before it could gain momentum and convinced workers to remain on the job. He then fired the organizers and had them expelled from the department.[52] In 1927 cane loaders refused to comply with a new method of payment requiring them to work more for less money. The Aspíllagas explained that all other plantations on the north coast had switched to the new system, and, after a month of haggling, loaders eventually gave in.[53]

In general, the Aspíllagas did not view labor disputes as emanating from legitimate grievances, but rather from the spread of poisonous working-class ideologies and trade unionism. This accounts for their great concern over outside agitators, particularly union organizers and prolabor journalists. These persons represented a genuine threat to Aspíllaga interests. They were alarmed, therefore, when, in 1921, several contractors, *mayordomos*, and twenty-five workers requested permission to form a mutual aid society at Cayaltí. Although the proposed charter was dedicated solely to the promotion of good will and fellowship, Antero saw the society as a dangerous precedent with nefarious consequences for the family's interests. He explained his reasons for rejecting the request to his son:

The terms of the organization and of the proposal we find correct and mannerly for the administration and the estate. The end that they pursue appears very saintly and good. But as behind the cross one can find the Devil, and as we have already agreed, for no manner or reason should we consent or permit institutional societies, clubs on the estate that carry the danger that they can serve as foci of pretentious intriguers and . . . pernicious agitators.[54]

Management was also concerned about the activities of radicals in the nearby town of Saña, who threatened to inculcate their workers with dangerous ideas. They requested the assistance of local political authorities in crushing the Centro Socialista de Saña and expressed concern over the painting of political slogans that praised the Russian Revolution and social revolution generally.[55]

A more serious threat to labor tranquility at Cayaltí, however, came when strikes broke out on neighboring estates. Recent history had shown that disturbances could spread rapidly from one estate to another, and that no plantation was immune to potential violence. The most threatening situation for Cayaltí developed during the 1931 strike in the nearby Lambayeque Valley.

In response to the Depression, Cayaltí had released some 150 workers and reduced wages, actions likely to produce discontent in the work force. When the strike erupted at Pátapo, the Aspíllagas helped to orchestrate its suppression by the government, as we have seen. At the same time, they took measures to prevent the spread of the strike to Cayaltí, including the doubling of security to suppress the dissemination of dangerous materials, especially the newspaper *El Trabajador*, and the entry of the ubiquitous outside agitator.[56] They succeeded in stopping a truck driver from Saña from passing out copies of *El Trabajador* and detained two workers caught signing up men for a Chiclayo union. Management expelled the troublemakers from the plantation and arranged for their departure from the department. Ismael Aspíllaga Anderson, taking pride in the lack of labor strife at Cayaltí, then granted an interview to a local paper in which he stated that his workers were paid well and treated fairly. The interview brought a response, in the form of a letter written to *El Trabajador*, by someone who claimed to be a worker from Cayaltí. The writer sarcastically accused Ismael of exaggerating wage scales and living conditions and asserted that Cayaltí's workers favored unionization. He ended by saluting the proletariat and signed himself "Marejildo Izquierdo" ("Marejildo Leftist").[57]

It is impossible to know whether the letter was truly written by a worker, or whether it was the work of the paper's editors, labor organizers, or strikers on other estates. It is possible that there existed sentiment for unionization at Cayaltí born of socialist thought and resentment toward the Aspíllagas. However, the course of events demonstrates that such beliefs were given little practical expression, especially in comparison with other plantations. Indeed, in the history of labor relations during these years, what stands out is the success that the Aspíllagas had in suppressing the development of a working-class movement on their estate.

Conclusion and Postscript

The period from 1912 into the 1930s witnessed a growing confrontation between labor and capital on north coast sugarcane plantations. A series of strikes rocked regional estates, with the most serious conflicts occurring at Casa Grande in 1912, Roma in 1921, Chicama Valley estates and Pátapo in 1931. The central issue in each case was higher wages, as laborers fought for a larger share of planters' profits. The dichotomy between falling wages and rising profits was particularly acute during the First World War, a period when strikes broke out on practically all regional estates.

These conflicts did not occur in isolation from one another. Strikes in the Chicama and Lambayeque valleys frequently spread to neighboring estates, and sometimes even to adjacent valleys. Moreover, urban workers and labor organizers from nearby cities sometimes tried to organize plantation workers, and the prolabor press supported strikers and unionization. This was indicative of larger changes within Peruvian society, as a working-class movement developed during these years to challenge the coastal elite.

On the northern coast, planters successfully resisted this challenge, but only through the use of extreme force. Planters enjoyed the support of Civilista governments, especially those headed by sugar planters, like José Pardo. These executives did not hesitate to send in the troops to crush strikes. After a short period of uncertainty, planters also received the support of Leguía in suppressing strikes. The dictator, despite his political differences with many north coast planters, shared their fear of the working class.

Nevertheless, the turmoil on the plantation left a legacy. Unions had been formed, workers from various estates had joined forces to demand higher wages and improved living conditions, and a prolabor political movement, APRA, had arisen in the region. Force could control these developments for the immediate future, but they would resurface years later as powerful instruments of lasting change.

Cayaltí did not completely escape the violence of the early twentieth century. Minor strikes periodically broke out on the estate, and the Aspíllagas were justifiably concerned over the spread of the working-class movement to their estate. However, they were successful at preventing serious strikes and the development of unions.

These successes should be attributed in large part to the Aspíllagas' program of social control. Beginning in the early twentieth century, they focused on defusing labor conflict through paternalistic gestures: they adopted a conciliatory policy on wage increases, kept the price of staples relatively low, guarded against the dissemination of socialist thought, and screened new recruits. It was a program that combined compromise with vigilance, and it worked because Cayaltí retained a system of production more responsive to social control and because of the managerial skill of the Aspíllagas. Like other planters, of course, the owners of Cayaltí also enjoyed the support of the government. Although they did not rely heavily on troops, they had authorities exile labor organizers and prolabor journalists from the department.

The support of the government also proved crucial in containing APRA and the working-class movement in the region for the remainder of the decade. Following the assassination of President Sánchez-Cerro in 1933, General Oscar Benavides took control of the executive and governed as a military dictator for six years. During this period, APRA and trade unionism were suppressed.[58]

When Benavides stepped down in 1939 he was replaced by Manuel Prado, a member of the elite. Prado's administration (1939-1945) coincided with a period of general prosperity, as the demand for Peruvian exports increased during the Second World War. Although APRA and unions remained illegal, the groundwork was laid for their legalization after the next presidential election.[59]

In 1945 José Luis Bustamante was elected president with the open support of APRA, which won a large number of seats in the national Congress. The Aprista leadership quickly organized a national union of sugar workers in affiliation with the Confederación de Trabajadores Peruanos (Confederation of Peruvian Workers).[60] At Cayaltí, the Aspíllagas were in a poor position to deal with this new threat. In 1943 the family had packed its belongings and turned the administration of the estate over to employees, thereby losing all personal touch with workers and direct control over labor relations. In so doing, they removed the linchpin in their regime of social control at the same time that efforts to unionize sugar workers were intensified.[61]

In the mid-1940s unions were established on almost all north coast sugarcane plantations, including Cayaltí. As a longtime employee of the estate lamented, "What a shame it is that the Aspíllagas don't go to their plantation, because the *Superintendent* and his new one at Cayaltí, *Elías* [the head of the union], are ruining the plantation, and in the long run it is the poor workers who will pay the consequences."[62] The new style of the Aspíllagas, he said, was to hire lawyers to negotiate with the union, rather than to deal directly with workers themselves. He longed for the personal style of Ismael and Luis Aspíllaga Anderson, who were no longer active in running the estate.[63]

With their personal control over labor relations severely weakened, the Aspíllagas now had to rely more on the government to control workers. As long as APRA remained powerful in Lima, they would have to live with unions. But as the coalition between Bustamante and APRA began to unravel, they and other planters began to exert pressure on the Labor Ministry to withdraw recognition of selected unions. The ministry finally complied with Cayaltí's request, and the union and its officers were expelled from the estate.[64]

Nevertheless, the Aspíllagas and other planters still feared the outbreak of strikes and the return of unions, particularly under the strains of the postwar recession. They created a secret insurance fund to guard against strike damage, but recognized that a better safeguard rested with a political solution.[65]

It is well known that sugar planters, including the Aspíllagas, were among the organizers of the coup d'état that toppled the crumbling Bustamante administration and ushered into power General Manuel Odría (1948–1956). During Odría's dictatorship, APRA was forced underground and unions were suppressed. Once again, sugar planters enjoyed the political protection of the central government and the army.[66]

Nevertheless, labor relations at Cayaltí had been unalterably changed during the 1940s. The seed of unionization had been planted, and the plantation administration now relied more on force to solve labor problems, including the stationing of the Guardia Civil on the estate.

It was under these circumstances that Cayaltí suffered its worst labor confict. To offset rampant inflation, in 1950 the government issued a decree raising the salaries of all workers. When the administration of Cayaltí neutralized the pay hike by raising prices in the plantation store, workers went out on strike. Police reinforcements were called in, and there followed a series of arrests and the death of a worker. Just when the strike seemed to have been broken, the police inexplicably turned and fired on workers who had assembled at the Guardia Civil post and then, firing indiscriminately, pursued them throughout the plantation. At least 120 workers were killed, and many others, burning cane fields in their wake, fled the estate.[67]

Years later, a worker recalled, "They gathered the dead and wounded with company trucks and took them directly to La Guitarra Mountain where a pit had been dug and there they were thrown." A friend of his drove one of the trucks and "he became ill from the horror of what he had seen and died without recovering."[68] Another eyewitness recalled the immediate aftermath of the conflict:

> Afterward, all was calm. The company had the support of all the authorities. They threatened the people who complained with dismissal or being shot. The police took the leaders away and nothing more was heard of them. The only thing heard was the crying of many old women, daughters, and wives asking about their dear ones. In the end, it was like an earthquake: senseless. There was calm, but, yes, there was this hate.[69]

The administrator of the plantation blamed the strike on the rise in prices, but believed that the violence could have been avoided if the Aspíllagas had been on the estate to negotiate with workers.[70] The personal touch, however, had long since been absent from labor relations at Cayaltí. It was now subject to the same bloody conflicts between labor and capital that had characterized the history of the Chicama Valley estates since 1912, and most Lambayeque plantations for decades.

Conclusion

In the decade following the disastrous War of the Pacific, the economic and political recovery of Peru was predicated on the resurgence of the agricultural and mining industries as well as on the return to civilian rule under the direction of the coastal elite. The sugar industry and sugar planters played important roles in this process. A largely new group of planters, many of recent immigrant origin, led the development of the industry and benefited from connections with foreign and domestic merchant houses. They acquired large estates on the northern coast, between the cities of Trujillo and Chiclayo, and invested heavily in land consolidation and technological improvements. By the late nineteenth century, sugar production in the region had increased significantly, making sugar one of the nation's leading exports. Sugar planters used their newly acquired wealth to gain entrance into the national elite and into positions of political importance. Two sugar planters, in fact, José Pardo and Eduardo López de Romaña, served as presidents of Peru during the period known as the República Aristocrática.

The initial success of sugar planters was achieved during a period of adversity, for, until the outbreak of the First World War, these entrepreneurs guided their estates through periods of stagnation caused by low demand for their product on the world market. They demonstrated considerable skill at acquiring capital and lowering the cost of production through labor-saving technological innovations.

The boom period for the industry occurred during the war years, when European sugar beet producers were forced out of the market, thereby reducing supplies and driving the price of sugar upwards. This was the period of great profit-taking for the sugar elite. With the end to hostilities, however, European producers returned to the market, and the price of sugar gradually declined to prewar levels. This was also the period when the elite lost control of the government to the dictator Leguía, who seized power in 1919 and remained in control until 1930. Leguía's fall from the presidency also coincided with the onset of the Great Depression, during which sugar prices fell to record lows and planters were faced with heavy losses.

An important, controversial aspect of this period in Peruvian history concerns the relative degree of direct foreign control over the sugar industry. All students of the industry agree that it depended on the export market for survival. However, Peter F. Klarén and others have also argued that the sugar industry, much like the copper and petroleum industries, was largely controlled by foreign corporations. This conclusion is based largely on the history of the Chicama Valley, where the largest plantations were owned by W. R. Grace & Co. of New York and the Gildemeister family. Nevertheless, as Klarén points out, the Gildemeisters are not easily classified as either foreign or Peruvian.[1] Moreover, outside of the Chicama Valley almost all large plantations were owned by Peruvians,[2] and together they far outdistanced the Grace estate in production.

It is also significant that Peruvian sugar planters did not receive all of their capital from foreign sources. Although British capital was important, the industry was initially capitalized with money generated domestically during the guano boom, and it later received capital from domestically chartered banks as well as from profits.

In an important sense, then, the sugar industry was an exception to the general pattern of economic development during these years. Namely, while other important sectors of the national economy fell into the hands of foreign firms, the sugar industry was largely controlled by nationals.[3] This gave planters a significant voice in molding the economic future of Peru, especially given their political strength.

Rosemary Thorp and Geoffrey Bertram have criticized sugar planters and other members of the national elite for not diversifying their investments and thereby wresting control of the national economy from foreign investors.[4] The Aspíllagas, Pardos, Gildemeisters, and others did make extensive investments in urban real estate, banks, insurance companies, and, on a much more modest level, in mining. It is true, however, that they never sought to buy out foreign corporations, systematically, because they never saw the need for it. Their prosperity had been built on linkages with foreign markets and merchants, and they welcomed such ties and strove to improve them. They wanted to learn from more experienced capitalists, such as the Kendalls, and from foreign managers and technicians. Their vision of Peru did not include an economy controlled by nationals. They saw no short-term nor long-term benefit for themselves without their traditional ties with foreign interests.

During the República Aristocrática, sugar planters grew rich while holding high political office as members of the Civilista party. During this period, they also welcomed foreign corporations into the country and stood by as these multinationals hauled profits out of Peru by the boatload. This was a similar structural pattern, on the surface at least, to what happened during the administration of Porfirio Díaz in Mexico, when a small elite dominated politics and foreign interests seized control of the petroleum and mining industries.

The Porfiriato ended with the Mexican Revolution, which overthrew the oligarchy and sought to end the predominance of foreign capital in the national economy. The República Aristocrática did not suffer a similar fate, but the elite did begin to lose control over national politics during the First World War. The Civilista party developed dangerous splits in its leadership that contributed to the defeats of Antero Aspíllaga Barrera in the presidential elections of 1912 and 1919. Both elections were important turning points in Peruvian history: the first because it demonstrated the Civilistas' vulnerability and the political threat of the working class, and the second because it ushered into power Augusto B. Leguía.

The war years also saw the rise of a working-class movement in the cities and in the countryside. Sugar planters felt that they were unfairly portrayed in the working-class press as greedy capitalists, and were also let down by some of their party leaders, who failed to deal forcefully enough with the threat from the dangerous classes. Naturally, planters were most concerned with the actions of workers on their own estates.

In discussing their workers, planters help to reveal the character and morality of capitalist development in Peru. For example, the ambition of young Antero and Ramón Aspíllaga Barrera to become heroes hinged on their ability to turn Cayaltí into a prosperous plantation during a period of chaos. If that required treating their Chinese wage laborers as slaves, then so be it. Their desire for wealth and power were overriding concerns.

The discussion of social relations of production raises questions of thematic importance for students of rural labor in Latin America. Beginning with Engels, scholars have recognized that forms of "bondage" can exist within predominantly capitalistic systems of production.[5] Moreover, many Latin Americanists have taken this position a step farther by emphasizing the importance of extraeconomic coercion in the formation of wage-labor regimes on haciendas and plantations.[6] This study also finds that coercion was an important feature of labor mobilization and control, but demonstrates that its importance decreased over time.

At Cayaltí, labor systems gradually evolved toward a regime of free wage labor. In earlier stages, planters relied heavily on extraeconomic coercion to recruit and control laborers. However, accommodation and manipulation gradually replaced force and indebtedness as the plantation community grew larger and more complex, laborers became more mobile and aggressive, and the polity stabilized.

The first stage in the development of wage labor extended from 1875, the year after the trade in Chinese indentured servants ended, into the early 1880s. This stage witnessed little change for laborers, as indentured servants merely had their contracts extended or were rehired under short-term arrangements at token wages. A minority, however, were hired as noncontract laborers at higher wages.

The second stage, spanning the period from roughly 1880 to 1890, saw the emergence of Chinese laborers contracted to Chinese merchants. These labor brokers sold the services of their countrymen to planters in return for the right to operate stores on the plantations and to have their laborers' wages paid through them. Contracted laborers grew in number as the decade advanced, although noncontracted Chinese and Peruvian wage laborers constituted sizable minorities.

The Chinese were subjected to a harsh regime of social control, which was somewhat harsher during the first stage. Their treatment reflected severe labor shortages, intense racism, and the temporary breakdown of public authority. Violence, intimidation, and indebtedness were all common control mechanisms planters employed.

The Chinese experience in Peru is an important chapter in the nation's history, but very few studies exist on this topic. This analysis, in fact, is the only one that discusses social and economic conditions in any depth. There is obviously considerable room for future research on this topic, including studies comparing the Chinese experience in different parts of the Americas. Chinese sugar workers in Cuba, for example, seem to have lived under a regime of social control similar to that experienced by their countrymen in Peru.[7]

Beginning in the 1880s, plantations on the northern coast of Peru began to recruit peasants from the nearby highlands to replace their aging Chinese laborers. A gradual process of labor substitution ensued, with Peruvians initially taking over jobs that required more strength, and the Chinese continuing in more-skilled positions, such as tractor drivers. Once again, something similar occurred in Cuba, where the Chinese frequently manned machinery while black slaves did back-breaking labor in the fields.[8]

The traditional interpretation of labor contracting (expressed in the work of Indianist writers, the early writing of Peter F. Klarén, and that of Ernesto Yepes del Castillo) emphasizes the importance of extraeconomic coercion. This study demonstrates, however, that labor recruitment involved the complex interaction of force and manipulation with economic incentives and accommodation. Peasants had ample reasons for wanting to leave the sierra, and plantations offered them material rewards in the form of advances, cash wages, food rations, and a variety of social services. This explains why many highlanders migrated to the coast of their own volition. Contractors did have to meet labor quotas, though, and this sometimes caused them to trick peons into signing employment contracts, or to force tenants and subtenants on their highland estates to fulfill labor obligations by working on the coast.

There is also no doubt that laborers were subjected to a regime of debt peonage on plantations. However, at Cayaltí debt peonage never served as a master strategy to form a permanent work force. In fact, contrary to the traditional interpretation, peonage was not an efficient system of social control. Planters and contractors both complained about the large sums of money that they had to advance to peons to get them to work, and indebted laborers sometimes ran away and could not be recaptured. In addition, the idea of a peon working a lifetime on a coastal estate, weighed down with debts, was simply impractical. After several years of hard labor in an insalubrious climate, productivity declined and the work force had to be replenished. Planters also found that their ability to maintain workers was influenced by forces beyond their control, namely the price of sugar on the world market. This variable was the primary determinant of profit margins, and hence of the ability to meet wage bills.

Labor contracting evolved through two general stages. The first, encompassing the period from the late 1880s until the First World War, witnessed the replacement of Chinese laborers with Peruvian peons. At first, there was a rapid turnover in the work force, but after a decade or so there developed a tendency for some contracted workers to remain on the estate for years at a time. Some of these workers even brought their families with them, or acquired second families on the coast.

The outbreak of the First World War marks an important watershed in the history of labor relations. The work force now began to show signs of increasing duality as a large number of noncontracted workers, *peones libres*, appeared on the estates. These laborers, who constituted a majority at Cayaltí by 1924, severed their ties with the highlands and settled on the coast as full-time wage laborers. They sold their labor directly to planters without the services of contractors and came close to being free wage laborers. Nevertheless, they could still receive loans from planters, which might bind them to estates, and were occasionally subjected to other forms of coercion.

After the changeover to Peruvian labor, the Aspíllagas devised more complex methods of control. Debt peonage, violence, and intimidation all remained part of their strategy, but they came to rely more heavily on accommodation and manipulation. The owners of Cayaltí sought to accommodate workers by offering them improved housing and medical care, fair prices on goods, and food rations. They also attempted to transform first-generation peons into dutiful and efficient laborers through work incentives and paternalistic gestures such as recreational facilities. Early industrialists in Great Britain and the United States who, like the Aspíllagas, were interested in improving production and providing a more secure environment for their investments, employed similar strategies of control.

The shift away from violent methods of control should also be seen in the context of the development of a working-class movement. The owners of Cayaltí firmly believed that violence begot violence and they cautioned *mayordomos* to rely more on tact, intellect, and manipulation to keep things quiet. The outbreak of strikes on neighboring plantations caused the Aspíllagas to screen new recruits, double plantation security, and, in general, adopt a more conciliatory attitude toward laborers rather than risk a major confrontation.

The Aspíllagas largely succeeded in escaping the violence that characterized labor relations on neighboring plantations. This should be attributed in part to their skill at defusing explosive situations and maintaining an effective system of control, and in part to their failure to keep pace technologically. In other words, their more archaic system of production offered a milieu more conducive to the implementation of paternalistic gestures whose origins lay in preindustrial social relations of production.

The Aspíllagas and other planters also benefited from the support of the state in controlling workers, particularly in the suppression of unions and strikes. This was especially important during the strikes that rocked the Chicama Valley in 1912, 1921, and 1931. On the surface, the politics of social control changed after 1931, as the military assumed a greater role in the direction of the Peruvian state, however, members of the elite remained influential as politicians, political advisers, newspaper publishers, and corporate leaders. In fact, the military and the oligarchy tended to have similar views concerning the economy, the need to suppress APRA, and the desirability of maintaining good relations with the United States and overseas corporations.

APRA continued to represent the interests of sugar workers and succeeded in establishing unions on many plantations during the Bustamante administration and after 1956. However, it never gained control of the presidency—either by revolution or election—and increasingly chose to enter into the politics of compromise with moderates and conservatives.[9]

By the 1960s APRA had completely shed its reformist image and was openly supporting policies that benefited the oligarchy. For example, during the first Belaúnde administration (1963–1968) APRA backed the devaluation of the sol (a policy that benefited exporters), opposed expropriation of foreign-owned petroleum companies (in direct opposition to its original anti-imperialist platform), and voted against a protectionist tariff. For our purposes, APRA's most significant policy reversal occurred when it helped to sabotage an effective agrarian reform law in the legislature. In fact, "Some of the amendments specifically introduced by the Apristas excluded the large sugar plantations from the application of the Agrarian Reform Act so long as it can be shown that the area covered permits an adequate use of the machinery."[10]

APRA's desertion of sugar workers left them without meaningful political support, and a decisive break with the past occurred in 1968, when General Juan Velasco Alvarado overthrew the democratic government of Fernando Belaúnde Terry and installed a revolutionary junta. One of his first major acts was to confiscate coastal sugar plantations, an important source of income for the oligarchy, and to transform them into cooperatives.

The Pardos, the Gildemeisters, the de la Piedras, the Larcos, indeed all of the sugar families who had played such an important role in the molding of modern Peru, were now without one of their principal sources of wealth. Although they received compensation in the form of credits, their economic loss was substantial.

The transition from plantation to cooperative was not an easy one. Problems arose over mismanagement, conflicts between workers and technicians, political interference, and competition for membership. Still, co-ops did result in higher wages for workers and increased production. They also substantially weakened the oligarchy, which loomed as a major political threat to the Velasco government.[11]

The fate of the sugar cooperatives lies in the political economy of Peru. The recent demise of the revolutionary junta and the re-election of Fernando Belaúnde Terry to the presidency represents a dramatic change in political and economic philosophy. Will the sugar oligarchy return, or a new one rise to take its place? If either happens, planters will likely have to devise more intricate and effective methods of control to dominate workers who have now shared in the cooperative experience.

Notes

Introduction: Modern Peru, Plantation Agriculture, and Social Control

1. Rosemary Thorp and Geoffrey Bertram, *Peru, 1890–1977: Growth and Policy in An Open Economy* (New York: Columbia University Press, 1978), chap. 15; Abraham F. Lowenthal, ed., *The Peruvian Experiment: Continuity and Change under Military Rule* (Princeton: Princeton University Press, 1975).

2. Jesús Chavarría, "La desaparición del Perú colonial (1870–1919)," *Aportes*, no. 3 (Jan. 1972), pp. 121–153; Dennis L. Gilbert, *The Oligarchy and the Old Regime in Peru* (Ithaca, N.Y.: Cornell University Dissertation Series in Latin America, 1977), chap.1; Julio Cotler, *Clases, estado y nación en el Perú* (Lima: Instituto de Estudios Peruanos, 1978), chap. 3.

3. Kenneth Duncan and Ian Rutledge, eds., *Land and Labour in Latin America: Essays on the Development of Agrarian Capitalism in the Nineteenth and Twentieth Centuries* (Cambridge: Cambridge University Press, 1977). For a provocative article that raises many relevant questions, see Arnold J. Bauer, "Rural Workers in Spanish America: Problems of Peonage and Oppression," *Hispanic American Historical Review* 59, no. 1 (Feb. 1979): 34–64.

4. Bauer, "Rural Workers."

5. Humberto Rodríguez Pastor, "El Archivo del Fuero Agrario, Lima, Perú," *Latin American Research Review* 14, no. 3 (1979): 202–207.

Chapter 1: The Physical and Historical Setting

1. David A. Robinson, *Peru in Four Dimensions* (Lima: American Studies Press, 1964), p. 157; Delbert Fitchett, "Defects in the Agrarian Structure as Obstacles to Economic Development: A Study of the Northern Coast of Peru," (Ph.D. diss., University of California, Berkeley, 1962), pp. 147–148.

2. Susan E. Ramírez-Horton, "Land Tenure and the Economics of Power in Colonial Peru: A Social History of the Hacienda in Lambayeque" (unpublished MS, 1981). Professor Ramírez kindly gave me permission to read and to cite her manuscript, which promises to be a significant contribution to Peruvian historiography.

3. Claude Collin Delavaud, *Les régiones côtières du Pérou septentrional* (Lima: Institut Français d'Etudes Andines, 1968); Robinson, *Peru in Four Dimensions*; Emilio Romero, *Geografía económica del Perú*, 3d ed. (Lima: University of San Marcos, 1961); Peru, Ministerio de Fomento, *Estadística de la industria azucarera en el Perú* (Lima, 1912).

4. Douglas E. Horton, "Haciendas and Cooperatives: A Preliminary Study of Latifundist Agriculture and Agrarian Reform in Northern Peru," Land Tenure Research Paper, no. 53 (Madison, Wis.: Land Tenure Center, 1973), pp. 6–7.

5. Ibid., p. 4.

6. Collin Delavaud, *Pérou septentrional*, pp. 363–367; chap. 3 for a discussion of land disputes between Saña and Cayaltí; *Censo general de la República del Perú, formado en 1876, Vol. V, Huanuco, Ica, Junin, Lambayeque, La Libertad* (Lima: Imp. del Teatro-Portal de Agustín, 1878), hereinafter cited as *Censo de 1876*.

7. For a discussion of pre-Columbian civilizations in the region, see Robert G. Keith, *Conquest and Agrarian Change: The Emergence of the Hacienda System on the Peruvian Coast* (Cambridge, Mass.: Harvard University Press, 1976), chap. 1.

8. *Encomenderos* held the royal grant of *encomienda*, which permitted them to extract goods and services from designated Indian communities.

9. Keith, *Conquest and Agrarian Change*; Ramírez-Horton, "Land Tenure," chap. 3.

10. Keith, *Conquest and Agrarian Change;* Ramírez-Horton, "Land Tenure," p. 100.

11. Ramírez-Horton, "Land Tenure," pp. 121–129, 134–137.

12. Ibid.; Frederick P. Bowser, *The African Slave in Colonial Peru, 1524–1650* (Stanford, Cal.: Stanford University Press, 1974).

13. Ramírez-Horton, "Land Tenure," pp. 164–172.

14. Ibid., pp. 176–177.

15. Bowser, *The African Slave.*

16. In many parts of Latin America the recovery of the Indian population dates from the eighteenth century. However, Ramirez-Horton's study of the northern coast of Peru shows that some Indian communities began to recover after 1650 (see Ramírez-Horton, "Land Tenure," p. 244, and appendix 7).

17. Ibid., chap. 6.

18. Ibid., pp. 316–318; Nicholas P. Cushner, *Lords of the Land: Sugar, Wine, and Jesuit Estates of Coastal Peru, 1600–1767* (Albany: State University of New York Press, 1980).

19. Ramírez-Horton, "Land Tenure," p. 319.

20. Nils Jacobsen, "The Development of Peru's Slave Population and its Significance for Coastal Agriculture, 1792–1854," (unpublished, 1974), p. 68.

21. Guillermo Céspedes del Castillo, "Lima y Buenos Aires. Repercusiones económicas y políticas de la creación del Virreinato de la Plata," *Anuario de Estudios Americanos* 3 (1946): 669–874.

22. J. R. Fisher, *Silver Mines and Silver Miners in Colonial Peru, 1776–1824* (Liverpool: Centre for Latin American Studies, 1977).

23. Ramírez-Horton, "Land Tenure," pp. 313–315.

24. Ibid., pp. 330, 343.

25. Manuel Burga, *De la encomienda a la hacienda capitalista: El valle de Jequetepeque del siglo XVI al XX* (Lima: Instituto de Estudios Peruanos, 1976), pp. 134–143.

26. Ramírez-Horton, "Land Tenure," pp. 347–348, 374.

27. Ibid., p. 357.

28. Ibid., pp. 357–376.

29. Jacobsen, "Peru's Slave Population," pp. 11–12, 20, 32–33, 82.

30. Burga, *El Valle de Jequetepeque*, p. 148.

31. Ibid., pp. 150–151.

32. *El Comercio* (18 August 1841); Santiago Távara, *Abolición de la esclavitud en el Perú* (Lima: Imp. del Comercio), p. 12; Flora Tristán, *Peregrinaciones de una paria* (Lima, 1946), p. 414; Jacobsen, "Peru's Slave Population," p. 70.

33. Jacobsen, "Peru's Slave Population," table 15, pp. 70–73.

34. Oscar Febres Villarroel, "La crisis agrícola en el Perú en el último del siglo XVIII," *Revista Histórica* 27 (1964): 181–182; Távara, *La esclavitud*, pp. 14–15; Jonathan V. Levin, *The Export Economies: Their Pattern of Development in Historical Perspective* (Cambridge, Mass.: Harvard University Press, 1960), p. 120; *El Comercio* (15 July 1841).

35. Pablo Macera, *Las plantaciones azucareras en el Perú, 1821–1875* (Lima: Biblioteca Andina, 1974), pp. lxvi–lxviii.

36. Levin, *The Export Economies*; Heraclio Bonilla, *Guano y burguesía en el Perú* (Lima: Instituto de Estudios Peruanos, 1974); W. M. Mathew, *The House of Gibbs and the Peruvian Guano Monopoly* (London: Royal Historical Society, 1981). Some of the early consignment contracts were granted to Peruvians. The Peruvian government departed from the consignment system in 1869, when it signed an agreement with Dreyfus Brothers & Co. of Paris to sell two million tons of guano in Europe, (see Levin, *The Export Economies*, pp. 98–99).

37. Bonilla, *Guano*; Mathew, *House of Gibbs*; Ernesto Yepes del Castillo, *Perú, 1820–1920: Un siglo de desarrollo capitalista* (Lima: Instituto de Estudios Peruanos, 1972), chap. 2; Watt Stewart, *Henry Meiggs, Yankee Pizarro* (Durham, N.C.: Duke University Press, 1946); Shane Hunt, "Growth and Guano in Nineteenth Century Peru," Discussion Paper no. 34 (Princeton, N.J.: Woodrow Wilson School). The value of Peruvian currency fluctuated. In 1863 Peru changed from the peso to the sol. The sol was made of silver and weighed 25 grams, 0.900 fine (see table N.1 for conversion figures).

Table N.1
Conversion Table for Sol

Date	Pence per Sol	U.S. Cents per Sol
1883	39.67	
1886	36.00	
1887	34.50	
1888	33.25	
1889	32.50	
1890	36.25	
1891	34.25	
1892	30.25	
1893	27.00	
1894	22.00	
1895	22.75	

Table N.1 (continued)

Date	Pence per Sol	U.S. Cents per Sol
1896	23.25	
1897–1912		48.50
1913		47.70
1914		47.20
1915		42.30
1916		48.20
1917		49.90
1918		52.30
1919		49.20
1920		45.90
1921		36.00
1922		38.60
1923		41.10
1924		40.50
1925		40.00
1926		37.20
1927		37.30
1928		39.70
1929		40.00
1930		35.30

Sources: William A. Bollinger, "The Rise of U.S. Influence in the Peruvian Economy, 1869 to 1921" (M.A. thesis, U.C.L.A., 1971), pp. 212, 273; I. G. Bertram, "Development Problems in an Export Economy: A Study of Domestic Capitalists, Foreign Firms and Government in Peru, 1919–1930" (Ph.D. diss., Oxford University, 1974), p. 36; Rosemary Thorp and Geoffrey Bertram, *Peru, 1890–1977: Growth and Policy in an Open Economy* (New York: Columbia University Press, 1978), table 3.2, p. 29.
Note: The change from pence to cents reflects the emergence of the United States as Peru's principal trading partner.

38. *Las plantaciones azucareras*, p. lxv; W. M. Mathew, "The Imperialism of Free Trade: Peru, 1820–1870," *The Economic History Review*, second series, 21, no. 3 (December 1968): 575, discusses graft during the Echenique administration.
39. *Libertos* were children of slaves born after 28 July 1821, who were technically free but had to work for their parents' masters up to the age of 20, if female, and 24, if male.
40. Jacobsen, "Peru's Slave Population," pp. 49, 77–79; Macera, *Las plantaciones azucareras*, pp. lxv, xxii, and chap. 3.
41. Macera, *Las plantaciones azucareras*, p. lxv.
42. Ibid., pp. lxvii, xxii, chap. 3.
43. Ibid., p. lxv; Jacobsen, "Peru's Slave Population," pp. 77–79.

Chapter 2: Planters and Capital, 1860–1933
   1. Dennis Gilbert has defined the Peruvian oligarchy in the following way:

The oligarchy is an elite group of families at the apex of Peru's propertied class which (a) controls certain strategic resources (coastal land and mines oriented toward export production, commercial banks and newspapers), (b) is extensively linked by ties of kinship and affinity both internally and with the most prestigious stratum of upper-class Lima society, with which it is closely identified, and (c) has built its substantial political and economic power on these bases. (*The Oligarchy and the Old Regime in Peru* [Ithaca, N.Y.: Cornell University Dissertation Series in Latin America, 1977], p. 340).

2. Jesús Chavarría, "La desaparición del Perú colonial (1870–1919)," *Aportes*, no. 23 (Jan. 1972), pp. 124–129; Julio Cotler, *Clases, estado y nación en el Perú* (Lima: Instituto de Estudios Peruanos, 1978), chap. 2.

3. Steve Stein, *Populism in Peru: The Emergence of the Masses and the Politics of Social Control* (Madison: University of Wisconsin Press, 1980), pp. 27–28.

4. Ibid.

5. Cotler, *Clases, estado y nación*, pp. 129–130; Chavarría, "La desaparición," p. 134.

6. Chavarría, "La desaparición"; Manuel Burga and Alberto Flores Galindo, *Apogeo y crisis de la República Aristocrática* (Lima: Ediciones "Rikchay Peru," 1979), pp. 88–94.

7. Rory Miller, "The Coastal Elite and Peruvian Politics, 1895–1919," *Journal of Latin American Studies* 14, no. 1 (May 1982): 97–120.

8. Gilbert, *The Oligarchy*, pp. 20–89; Stein, *Populism in Peru*, pp. 40–48. In 1919 Leguía won the election but seized the presidency in a coup d'état before he was installed in office. This allowed him to dissolve Congress and subsequently build an infrastructure for his dictatorship.

9. Bill Albert, *An Essay on the Peruvian Sugar Industry, 1880–1920, and the letters of Ronald Gordon, Administrator of the British Sugar Company in Cañete, 1914–1920* (Norwich: School of Social Studies, University of East Anglia, 1976), p. 6a, table 1.

10. Rafael Larco Herrera, *Memorias* (Lima: Empresa Editorial Rímac, 1947), pp. 9–10.

11. Peter F. Klarén, *Modernization, Dislocation, and Aprismo: Origins of the Peruvian Aprista Party, 1870–1932*, Latin American Monographs, no. 32 (Austin, Tex.: Institute of Latin American Studies, 1973), pp. 6–7; Larco Herrera, *Memorias*, pp. 10, 12, 15; Hermilio Valdizán, *Víctor Larco Herrera, el hombre-la obra* (Santiago de Chile: Nascimiento, 1934), p. 21. For a discussion of land consolidation in the Chicama Valley, see chap. 3.

12. Gilbert, *The Oligarchy*, pp. 55, 77–79.

13. Albert, *The Peruvian Sugar Industry*, p. 48a.

14. Klarén, *Modernization*, pp. 9, 15; Albert, *The Peruvian Sugar Industry*, p. 49a.

15. See chap. 3.

16. *Perú, 1820–1920: Un siglo de desarrollo capitalista* (Lima: Instituto de Estudios Peruanos, 1972), pp. 127–128; I. G. Bertram argues that the Gildemeisters were Peruvians (see "Development Problems in an Export Economy: A Study of Domestic Capitalists, Foreign Firms and Government in Peru, 1919–1930" [Ph.D. diss., Oxford University, 1974], p. 72).

17. Klarén, *Modernization*, p. 81.

18. Gilbert, *The Oligarchy*, p. 41, n. 7; *El Economista* (Lima) (30 Sept. 1910);

Gildemeister folder, AFA; Carlos Malpica, *Los dueños del Perú*, 6th ed. (Lima: Ediciones Peisa, 1974), pp. 99–103.

19. Klarén, *Modernization*, p. 9; William A. Bollinger, "The Rise of U.S. Influence in the Peruvian Economy, 1869 to 1921," (M.A. thesis, U.C.L.A., 1971). Bill Albert notes that

an interesting feature of Cartavio was that although the hacienda was managed by Grace, from 1889 to World War I the mill was operated by a Peruvian syndicate, the Ingenio Central de Cartavio. This company was established in Lima in 1899, with capital of 110,000 pounds sterling and under the direction of Antero Aspíllaga, the [co-] owner of Cayaltí. It is not immediately clear why Grace entered into this arrangement, but it is significant in showing that Peruvian entrepreneurs and capital were involved in developing what has generally been considered as a totally foreign owned enterprise. In 1914, Grace began to erect a new mill and it would seem that the Peruvian company was wound up at about this time, being superceded by the Compañia Agrícola Carabayllo, wholly owned by the Grace organization (*The Peruvian Sugar Industry*, p. 50a).

20. Gilbert, *The Oligarchy*, p. 41, n. 7.

21. See chap. 3; Claude Collin Delavaud, *Lés régions côtières du Pérou septentrional* (Lima: Institut Français D'Etudes Andines, 1968), p. 319; Pablo Macera, *Las plantaciones azucareras en el Perú, 1821–1875* (Lima: Biblioteca Andina, 1974), p. clxiii; Gilbert, *The Oligarchy*, p. 77, table 1–1.

22. Gilbert, *The Oligarchy*, pp. 55, 77, table 1–1.

23. Manuel Pardo himself never ran Tumán. In the twentieth century, Alfredo Ferreyros, a highly qualified technocrat, sometimes managed the estate. There has been some disagreement over exactly how the Pardo family acquired Tumán. Some have said that the government gave it to Manuel Pardo, but the Pardos themselves say that Felipe Barreda y Aguilar purchased the estate in 1872 for his daughter Mariana Barreda de Pardo, the wife of Manuel Pardo (see Jorge Basadre, *Introducción a las bases documentales para la Historia de la República del Perú con algunas reflexiones*, vol. 1 [Lima: P. L. Villanueva, 1971], pp. 409–410).

24. Douglas E. Horton, "Haciendas and Cooperatives: A Preliminary Study of Latifundist Agriculture and Agrarian Reform in Northern Peru," (Land Tenure Research Paper, no. 53, Madison, Wis.: Land Tenure Center, 1973), p. 8; Ricardo A. Miranda Romero, *Vda. de Piedra e Hijos, S. A. y entidades afiliadas* (Lima[?]: Imp. de Politécnico Nacional "José Pardo," 1959), pp. 10–19, 27–29; Gilbert, *The Oligarchy*.

25. Carlos J. Bachmann, *Departamento de Lambayeque. Monografía Histórico-Geográfica* (Lima: Imp. Torres Aguirre, 1921), p. 179; Rafael L. Barahona, *Juicio de Doña Rosa Ramos de Alamos y otros con La Compañia de Azúcar de Chiclayo* (Valparaíso, 1915), pp. 19–22; *El Peruano* (Lima) (16 October 1874); Macera, *Las plantaciones azucareras*, p. clxi; Enrique L. Espinoza, "Estadística Lambayeque," *Boletín del Ministerio de Fomento* 3, no. 9 (September 1905): 78; Klarén, *Modernization*, p. 21; Gilbert, *The Oligarchy*.

26. Manuel Burga, *De la encomienda a la hacienda capitalista* (Lima: Instituto de Estudios Peruanos, 1976), pp. 175–192. Burga gives the purchase price in pesos. Although the currency changed from pesos to soles in 1863, pesos remained in circulation and some transactions were made in this medium of exchange.

27. *La Prensa* (12 March 1951); Gilbert, *The Oligarchy*, p. 162.

28. "Patente de Navegación," 13 October 1852, private archive, Lima, courtesy of Dennis Gilbert.

29. Gilbert, *The Oligarchy*, p. 162. The Aspíllaga correspondence from Palto is housed at the AFA.

30. *El Peruano* (16 February 1886), quoted in Gilbert, *The Oligarchy*, p. 163. Gilbert also gives figures in pesos rather than soles.

31. *El Comercio* (21 May 1862), quoted in Gilbert, *The Oligarchy*, p. 163.

32. Carlos Camprubi, *Historia de los bancos en el Perú (1860–1879)*, vol. 1 (Lima: Editorial Lumen, 1957), pp. 3; 52, n. 106; 53; 212.

33. Gilbert, *The Oligarchy*, p. 164, presents the details of the business arrangement. The purchase date is in the memorandum dated 12 February 1946, AFA.

34. RAF to RAB, 11 September 1871, private archive, Lima, courtesy of Dennis Gilbert; Gilbert, *The Oligarchy*, p. 165; Oscar Bermúdez, *Historia del salitre desde sus orígenes hasta la Guerra del Pacífico* (Santiago de Chile: Universidad de Chile, 1963), pp. 261–264. See the *tradición* "María Abascal," in which (according to Camprubi) the merchant is Zaracóndegui.

35. Memorándum, 12 February 1946, AFA; RAB to AAB, 27 August 1875, AFA; RAB to AAB, 30 December 1875, AFA; AH to AH, 4 March 1886, AFA.

36. Gilbert, *The Oligarchy*, chap. 3.

37. RAB to AAB, 21 September 1875, AFA.

38. AH to AH, 28 May 1878, AFA.

39. RAB to IAB, 26 July 1881, AFA; AH to AH, 30 February [sic] 1885, AFA; AH to AH, 6 July 1889, AFA. Sugar technology is discussed in chap. 3.

40. See chap. 5.

41. RAB to IAB, 26 July 1881, AFA; AH to AH, 4 October 1880, AFA; AH to AH, 6 July 1889, AFA; AAB to AH, 1 November 1880, AFA. The Aspíllagas had to pay a tribute of from 4,000 to 6,000 paper soles per month. See chap. 3 for the sale of plantations on the north coast after the War of the Pacific.

42. Gilbert, *The Oligarchy*, p. 165.

43. Ibid., pp. 168–169.

44. Ibid., pp. 170–171.

45. Ibid.

46. Ibid., pp. 174–175.

47. Ibid., pp. 175–176.

48. Ibid., pp. 207–208.

49. Camprubi, *Los bancos*, pp. 61–63, 85, 91, 119–120.

50. RAB to AAB, 27 August 1875, AFA.

51. Heraclio Bonilla, *Guano y burguesía en el Perú* (Lima: Instituto de Estudios Peruanos, 1974), pp. 100–108, 146.

52. Camprubi, *Los bancos*, pp. 169–171.

53. Ibid., pp. 169–211; Yepes del Castillo, *Peru*, p. 134.

54. Yepes del Castillo, *Peru*, p. 131; Bertram, "Development Problems," p. 25.

55. Bertram, "Development Problems," p. 26; Yepes del Castillo, *Perú*, pp. 163–165, 175; Antonello Gerbi, *El Perú en marcha* (Lima: Banco Italiano, 1941), pp. 333–385, for a general discussion of banks in Peru.

56. Yepes del Castillo, *Perú*, p. 175.

57. Gilbert, *The Oligarchy*, p. 169.

58. *Extracto estadístico del Perú, 1928* (Lima: Dirección Nacional de Estadística, 1929), p. 36.

59. The British firm of Gibbs & Co. had already experimented with the importation of Peruvian sugar to Great Britain in the 1830s.

60. AH to AH, 7 August 1876, AFA; AH to AH, 11 August 1876, AFA.

61. Camprubí, *Los bancos*, p. 3.

62. AH to AH, 27 August 1895, AFA.

63. AAB to RAB, 30 January 1917, AFA. All three mortgages were paid off by 1917.

64. AH to AH, 7 April 1887 (a), AFA. All translations are mine, unless otherwise noted.

65. Klarén, *Modernization*, p. 15.

66. See chap. 2, p. 27.

67. Bollinger, "U.S. Influence." Of course, after 1900 many Peruvian planters began to invest in finance and urban property within Peru, and profits from these concerns could have been invested in their estates. However, their fortunes were not as large as those of foreign corporations and could be considered more vulnerable because they were concentrated within one country. See Gilbert, *The Oligarchy*, for a discussion of the investments of north coast planters.

68. Bertram, "Development Problems," pp. 26–27, cited in Albert, *The Peruvian Sugar Industry*, p. 84a.

69. I discuss the organization of labor in chap. 4, labor supply in chaps. 5 and 7, and technology and markets in chap. 3.

70. Albert, *The Peruvian Sugar Industry*, p. 5a. The principal markets for Peruvian sugar were Great Britain and Chile.

71. Ibid., pp. 16a, 117a–126a.

72. I discuss differences in size and technology in chap. 3.

73. C. D. Scott, "The Political Economy of Sugar in Peru," (unpublished, 1974), p. 16, n. 1. Scott obtained his information via a personal communication with R. J. Lockett in August of 1972. The Locketts had a long association with the Peruvian sugar industry.

74. On the reduction of cost of production, see the balance of July 1941 in the Gildemeister folder, AFA. There is also a great deal of information on the Gildemeisters' holdings in Chile in this folder. The Gildemeisters' hold over the Chilean market is discussed in RAA to Señores Aspíllaga Anderson Hermanos, S. A., 24 August 1929, AFA. It was also mentioned in an interview between William Albert and Gustavo Aspíllaga Anderson on 26 March 1974 in Lima. Professor Albert kindly shared this information with me.

75. *Seven Interpretive Essays on Peruvian Reality*, trans. Marjory Urquidi (Austin: University of Texas Press, 1971), pp. 17, 20, 21.

76. Klarén, *Modernization*, pp. 142–143.

Chapter 3: Land and Technology, 1860–1933

1. See chap. 1.

2. Manuel Pasapera, ed., *Ley de aguas con sus antecetes. Código y Reglamento Aguas* (Lima: Imp. y Librería de San Pedro, 1902).

3. Ibid.; Peter F. Klarén, *Modernization, Dislocation, and Aprismo: Origins of the Peruvian Aprista Party, 1870–1932*, Latin American Monographs, no. 32 (Austin, Tex.: Institute of Latin American Studies, 1973), pp. 56–57; VAT to AH, 30 August 1907, AFA.

4. Klarén, *Modernization,* chap. 1.
5. Ibid.; *La Reforma* (22 August 1917).
6. Klarén, *Modernization,* chap. 1; Carlos Malpica, *Los dueños del Perú,* 6th ed. (Lima: Ediciones Peisa, 1974), pp. 99–102.
7. Klarén, *Modernization,* chap. 1.
8. Ibid.
9. Ibid., pp. 17–18; Bill Albert, *An Essay on the Peruvian Sugar Industry, 1880–1920 and the Letters of Ronald Gordon, Administrator of the British Sugar Company in Cañete, 1914–1920* (Norwich, England: School of Social Studies, University of East Anglia, 1976), p. 50a, n. 5, and table 1.
10. VAT to AH, 30 August 1907, AFA; chap. 2.
11. The first mention of the land dispute is in AH to AH, 3 November 1876, AFA. For the riot and its aftermath, see BAB to AH, 8 May 1913, AFA; AAB to AH, 10 July 1913, AFA; VAT to AH, 29 August 1913, AFA; Samuel Alva, Gobernador Comisario del Distrito de Saña to AH, 4 May 1913, AFA.
12. AAB to RAB and BAB, 23 October 1913, AFA; AAB to RAB and BAB, 30 October 1913, AFA. Prefects were presidential appointments.
13. AH to AH, 30 May 1893, AFA; AH to AH, 12 May 1896, AFA.
14. AH to AH, 12 May 1896, AFA.
15. Federico Costa y Laurent, *Reseña historia de los ferrocarriles del Perú* (Lima: Carlos Fabbri-Mercaderes, 1908), p. 28; Alejandro Garland, *Las vías de comunicación y la futura red ferroviaria del Perú* (Lima: Imp. de La Industria, 1906), p. 24; BAB to AAB, October 1900, AFA, no day given.
16. *Memorial que presenta el sindicato de la "Empresa del Muelle y Ferrocarril del valle de Chicama," á la representación nacional* (Lima: Librería e Imp. Gil, 1917); Klarén, *Modernization,* pp. 71–78.
17. Antonio Raimondi, *El Perú* (Lima: Editores Técnicos Asociados, 1965), vol. 1, p. 323.
18. George R. Fitz-Roy Cole, *The Peruvians at Home* (London: Kegan, Paul, Trench & Co., 1884), p. 129; RAB to AAB, 21 September 1875, AFA; AH to AH, 7 October 1887, AFA. Cayalti's mill contained the latest technological improvements: see Noel Deerr, *The History of Sugar* (New York: American Book, 1949), vol. 1, pp. 559–560.
19. Albert, *The Peruvian Sugar Industry,* p. 65a, passim.
20. AH to AH, 26 April 1889, AFA; VAT to AH, 23 August 1915, AFA.
21. Thomas Colston to the Aspillagas, 3 January 1908, in Pablo Macera, ed. *Cayalti 1875–1920: Organización del trabajo en una plantación azucarera del Perú* (Lima: Seminario de Historia Rural Andina, 1973).
22. VAT to AH, 23 February 1915, AFA.
23. AAB to RAB and BAB, 3 January 1917, AFA; AAB to RAB and BAB, 6 March 1917, AFA.
24. VAT to AH, 23 February 1915, AFA.
25. AAB to RAB and BAB ("Queridos Hermanos"), 23 May 1917, AFA; AAB to RAB and BAB, 26 May 1917, AFA.
26. RAB to AAB, 21 September 1875, AFA; AH to AH, 7 October 1887, AFA.
27. AH to AH, 22 May 1889, AFA; AH to AH, 10 June 1901, AFA.
28. AH to AH, 31 January 1906, AFA.

29. AH to AH, 12 May 1911, AFA; BAB to RAB, 12 May 1911, AFA.

30. AH to AH, 30 December 1887, AFA; AH to AH, 30 August 1888, AFA; AH to AH, 12 May 1911, AFA; AH to AH, 16 May 1911, AFA.

31. AAB to AH, 2 January 1882, AFA; AH to AH, 4 November 1887, AFA; AAB to RAB and IAB, 10 October 1884, AFA; AH to AH, 5 August 1887, AFA.

32. Thomas Colston to RAB, August 1886, AFA, no day given; BAB to AAB, October 1900, AFA, no day given.

33. Same as note 32.

34. AH to AH, 18 January 1889, AFA.

35. AH to AH, 5 June 1889, AFA; AH to AH, 3 October 1889, AFA.

36. AH to AH, 16 May 1889, AFA; AH to AH, 22 May 1889, AFA; AH to AH, 22 June 1889, AFA; AH to AH, 8 August 1889, AFA; AH to AH, 3 October 1889, AFA; AH to AH, 1 May 1890, AFA; table 32, chap. 4.

37. AH to AH, 21 September 1879, AFA.

38. AH to AH, 27 January 1894, AFA.

39. Klarén, *Modernization*, p. 15; *Boletín del Ministerio de Fomento*, various years; BAB to AH, 26 October 1908, AFA; AAB to RAB and BAB, 6 July 1908, AFA; AAB to RAB and BAB, 2 February 1917, AFA.

40. VAT to AH, 23 February 1915, AFA.

41. AH to AH, 21 January 1898, AFA.

42. AH to AH, 11 February 1898, AFA; VAT to AH, March 1907, AFA, no day given; AH to AH, 11 February 1898, AFA; AAB to RAB and BAB, 6 March 1917, AFA.

43. See chap. 2 for a brief description of the political career of Antero Aspíllaga Barrera. In the plantation correspondence, fewer letters are written by Antero as time goes on.

44. See tables 6 and 10.

45. Gilbert, *The Oligarchy and the Old Regime in Peru* (Ithaca, N.Y.: Cornell University Dissertation Series in Latin America, 1977), pp. 219–220.

Chapter 4: The Organization of Labor at Cayaltí

1. Cayaltí correspondence.

2. Presupuesto de los gastos mensuales de la Hacienda Cayaltí, 1 April 1882, AFA; Dirección general para los empleados de esta Hacienda, en las oficinas y en el campo, January 1882, AFA.

3. Same sources as note 2; AH to AH, 5 April 1890, AFA; AH to AH, 26 February 1896, AFA; AH to AH, 18 March 1896, AFA; AH to AH, 28 July 1896, AFA.

4. Cayaltí correspondence; AH to Thomas Colston, 26 June 1890, AFA.

5. Presupuesto de los gastos mensuales de la Hacienda Cayaltí, 1 April 1882, AFA; Direcciones para el empleado á cuyo cuidado se encarga la sección Centrífugas, January 1882, AFA.

6. Presupuesto de los gastos mensuales de la Hacienda Cayaltí, 1 April 1882, AFA; Obligaciones de mayordomos, corte de caña, 18 April 1882, AFA; Obligaciones principales de los mayordomos de las carretas de cañas, 29 March 1882, AFA; Instrucciones para el servicio de Don Gregorio Ugaz, mayordomo del ganado del trabajo en esta Hacienda, 6 October 1882, AFA; Obligaciones de los

mayordomos, sembrio de caña, 17 April 1882, AFA; Obligaciones de los mayordomos, del riego de la Hacienda Cayaltí, 18 April 1882, AFA.

7. AH to AH, 2 June 1896, AFA; AH to AH, 3 May 1893, AFA.

8. Presupuesto de los gastos mensuales de la Hacienda Cayaltí, 1 April 1882, AFA.

9. AH to AH, 6 July 1889, AFA.

10. AH to AH, 18 August 1891, AFA; AH to AH, 10 May 1892, AFA.

11. AH to AH, 22 June 1889, AFA; AH to AH, 26 March 1892, AFA; AH to AH, 22 September 1896, AFA; AH to AH, 7 July 1897, AFA; AH to AH, 17 June 1901, AFA.

12. AH to AH, 18 August 1891, AFA; AH to AH, 7 January 1891(a), AFA; AH to AH, 9 April 1892, AFA.

13. See AH to Thomas Colston, 26 June 1890, AFA.

14. See table 33; AH to AH, 30 December 1887, AFA; AH to AH, 4 November 1898, AFA; AH to AH, 1 February 1899, AFA; AH to AH, 20 February 1890, AFA.

15. See table 33; AH to AH, 20 February 1890, AFA; AH to AH, 11 July 1889(b), AFA; AH to AH, 14 May 1886, AFA.

16. Instrucciones para el mayordomo encargado del sembrio de caña, 17 April 1882, AFA.

17. Thomas Colston to AH, 19 March 1912, AFA; AH to AH, 7 April 1887(a), AFA; AH to AH, 12 April 1889, AFA; AH to AH, 19 October 1889, AFA; AH to AH, 23 January 1890(a), AFA; AH to AH, 17 January 1893, AFA.

18. Instrucciones para el mayordomo encargado del sembrio de caña, 17 April 1882, AFA; AH to AH, 29 April 1879, AFA; AH to AH, 3 November 1887, AFA; AH to AH, 4 November 1887, AFA.

19. Instrucciones para el mayordomo encargado del sembrio de caña, 17 April 1882, AFA; Instrucciones para los mayordomos del riego de la Hacienda Cayaltí, 18 April 1882, AFA.

20. Cayaltí drew water from three acequias madres, which together extended for over 50 kilometers.

21. N. Salcedo to AH, 13 September 1902, AFA; VAT to AH, 18 June 1907, AFA; AH to AH, 4 June 1878, AFA; AH to AH, 9 July 1878, AFA; AH to AH, 17 April 1879, AFA; AH to AH, 5 June 1889(a), AFA.

22. AH to AH, 6 January 1890, AFA; George R. Fitz-Roy Cole, The Peruvians at Home (London: Kegan, Paul, Trench & Co., 1884), p. 134; unsigned letter dated 30 January 1888, AFA; AH to AH, 4 June 1878, AFA; AH to AH, 9 July 1878, AFA; AH to AH, 5 June 1889(a), AFA; AH to AH, 18 May 1892, AFA; AH to AH, 17 January 1893, AFA.

23. AH to AH, 5 June 1889(a), AFA.

24. Cole, Peruvians at Home, p. 134.

25. Instrucciones para el mayordomo encargado del sembrio de caña.

26. Ibid.

27. N. Salcedo to AH, 12 August 1899, AFA; AAB to RAB and IAB, 5 December 1884, AFA; AH to AH, 29 January 1898, AFA.

28. AH to AH, 30 May 1893, AFA.

29. Cayaltí correspondence.

30. Instrucciones para los mayordomos, corte de caña, 18 April 1882, AFA; AH to AH, 17 May 1899, AFA; AH to AH, 21 January 1898, AFA; and chap. 3, section on technology.

31. See table 33. Sometimes there were significantly more haulers than this table shows. For example, there were sixty in June of 1889: AH to AH, 22 June 1889, AFA.

32. RAB to AAB, 10 September 1875, AFA; AH to AH, 18 January 1889, AFA; AH to AH, 27 February 1894, AFA; AH to AH, 10 February 1898, AFA; AH to AH, 5 March 1898, AFA; AH to AH, 2 January 1899, AFA.

33. AAB to AH, 2 January 1882, AFA; AH to AH, 4 November 1887, AFA.

34. AH to AH,16 May 1889, AFA; AH to AH, 22 May 1889, AFA; AH to AH, 22 June 1889, AFA; AH to AH, 8 August 1889, AFA; AH to AH, 3 October 1889, AFA; AH to AH, 1 May 1890, AFA; table 33.

35. In more recent times, *bagazo* has been used in making paper products, such as toilet paper.

36. Direcciones para el empleado á cuyo cuidado se encarga la sección Centrifugas, January 1882, AFA; Noel Deerr, *The History of Sugar*, 2 vols. (New York: American Book, 1949), p. 2:559 (vacuum pans), pp. 2:573–574 (centrifugal). Also various photographs in *Album 1900*, Biblioteca Nacional (Lima), copies of which are in my possession.

37. AH to AH, 24 January 1893, AFA.

38. Instrucciones para el servicio de Don Gregorio Ugaz, Mayordomo del Ganado del Trabajo en esta Hacienda, 6 October 1882, AFA.

39. Table 24; RAB to AAB, 31 August 1875, AFA; AH to AH, 9 January 1877, AFA; AAB to AH, 12 October 1881, AFA; AH to AH, 27 February 1882, AFA; Escala de pagos á los artesanos, Hacienda Cayaltí, 15 January 1882, AFA.

40. AH to AH, 28 May 1878, AFA; AH to AH, 25 June 1878, AFA; AH to AH, 20 August 1878, AFA; AH to AH, 13 July 1888, AFA.

41. AH to AH, 8 October 1888, AFA; AH to AH, 14 February 1893, AFA.

42. AH to AH, 14 February 1893, AFA.

43. Workers' wages will be analzyed in the context of labor demand and supply in later chapters.

Chapter 5: The Chinese Worker, 1875–1900

1. Arnold J. Bauer, "Rural Workers in Spanish America: Problems of Peonage and Oppression," *Hispanic American Historical Review* 59, no. 1 (February 1979): 34–64; Brian Loveman, "Critique of Arnold J. Bauer's 'Rural Workers in Spanish America: Problems of Peonage and Oppression,' " *Hispanic American Historical Review* 59, no. 3 (August 1979): 478–486; and Bauer's reply in the same issue, pp. 486–490; Jonathan M. Wiener, "Class Structure and Economic Development in the American South, 1865–1955," *American Historical Review* 84 (October 1979): 970–993; and comments by Robert Higgs and Harold D. Woodman, pp. 993–1002, and Wiener's reply in the same issue, pp. 1002–1006.

2. Arnold J. Meagher has defined indentured servitude as follows:

Indenture was originally a deed or contract between two or more parties written on one piece of parchment or paper and cut in two in a serrated or zigzag line so that when brought together the two edges tallied showing that they were parts of the same original document. Later indenture came to denote a legal instrument for binding an apprentice or servant to his master, or a contract by which a person bound himself to service ("The Introduction of Chinese Laborers to Latin America: The 'Coolie Trade,' 1847–1874" (Ph.D. diss., University of California, Davis, 1975), p. 1., n. 1.

3. Watt Stewart, *Chinese Bondage in Peru. A History of the Chinese Coolie in Peru, 1849–1874* (Durham, N.C.: Duke University Press, 1951), p. 13; Juan de Arona [Pedro Paz-Soldán y Unánue], *La inmigración en el Perú: Monografía histórico-crítica*, 2d ed. (Lima: Academia Diplomática del Perú, 1947), pp. 52–53.

4. Stewart, *Chinese Bondage*, p. 8; Arona, *La inmigración*, p. 7.

5. Stewart, *Chinese Bondage*, p. 10.

6. Ibid.; Arona, *La inmigración*, p. 53; Gustavo Pons Muzzo, *Historia del conflicto entre el Perú y España (1864–1866)* (Lima: Colegio San Julián, 1966), p. 45.

7. Meagher, "Introduction of Chinese Laborers," pp. 4, 42, 239, n. 1; Stewart, *Chinese Bondage*, pp. 20–23.

8. Meagher, "Introduction of Chinese Laborers," pp. 50–55.

9. Ibid., pp. 59, 62, 68–69, 72–73.

10. Ibid., pp. 70, 73–78; Stewart, *Chinese Bondage*, pp. 37–38.

11. Stewart, *Chinese Bondage*, p. 19.

12. Ibid., p. 82–83; Meagher, "Introduction of Chinese Laborers," p. 155a.

13. Meagher, "Introduction of Chinese Laborers," pp. 161–163.

14. Meagher has documented sixty-eight mutinies, "Introduction of Chinese Laborers," pp. 176, 185.

15. Ernst W. Middendorf, *Perú. Observaciones y estudios del país durante una permanencia de 25 años*, 2 vols., trans. Ernesto More (Lima: Universidad Mayor de San Marcos, 1973), pp. 1:169–170.

16. Arona, "La inmigración," p. 61; Stewart, *Chinese Bondage*, pp. 26, 63.

17. Meagher discusses the increased demand for coolies and the growing difficulties in recruitment, "Introduction of Chinese Laborers," pp. 71–73.

18. Stewart, *Chinese Bondage*, pp. 20–23.

19. [Domingo Elías and Juan Rodríguez], *Inmigración de Chinos, ventajas que proporciona al país* (Lima: Imprenta de José Masias, 1851).

20. Ibid.

21. Stewart, *Chinese Bondage*, pp. 22–23.

22. Ibid.

23. Ibid., p. 25; see chaps. 1 and 2 for discussions of the agricultural development of the coast durng the mid-nineteenth century. From 1862 to 1864 Peruvians also imported 3,634 Polynesian islanders as contract laborers. However, 3,215 of them died, mostly from disease. The few who returned introduced smallpox to the islands, which resulted in an additional 2,950 deaths. In 1864 the Peruvian government paid $24,271.84 to France as compensation for wrongs committed against her nationals and protected subjects in Polynesia. Of this sum, $13,124.17 was sent to Tahiti in 1866 for distribution among the islanders (H. E. Maude, *Slavers in Paradise: The Peruvian Slave Trade in Polynesia, 1862–1864* (Stanford: Stanford University Press, 1981), pp. 165–166; table 5, p. 190; table 6, p. 191). The Peruvian government also paid Peruvian importers 50 soles for each immigrant who had died in Peru: See Stewart, *Chinese Bondage*, pp. 28–29.

24. Meagher, "Introduction of Chinese Laborers," pp. 307–310, 331; Robert L. Irick, *Ch'ing Policy toward the Coolie Trade, 1847–1878* (Taipei: Chinese Materials Center, 1982).

25. Meagher, "Introduction of Chinese Laborers," pp. 324–326; Stewart, *Chinese Bondage*, chap. 7.

26. Meagher, "Introduction of Chinese Laborers," pp. 333–334.

27. Stewart, "Chinese Bondage," chaps. 6 and 7.

28. See chap. 3 for a discussion of technological change.

29. AAB to RAF, 14 June 1875, AFA.

30. Aspíllagas y Cía. to Señores Zaracóndegui y Cía., 2 August 1864, AFA; AAB to RAF, 14 June 1875, AFA; AAB to RAF, 5 July 1875, AFA.

31. RAB to AAB, 24 December 1875, AFA.

32. Ibid.; AH to AH, 7 April 1876, AFA. In 1881 the average yearly wage was 48.60 soles: AH to AH, 14 November 1881, AFA.

33. AH to AH, 18 December 1877, AFA.

34. AH to AH, 28 August 1885, AFA.

35. AH to AH, 7 April 1876, AFA.

36. AH to H. Seymour Geary, 12 May 1877, AFA.

37. AH to AH, 12 February 1878, AFA.

38. AH to AH, 25 November 1878, AFA.

39. AAB to IAB, 3 May 1881, AFA.

40. See chap. 2 for a discussion of the impact of the Chilean invasion on Cayaltí.

41. AAB to IAB, 16 February 1881, AFA; AAB to IAB, 6 March 1881, AFA; RAB to IAB, 16 March 1881, AFA; AAB to IAB, 29 March 1881, AFA; AAB to IAB, 26 April 1881, AFA; AAB to IAB, 28 June 1881, AFA; AAB to IAB, 7 June 1881, AFA; AAB to AH, 6 September 1881, AFA; AH to AH, 27 September 1881, AFA; AAB to AH, 7 February 1882, AFA. The Aspíllagas generally made the Chinese repay the cost of the passage from Lima to Cayaltí.

42. Unsigned letters dated 18 March 1884, AFA; 31 March 1884, AFA; 18 May 1884, AFA; 19 May 1884, AFA; 1 June 1884, AFA.

43. AAB to AH, 14 November 1881, AFA.

44. Contract between Cayaltí and "El Asiático," D. Asian, October 1884, AFA.

45. AH to AH, 17 July 1889, AFA; AH to AH, 26 February 1885, AFA.

46. AAB to RAB and IAB, 15 October 1884, AFA.

47. Contract dated October 1884, AFA.

48. See chap. 7.

49. AH to AH, 9 June 1891, AFA.

50. AH to AH, 22 March 1892, AFA. Baldomero is indentifiable by his handwriting.

51. AH to AH, 1 November 1892, AFA.

52. AH to AH, 12 October 1889, AFA; AH to AH, 15 February 1890, AFA; AH to AH, 7 June 1893, AFA; AH to AH, 11 November 1897, AFA.

53. AH to AH, 24 January 1893, AFA.

54. AH to AH, 24 September 1895, AFA; AH to AH, 23 April 1895, AFA.

55. AH to AH, 16 November 1895, AFA.

56. AH to AH, 8 March 1897, AFA.

57. AH to AH, 24 January 1899, AFA.

58. AH to AH, 10 March 1899, AFA.

59. VAT to AH, 12 September 1907, AFA.

Chapter 6: Culture and Social Control, 1865–1905
1. See chap. 5.
2. AAB to AH, 9 December 1884, AFA; AH to AH, 29 July 1887, AFA; AH to AH, 19 August 1887, AFA.
3. AAB to AH, 9 December 1884, AFA.
4. AH to AH, 10 August 1888, AFA.
5. AH to AH, 9 February 1892, AFA; AH to AH, 14 February 1899, AFA.
6. AH to AH, 8 October 1886, AFA; AH to AH, 19 May 1876, AFA; AAB to IAB, 7 June 1881, AFA; AH to AH, 7 December 1888, AFA; AH to AH, 18 March 1896, AFA.
7. AH to AH, 14 October 1878, AFA; unsigned letter dated 12 April 1882, AFA; AAB to RAB, 15 October 1884, AFA.
8. See chap. 5.
9. Ibid.
10. AH to AH, 27 June 1894, AFA.
11. Ibid.; AH to AH, 12 June 1898, AFA.
12. Unsigned letter dated 10 January 1899, AFA.
13. AH to AH, 13 December 1897, AFA.
14. AH to AH, 28 December 1877, AFA; AH to AH, 11 June 1878, AFA; AH to AH, 7 December 1888, AFA; AH to AH, 27 September 1897, AFA; AH to AH, 13 December 1897, AFA; AH to AH, 4 January 1898, AFA.
15. Aspíllagas y Cía. to Señores Zaracóndegui y Cía., 1 January 1865, AFA.
16. See album, *República Peruana* 1900, Biblioteca Nacional (Lima).
17. Ernst W. Middendorf, *Perú. Observaciones y estudios del país y sus habitantes durante una permanencia de 25 años*, 2 vols., trans. Ernesto More (Lima: Universidad Mayor de San Marcos, 1973), p. 1:274.
18. See chap. 5.
19. On vegetables, see Middendorf, *Observaciones y estudios*, p. 1:262.
20. AH to AH, 3 October 1899(b), AFA; AH to AH, 19 October 1899, AFA.
21. See chap. 5; Middendorf, *Observaciones y estudios*, p.1:174; Juan Pérez de la Riva, *El barracón: Esclavitud y capitalismo en Cuba* (Barcelona: Editorial Crítica, 1975), p. 70.
22. Middendorf, *Observaciones y estudios*, p.1:174; Alfredo Sacchetti, "Inmigrantes para el Perú," *Boletín del Ministerio de Fomento* 3, no. 3 (March 1905): 70; Pérez de la Riva, *El barracón*, p. 71.
23. Middendorf, *Observaciones y estudios*, p. 1:174; AAB to IAB, 16 February 1881, AFA; AH to AH, 1 November 1892, AFA; conversation with Señor Humberto Rodríguez Pastor, who has done research on the Chinese at Palto.
24. Sachetti, "Inmigrantes," p. 70.
25. AH to AH, 15 February 1879, AFA.
26. Middendorf, *Observaciones y estudios*, p. 2:262.
27. Chinese religion is, of course, a complex subject. Two introductory studies are C. K. Yang, *Religion in Chinese Society* (Berkeley & Los Angeles: University of California Press, 1967), and Lawrence G. Thompson, *Chinese Religion: An Introduction* (Belmont, Cal.: Dickenson Publishing, 1969). On the use of shrines in

the home, see Yang, *Religion*, pp. 28–29; and on laymen's religion, see Thompson, *Chinese Religion*, pp. 97–98.

28. Thomas J. Hutchinson, *Two Years in Peru with Exploration of its Antiquities*, 2 vols. (London: Sampson, Low, Marston, Low & Searle, 1873), p. 1:137.

29. AH to AH, 3 September 1895, AFA.

30. AH to AH, 18 December 1900, AFA. Achen became Pedro Aspillaga and Ajey took the name Antonio Aspillaga.

31. AH to AH, 30 January 1892, AFA; AH to AH, 7 February 1894, AFA.

32. There are no references to gambling by Peruvians in the Aspillaga correspondence. On gambling in China, the Rev. Justus Doolittle wrote in 1867,

The Chinese are noted gamblers, and have invented a great many methods of playing for amusement or for money. The shops opened for gamblers are very numerous in some streets and in some localities. There are several kinds of street gambling, on a small scale for money or for sweetmeats, candies, etc., which it is impossible to avoid noticing while passing along. (*Social Life of the Chinese* [New York: Harper & Brothers, 1867], pp. 1:283–284)

For the pervasive and persistent influence of gambling in Kwangtung Province (the original home of most Chinese in Peru), see Tsou Lu, *The Gambling Blight*, in *Collected Works of Tsou Lu* (Peking: Pei-hua Shu-chu, 1930), vol. 2, chap. 8, reference and translation courtesy of Edward A. Gargan.

33. AH to AH, 23 April 1895, AFA.

34. AH to AH, 8 April 1882, AFA.

35. AH to AH, 11 November 1887, AFA. For an additional refrence to gambling by Chinese, see AH to AH, 1 November 1892, AFA.

36. Jonathan Spence, "Opium Smoking in Ch'ing China," in *Conflict and Control in Late Imperial China*, ed. Frederick Wakeman, Jr., and Caroline Grant (Berkeley & Los Angeles: University of California Press, 1975).

37. *El Peruano* (Lima), 27 September 1877.

38. AH to AH, 19 May 1891, AFA; AH to AH, 16 June 1891, AFA.

39. See chap. 5 for a discussion of labor shortages and indebtedness among the Chinese.

40. AH to AH, 1 May 1885, AFA, for opium purchases; see chap. 3 for sugar marketing.

41. AH to AH, 12 May 1876, AFA; AH to AH, 7 August 1879, AFA.

42. AAB to RAB, 2 August 1875, AFA.

43. AH to AH, 7 September 1895, AFA.

44. AH to AH, 1 May 1885, AFA; AH to AH, 12 May 1891, AFA.

45. AH to AH, 18 April 1876, AFA; AH to AH, 24 April 1876, AFA; AH to AH, 8 May 1876, AFA; AH to AH, 11 March 1879, AFA; AH to AH, 3 November 1891, AFA.

46. AH to AH, 7 April 1876, AFA; AH to AH, 18 April 1876, AFA; AH to AH, 8 May 1876, AFA; AH to AH, 12 May 1876, AFA; AH to AH, 11 March 1879, AFA.

47. AH to AH, 28 October 1879, AFA; AH to AH, 13 January 1880, AFA; AH to AH, 21 July 1891, AFA; AH to AH, 11 April 1893, AFA.

48. See chap. 5.

49. Ibid.

50. Ibid.

51. Ibid.

52. AH to AH, 15 January 1895, AFA.

53. AH to AH, 1 November 1892, AFA; AH to AH, 16 November 1895, AFA.

54. See chap. 5.

55. On absenteeism, see chap. 5.

56. Henry E. Dobyns and Paul L. Doughty, *Peru: A Cultural History* (New York: Oxford University Press, 1976), pp. 169–170, 212.

57. Aspíllagas y Cía to Señores Zaracóndegui y Cía., 2 August 1864, AFA.

58. Summer was always the most insalubrious time of year: AH to AH, 31 March 1876, AFA; AH to AH, 29 March 1890, AFA; AH to AH, 8 March 1897, AFA.

59. AH to AH, 18 June 1878, AFA.

60. AH to AH, 8 May 1877, AFA; AH to AH, 15 March 1878, AFA; AH to AH, 22 March 1878, AFA; AH to AH, 21 May 1878, AFA; AH to AH, 9 July 1878, AFA; AH to AH, 25 March 1891, AFA; AH to AH, 20 February 1894, AFA; AH to AH, 19 May 1894, AFA; AH to AH, 23 May 1894, AFA; AH to AH, 5 June 1894, AFA.

61. AH to AH, 11 January 1878, AFA; AH to AH, 15 March 1878, AFA; AH to AH, 22 March 1878, AFA; AH to AH, 21 May 1878, AFA; AH to AH, 18 June 1878, AFA; AH to AH, 9 July 1878, AFA; AH to AH, 28 October 1878, AFA; AH to AH, 12 March 1886, AFA; AH to AH, 25 March 1891, AFA; AH to AH, 20 February 1894, AFA; AH to AH, 19 May 1894, AFA; AH to AH, 23 May 1894, AFA.

62. AH to AH, 5 April 1890, AFA; AH to AH, 12 April 1890, AFA; AH to AH, 10 May 1890, AFA.

63. AH to AH, September 1892, AFA, no day given; AH to AH, 15 October 1892, AFA.

64. AH to AH, 12 March 1878, AFA; AH to AH, 15 March 1878, AFA; AH to AH, 25 February 1879, AFA; AH to AH, 13 December 1898, AFA.

65. AH to AH, 22 March 1878, AFA; AH to AH, 21 May 1878, AFA; AH to AH, 9 July 1878, AFA; AH to AH, 28 October 1878, AFA.

66. Aspíllagas y Cía to Señores Zaracóndegui y Cía., 3 July 1864, AFA; AH to AH, 8 May 1876, AFA.

67. AH to AH, 21 May 1886, AFA. See chap. 5; it may very well be that the Chinese used herbal medicines of their own making, although I have no evidence of this.

68. AH to AH, 21 April 1876, AFA.

69. AH to AH, 21 April 1876, AFA; AH to AH, 8 May 1876, AFA.

70. AH to AH, 4 June 1878, AFA; AH to AH, 13 August 1878, AFA; AH to AH, 24 September 1878, AFA; AAB to AH, 6 September 1881, AFA.

71. AH to AH, 29 May 1894, AFA.

72. AH to AH, 14 January 1887, AFA.

73. AH to AH, 24 February 1894, AFA; AH to AH, 3 March 1894, AFA; AH to AH, 8 February 1896, AFA; AH to AH, October 1896, AFA, no day given.

74. AH to AH, 7 June 1897, AFA.

75. AH to AH, 16 October 1885, AFA; AH to AH, 21 May 1886, AFA.

76. For age of Chinese population, see AH to AH, 16 October 1885, AFA; also see chap. 5.

77. Aspíllagas y Cía to Señores Zaracóndegui y Cía., 6 September 1865, AFA.

78. AH to AH, 25 June 1878, AFA.

79. AH to AH, 19 November 1878, AFA; AH to AH, 25 November 1878, AFA.

80. AH to AH, 10 October 1888, AFA; AH to AH, 7 November 1888, AFA.

81. AH to AH, 14 August 1876, AFA.

82. Ibid.

83. AH to AH, 18 August 1876, AFA.

84. AH to AH, 1 September 1876, AFA.

85. AH to AH, 31 July 1877, AFA.

86. AH to AH, 3 August 1877, AFA.

87. AH to AH, 2 July 1886, AFA.

88. RAB to AAB, 12 November 1875, AFA.

89. AH to AH, 7 November 1888, AFA; AH to AH, 20 December 1888, AFA; AH to AH, 1 November 1892, AFA; AH to AH, 21 August 1895, AFA.

90. See chap. 5.

91. Chinese Commission Report of 1887, Biblioteca Nacional.

92. AH to AH, 30 [sic] February 1885, AFA.

93. AH to AH, 30 September 1887, AFA; AH to AH, 7 October 1887, AFA.

94. Chinese Commission Report of 1887, Biblioteca Nacional.

95. Ibid.

96. *Informe*, Chinese consul Ten Ayan, subprefect of Trujillo Lizardo Lavalle, interpreter P. A. Ponky, Biblioteca National; Jesús García y García to el ministro de gobierno, 21 August 1893, Biblioteca Nacional.

97. "La visita china," editorial, *El Tiempo* (1 October 1887), reprinted in *El Comercio* (15 October 1887).

98. *The Peruvians at Home* (London: Kegan, Paul, Trench & Co., 1884), pp. 139–140, 200.

99. RAF to RAB, 18 September 1870, private archive, Lima, courtesy of Dennis Gilbert. There is an essay on this rebellion by Humberto Rodríguez Pastor, but I have been unable to obtain it.

100. Jorge Basadre, *Historia de la República del Perú*, 4th ed., 2 vols. (Lima: Editorial Cultura Antártico, 1949), p. 2:225.

101. See chap. 2, pp. 31-32.

102. Ibid., p. 32.

103. AH to AH, 18 July 1876, AFA; AH to AH, 14 September 1877, AFA.

104. RAB to IAB, 26 July 1881, AFA.

105. RAB to AAB, 5 October 1875, AFA.

106. AH to AH, 4 March 1879, AFA.

107. RAB to AAB, 5 October 1875, AFA. Once the Aspíllagas returned a Chinese who had escaped from Tumán, but only because they wanted to befriend the Pardos: AH to AH, 28 August 1885, AFA.

108. AH to AH, 11 September 1877, AFA.

109. AH to AH, 18 February 1879, AFA.

110. AH to AH, 21 May 1876, AFA; RAB to AAB, 8 October 1875, AFA.

214   Notes to pages 113-118

111. AH to AH, 2 June 1877, AFA.
112. RAB to AAB, 8 October 1875, AFA.
113. AH to AH, 14 September 1877, AFA.
114. RAB to AAB, 5 October 1875, AFA.
115. Pérez de la Riva, *El barracón*, p. 67.
116. For a description of conditions on the guano islands, see Maude, *Slavers*, p. 136.
117. AH to AH, 8 May 1876, AFA; AH to AH, 12 May 1876, AFA; AH to AH, 18 July 1876, AFA; RAB to AAB, 4 January 1876, AFA; RAB to AAB, 25 January 1876, AFA; AH to AH, 4 June 1878, AFA. This was also the most common way of commiting suicide in Cuba: Pérez de la Riva, *El barracón*, p. 69.
118. AH to AH, 8 May 1876, AFA.
119. RAB to AAB, 4 Janaury 1876, AFA.
120. See chap. 3.
121. See chap. 2.
122. AH to AH, 28 May 1878, AFA.
123. AH to AH, 27 February 1895, AFA.
124. See AAB to RAB, 14 June 1875, AFA; AAB to IAB, 16 February 1881, AFA.
125. AH to AH, 8 May 1876, AFA; AH to AH, 8 April 1882, AFA; AH to AH, 11 November 1887, AFA.
126. AH to AH, 8 May 1876, AFA.
127. AH to AH, 24 January 1893, AFA.

Chapter 7: Labor Contracting, 1880–1933
1. Early works critical of *enganche* include Alberto Ulloa Sotomayor, "La organización social y legal del trabajo en el Perú" (Ph.D. diss., Universidad de San Marcos, 1916), chap. 11; Marco Aurelio Denegri, *La crisis del enganche* (Lima: San Martí, 1911); Francisco Mostajo, "Algunas ideas sobre la cuestión obrera (contrato de enganche) (Ph.D. diss., Universidad de Arequipa, 1913); and Dora Mayer de Zulen, *El indígena peruano o los cien años de república libre e independiente* (Lima: Imp. E. Z. Casanova, 1921). For more recent works, see Peter F. Klarén, *Modernization, Dislocation, and Aprismo: Origins of the Peruvian Aprista Party, 1870–1932*, Latin American Monographs, no. 32 (Austin, Tex.: Institute of Latin American Studies, 1973), pp. 26–28; Ernesto Yepes del Castillo, *Perú, 1820–1920: Un siglo de desarrollo capitalista* (Lima: Instituto de Estudios Peruanos, 1972), pp. 209–213. Klarén modified his interpretation to stress the importance of monetary reward after the early twentieth century in his essay "The Social and Economic Consequences of Modernization in the Peruvian Sugar Industry, 1870–1930," in *Land and Labour in Latin America*, ed. Kenneth Duncan and Ian Rutledge, p. 293 (Cambridge: At the University Press, 1977). Also see Peter Blanchard, "The Recruitment of Workers in the Peruvian Sierra at the Turn of the Century: The Enganche System," *Inter-American Economic Affairs* 33 (1980): 63–83.
2. For the postbellum southern United States, see Jonathan M. Wiener, "Class Structure and Economic Development in the American South, 1865–1955," *American Historical Review* 84 (October 1979): 970–993; and comments by

Robert Higgs and Harold Woodman, pp. 993–1002, and the reply by Wiener, pp. 1002–1006, in the same issue. In a revisionist essay, Arnold J. Bauer stresses the importance of the marketplace in *enganche*: "Rural Workers in Spanish America: Problems of Peonage and Oppression," *Hispanic American Historical Review* 59 (February 1979): 34–64. Brian Loveman disputes Bauer's overall analysis in "Critique of Arnold J. Bauer's 'Rural Workers in Spanish America: Problems of Peonage and Oppression,' " *Hispanic American Historical Review* 50 (August 1979): 478–486. See Bauer's reply in the same issue, pp. 486–490. For the period after 1940, C. D. Scott presents a modes-of-production analysis: "Peasants, Proletarianisation and the Articulation of Modes of Production: The Case of Sugar-Cane Cutters in Northern Peru, 1940–1969," *Journal of Peasant Studies* 3 (April 1976): 321–341. I discuss the relative importance of the marketplace, coercion, and debt peonage in "Capitalist Agriculture and Labour Contracting in Northern Peru, 1880–1905," *Journal of Latin American Studies* 12 (November 1980): 291–315.

3. AH to AH, 7 October 1898, AFA.

4. This included some fifteen thousand Chinese immigrants to Peru who, however, did not work on sugarcane plantations. See Peter Blanchard, "Asian Immigrants in Perú, 1899–1923," *North/South: Canadian Journal of Latin American Studies* 9 (1979): 60–75.

5. Standard contract, AFA (copy in my possession); BAB to Muy Queridos Hermanos, 6 May 1899, AFA.

6. Toraje Irie, "History of Japanese Migration to Peru," trans. William Himel, *Hispanic American Historical Review* 21, part 2 (November 1951): 648–723.

7. Ibid., pp. 635, 662–664; Blanchard, "Asian Immigrants"; Bill Albert, *An Essay on the Peruvian Sugar Industry, 1880–1920 and the Letters of Ronald Gordon, Administrator of the British Sugar Company in Cañete, 1914–1920* (Norwich: School of Social Studies, University of East Anglia, 1976), pp. 103a–105a.

8. Irie, *"Japanese Migration,"* p. 658; idem, *"History of Japanese Migration to Peru,* trans. William Himel, *Hispanic American Historical Review* 21, part 1 (August 1951): 447.

9. AH to AH, 9 April 1899, AFA; AH to AH, 13 April 1899, AFA.

10. AH to AH, 13 April 1899, AFA; AH to AH, 28 April 1899, AFA; AH to AH, 29 April 1899, AFA; AH to AH, 13 May 1899, AFA; AH to AH, 23 May 1899, AFA; AH to AH, 8 June 1899, AFA; AH to AH, 13 June 1899, AFA.

11. Francisco de Rivero, *Memoria o sean apuntamientos sobre la industria agrícola del Perú y sobre algunos medios que pudieran adoptarse para remediar su decadencia* (Lima: Imp. del Comercio, 1845); [Domingo Elías and Juan Rodríguez], *Inmigración de Chinos, ventajas que proporciona al país* (Lima: Imp. de José Masías, 1851).

12. Susan Ramirez-Horton, "The Sugar Estates of the Lambayeque Valley, 1670–1800: A Contribution to Peruvian Agrarian History" (M.A. thesis, University of Wisconsin, Madison, 1973), chap. 4.

13. AH to AH, 9 September 1879, AFA.

14. Chaps. 1 and 3; report on small farmers in the Lambayeque Valley by the Sociedad Nacional Agraria, 1937, AFA.

15. *Perú, Censo General de la República del Perú, formado en 1876, Vol. V,*

Huánuco, Ica, Junín, Lambayeque, La Libertad (Lima: Imp. del Teatro-Portal de San Agustín, 1878).
16. Gonzales, "Capitalist Agriculture," pp. 298–299.
17. AH to AH, 5 June 1899(a), AFA.
18. IAA to RAB, 5 November 1923, AFA. During the War of the Pacific the Aspillagas said that the number of workers from the coast increased at Cayaltí when the army was recruiting in the area, the implication being that plantation workers were protected from impressment: AAB to RAB and IAB, 19 November 1884, AFA. Further examples of hiring patterns for persons from the coast are in AAB to IAB, 13 June 1881, AFA; VAT to AH, 2 February 1912, AFA; AH to AH, 28 January 1887, AFA; AH to AH, 28 February 1893, AFA.
19. This is only the second example of which I am aware of urbanites being hired to work on plantations. During the Porfiriato, workers from Mexico City were recruited to labor on the henequen plantations of the Yucatán. See Friedrich Katz, "Labor Conditions on Haciendas in Profirian Mexico: Some Trends and Tendencies," *Hispanic American Historical Review* 54 (February 1974): 15–23.
20. AH to AH, 10 March 1894, AFA; AH to AH, 17 March 1894, AFA; AH to AH, 20 March 1894, AFA; AH to AH, 24 March 1894, AFA; AH to AH, 27 March 1894, AFA; AH to AH, 7 April 1894, AFA; AH to AH, 10 April 1894, AFA.
21. N. Salcedo to AH, 28 October 1899, AFA; AH to AH, 3 June 1899, AFA (also *enganche* contract attached to this letter); letter dated 13 June 1899, AFA.
22. Census of 1876; Perú, Ministerio de Hacienda y Comercio, *Dirección Nacional de Estadística. República del Perú, Censo Nacional de Población de 1940, Vol. II, Departamentos de Tumbes, Piura, Cajamarca, Vol. III, Departamentos de Lambayeque, La Libertad, Ancash* (Lima: Imp. Torres Aguirre, 1947).
23. Juan Saráchaga, Braulio Arana, and Carlos Dégola, eds., "Estadística física y política del Departamento de Cajamarca," in *Colección Fénix*, vol. 17 (Lima: Biblioteca Nacional, 1855).
24. Lewis Taylor, "Main Trends in Agrarian Capitalist Development: Cajamarca, Peru 1880–1976" (Ph. D. diss., University of Liverpool, 1979), p. 18, n. 1.
25. Ibid., pp. 18, 25–27.
26. Saráchaga, Arana, Dégola, eds., "Estadística," p. 24; Pelayo Puga, *La falta de brazos para la agricultura de la costa del Perú* (Lima: Librería Escolar e Imp. E. Moreno, 1903); BAB to AH, 16 February 1892, AFA.
27. Puga, *Falta de brazos*.
28. Interviews conducted by John Gitlitz in Cajamarca during the 1970s. Gitlitz kindly shared this information with me in a conversation in Lima on 5 September 1974.
29. Solomon Miller, "Hacienda to Plantation in Northern Peru: The Process of Proletarianization of a Tenant Farmer Society," in *Contemporary Change in Traditional Societies: Mexican and Peruvian Communities*, vol. 3, ed. Julian Steward, pp. 133–225 (Urbana: University of Illinois Press, 1967); Eulogio Eléspuru Berninzon, "La Provincia de Cajamarca," in *Ensayos Geográficos, Universidad Católica del Perú*, vol. 2 (Lima: Imp. Editora Peruana, 1939), pp. 146–162; archive of the Hacienda Chusgón, AFA; informe sobre mano de obra, Hacienda San Jacinto, 26 May 1945, AFA.

30. Scott, "Peasants," p. 330: "agents recruited from 'free' *minifundia* populations and not from the ranks of 'tied' hacienda peons."

31. Balances from 1945, Hacienda Cochabamba (section of Chusgón), AFA; VAT to AH, 20 March 1920, AFA; H. Zacharias to Señor Gerente de la Negociación Azucarera Laredo Ltda., 12 August 1928, AFA; Taylor, "Main Trends," p. 138.

32. Taylor, "Main Trends," pp. 117–136.

33. VAT to AH, 20 March 1920, AFA: Miller, "Hacienda to Plantation"; Scott, "Peasants," p. 328.

34. Memoria que presenta el Sub-Prefecto de la Provincia de Huamachuco á la Prefectura del Departamento, 26 May 1902, Biblioteca Nacional, Lima.

35. "Los hijos de Cutervo," *Proyectada Provincia de Cutervo* in *Colección Fénix*, vol. 17 (Lima: Biblioteca Nacional, 1904).

36. Gitlitz interview (see note 28); also see Taylor, "Main Trends," pp. 106–114.

37. Ibid.

38. Informe sobre mano de obra, Hacienda San Jacinto, 26 May 1945, AFA.

39. *Peasants* (Englewood Cliffs, N.J.: Prentice-Hall, 1966), p. 72.

40. Taylor, "Main Trends," p. 156.

41. BAB to AH, 16 February 1892, AFA.

42. AH to AH, 3 May 1897, AFA.

43. Carlos J. Bachmann, *Departamento de Lambayeque. Monografía histórico-geográfica* (Lima: Imp. Torres Aguirre, 1921), pp. 145–146; George R. Fitz-Roy Cole, *The Peruvians at Home* (London: Kegan, Paul, Trench & Co., 1884), pp. 136, 149. Both sources mention the Arbulu family as estate owners. Miguel Arbulu Gonzales appears as a labor contractor in Contratos de la Hacienda Pomalca, AFA; AH to AH, 24 June 1888, AFA; contracts between Eduardo Tiravante and the Hacienda Pomalca, 1 May 1912, and 20 June 1917, AFA.

44. *Enganche* contract, Daniel Orrego and Hacienda Pomalca, 26 January 1910, AFA; AH to AH, 8 February 1906, AFA; Manuel Coronado to Catalino Coronado, 29 September 1916, AFA; Manuel Coronado to Catalino Coronado, 21 September 1917, AFA.

45. Francisco Pérez Céspedes to AH, 4 September 1901, AFA.

46. Scott, "Peasants," p. 327.

47. Informe sobre la Hacienda Chusgón, 23 April 1958, AFA; Planillas of the Plantation Laredo, 1900–1908, AFA.

48. Contratos de la Hacienda Pomalca, AFA.

49. Ibid.; Cayaltí correspondence, AFA.

50. S. Tello to AH, 2 November 1919, AFA. In 1919 dollars, 50,000 soles equaled $24,000.

51. See note 31.

52. Scott, "Peasants," p. 328, for recruiting at markets; Miguel Coronado to Catalino Coronado, 22 August 1918, AFA; César Coronado to Catalino Coronado, 16 October 1918, AFA; AH to AH, 27 June 1889, AFA; AH to AH, 31 July 1889, AFA; AH to AH, 11 October 1892, AFA; interview with Galindo Bravo, CAP Pucalá, 27 June 1975. Bravo was originally contracted to work at Pucalá by Catalino Coronado. In 1975 he was a member of the Consejo de Administración, CAP Pucalá.

53. Correspondence of Catalino Coronado, AFA. This is also implied by the fact that many highlanders renewed their contracts on the coast.

54. Contratos de enganche, Hacienda Tumán, AFA; letter dated 19 June 1919, Cayaltí correspondence, AFA; Ulloa Sotomayor, "Organización social y legal." Sometimes peons had to pay interest on advances. See *enganche* contract between Cirilo Medina and Juan Vega, 18 January 1920, Contratos de enganche, Hacienda Tumán, AFA. In 1900 dollars, 50 soles equaled $24.25; 10 soles equaled $4.85; 10 centavos equaled $.0485.

55. Contratos de la Hacienda Pomalca, AFA; various contracts in the Cayaltí correspondence, AFA.

56. Chaps. 2 and 3.

57. See chap. 2 for the price of sugar and yearly profits.

58. AH to AH, 24 September 1878, AFA; AH to AH, 30 September 1878, AFA; AH to AH, 21 October 1878, AFA; AH to AH, 14 October 1879, AFA; Existencia de trabajadores, 8 June 1882, AFA; AAB to AH, 9 December 1884, AFA; AH to AH, 12 February 1885, AFA; AH to AH, 26 February 1885, AFA.

59. AH to AH, 20 July 1886, AFA; AH to AH, 29 March 1888, AFA; AAB to RAB and IAB, 10 October 1888, AFA.

60. AH to AH, 5 June 1888(a), AFA; AH to AH, 24 June 1888, AFA; AH to AH, 22 June 1889, AFA; AH to AH, 11 July 1889(a), AFA.

61. AH to AH, 7 May 1890, AFA; AH to AH, 12 November 1890, AFA; AH to AH, 19 January 1900, AFA; RAB to AH, 13 February 1892, AFA; AH to AH, 27 July 1892, AFA; AH to AH, 23 April 1895, AFA; AH to AH, 24 September 1895, AFA.

62. AH to AH, 16 October 1885, AFA; AH to AH, 23 September 1888, AFA; AH to AH, 3 October 1889(a), AFA; AH to AH, 15 November 1889, AFA; AH to AH, 16 November 1891, AFA; AH to AH, 16 February 1892, AFA.

63. AH to AH, 12 November 1890, AFA; AH to AH, 19 January 1900, AFA; BAB to AH, 13 February 1892, AFA; AH to AH, 27 July 1892, AFA; AH to AH, 24 September 1895, AFA; AH to AH, 23 April 1895, AFA.

64. Chaps. 2 and 3.

65. Chap. 3.

66. VAT to AH, 20 March 1920, AFA; H. Zacharias to Señor Gerente de la Negociación Azucarera Laredo Ltda., 12 August 1928, AFA.

67. VAT to AH, 23 February 1915, AFA; AAB to RAB and BAB, 19 January 1917, AFA.

68. Albert, *Peruvian Sugar Industry*, pp. 161a-162a, table 50a, p. 171a; Peter Blanchard, *The Origins of the Peruvian Labor Movement, 1883-1919* (Pittsburgh: University of Pittsburgh Press, 1982).

69. VAT to AH, 22 August 1916, AFA; VAT to AH, 1 September 1916, AFA.

70. AH to AH, 11 September 1914, AFA; letter dated 19 June 1919, AFA.

71. Chap. 3.

72. Letter dated 19 June 1919, AFA; LAA to RAA, 17 October 1924(b), AFA; RAA to Señores Aspíllaga Hermanos, S.A., 12 November 1929, AFA.

73. See table 36 for the reduction in the size of the work force. Worker militancy is discussed in chap. 9.

74. LAA to RAA, 4 November 1929, AFA; RAA to Señores Aspíllaga

Notes to pages 135-142   219

Anderson Hnos., S.A., 12 November 1929, AFA; LAA to RAA, 25 November 1929, AFA; RAA to Señores Aspíllaga Anderson Hnos., S.A., 10 March 1930, AFA; aviso from Cayaltí dated August 1930, AFA; IAA to Señor Cajero de la Hacienda Cayaltí, 9 August 1930, AFA; LAA to RAA, 3 June 1932, AFA; Dennis Gilbert, *The Oligarchy and the Old Regime in Peru* (Ithaca, N.Y.: Cornell University Dissertation Series in Latin America, 1977), chap. 3.

75. [IAA], "Situación topográfica," 1926, AFA.
76. VAT to AH, 21 September 1920, AFA; RAA to RAB, 3 July 1925, AFA; RAA to RAB, 6 July 1925, AFA.
77. For a discussion of merchandising at Cayaltí, see chap. 8.
78. AH to AH, 9 May 1899, AFA.
79. AH to AH, 13 January 1900, AFA.
80. See pp. 129–130; Bravo interview; Coronado correspondence, AFA. Laredo used the *ficha* system for rations in the early twentieth century, and Pucalá used both systems at various times in this century: see Planillas from Laredo, AFA; Bravo interview.
81. Coronado correspondence; Felipe Yanés Abarca, "Sistema de enganche, Distrito de Sorochuco-Hacienda Cayaltí" (B.A. thesis, Pontificia Universidad Católica del Perú, 1972).
82. AH to AH, 15 November 1892, AFA. In 1900 dollars, 100 soles equaled $48.50.
83. Coronado correspondence; Francisco Pérez Céspedes to AH, 24 November 1902, AFA; AH to AH, 13 December 1897, AFA.
84. For the management of the plantation store, see chap. 8.
85. Katz, "Labor Conditions."
86. See pp. 128–129, 133.
87. AH to AH, 14 October 1879, AFA.
88. AH to AH, 25 March 1891, AFA.
89. Francisco Pérez Céspedes to AH, 5 April 1902, AFA.
90. AH to AH, 25 March 1891, AFA.
91. See chap. 8 for a detailed discussion of health and health care.
92. See chap. 4 for a discussion of the organization of labor.
93. AH to AH, 25 July 1887, AFA. See chap. 8 for a detailed discussion of housing during this period.
94. AH to AH, 18 December 1906, AFA.
95. Scott, "Peasants."
96. VAT to AH, 14 October 1908, AFA.
97. AAB to AH, 1 May 1907, AFA; VAT to AH, 29 September 1908, AFA; VAT to AH, 14 October 1908, AFA.
98. See note 97; Francisco Pérez Céspedes to AH, 5 April 1902, AFA; VAT to AH, 30 August 1907, AFA; VAT to AH, 3 September 1907, AFA.
99. AH to AH, 18 November 1887, AFA; BAB to AH, 6 December 1902, AFA; Negrete Hnos. to AH, 12 June 1903, AFA; VAT to AH, 11 August 1908, AFA; VAT to AH, 14 October 1908, AFA; BAB to AH, 26 October 1908, AFA; Manuel Coronado to Catalino Coronado, 16 November 1917, AFA; Gregorio Castaños to Catalino Coronado, 10 March 1909, AFA; *enganche* contract between Eduardo Tiravante and Hacienda Pomalca, 20 June 1917, AFA (it was written into the contract

that, if a peon owed money to more than one contractor, the contractor "in possession" of the peon would have to pay off the outstanding debts to other contractors).

100. Letter from Huambos to Catalino Coronado, 9 December 1917, AFA. The other contractors involved were Tiravante and Arrascue.

101. Katz, "Labor Conditions"; Harry E. Cross, "Living Standards in Rural Nineteenth-Century Mexico: Zacatecas, 1820–80," *Journal of Latin American Studies* 19 (May 1979): 1–19.

102. Thomas Colston to AH, 14 October 1901, AFA.

103. Manuel E. Espinoza to José Ignacio Chopitea, 24 August 1903, AFA. For another example of peons running away because of excessive work loads, see Administrador de Tumán to Señor Sub-Prefecto e Intendiente de Policia de la Provincia de Chiclayo, 20 April 1907, AFA.

104. Frederick P. Bowser, *The African Slave in Colonial Peru, 1524–1650* (Stanford, Cal.: Stanford University Press, 1974); Carl N. Degler, *Neither Black nor White* (New York: Macmillan Co., 1971), pp. 47–52; R. K. Kent, "Palmares: An African State in Brazil," *Journal of African History* 6, no. 2 (1965): 161–175.

105. Chap. 5.

106. Negrete Hnos. to AH, 12 June 1903, AFA; S. Tello to AH, 26 October 1905, AFA; VAT to AH, 14 October 1908, AFA; BAB to AH, 26 October 1908, AFA; Manuel Coronado to Catalino Coronado, 9 August 1918, AFA.

107. See p. 141; Manuel Torres to Carlos Gutiérrez, 1 July 1907, AFA; M. Coronado to Catalino Coronado, 25 June 1915, AFA; Manuel Coronado to Catalino Coronado, 15 November 1918, AFA; V. Mires to Catalino Coronado, 25 March 1910, AFA; J. Orrego to Catalino Coronado, 22 September 1911, AFA; J. Orrego to Catalino Coronado, 10 March 1909, AFA; J. Orrego to Catalino Coronado, 15 September 1916, AFA; V. Mires to Catalino Coronado, 22 April 1910, AFA.

108. Scott, "Peasants," p. 328.

109. See p. 128.

110. VAT to AH, 14 October 1908, AFA.

111. Ibid.; N. Tello to AH, 29 November 1905, AFA; VAT to AH, 11 August 1908, AFA; Manuel Coronado to Catalino Coronado, 6 October 1916, AFA; V. Mires to Catalino Coronado, 18 February 1910, AFA; V. Mires to Catalino Coronado, 25 February 1910, AFA.

112. See pp. 129–130.

113. Yanés Abarca, "Enganche"; Hermongenes Banda to Catalino Coronado, 3 March 1918, AFA; Angel Dias to Catalino Coronado, 15 March 1918, AFA. The following are examples of cosigners being forced to pay a peon's loan: V. Mires to Catalino Coronado, 7 January 1910, AFA; V. Mires to Catalino Coronado, 6 May 1910, AFA.

114. V. Mires to Catalino Coronado, 7 January 1910, AFA; V. Mires to Catalino Coronado, 6 May 1910, AFA.

115. Manuel Anguello to Kai Krough, 23 January 1946, AFA; VAT to AH, 22 February 1921, AFA; RAA to RAB, 3 May 1926, AFA.

Chapter 8: The Plantation Community, 1890–1933

1. Solomon Miller, "Hacienda to Plantation in Northern Peru: The Processes

of Proletarianization of a Tenant Farmer Society," in *Contemporary Change in Traditional Societies: Mexican and Peruvian Communities*, vol. 3, ed. Julian Steward, pp. 133–225 (Urbana: University of Illinois Press, 1967).

2. AH to AH, 5 July 1887, AFA.

3. Censo de 1923, AFA.

4. AH to AH, 1 March 1890, AFA; RAB to IAB, 27 June 1900, AFA; AH to AH, 19 January 1900, AFA; BAB to AAB, RAB, and IAB ("Queridos Hermanos"), 25 April 1906, AFA; AAB to AH, 1 May 1907, AFA; AAB to RAB and BAB, 10 February 1915, AFA; AAB to RAB and BAB, 25 February, 1915, AFA; AAB to RAB and BAB, 5 March 1915, AFA; AAB to RAB and BAB, 19 March 1915, AFA; AAB to RAB and BAB, 11 May 1915, AFA; AAB to RAB and BAB, 6 January 1917, AFA; AAB to RAB and BAB, 25 January 1917, AFA.

5. AH to AH, 24 March 1894, AFA; AH to AH, 16 October 1894, AFA.

6. AAB to RAB, 10 February 1915, AFA; AAB to RAB and BAB, 10 April 1915, AFA.

7. AH to AH, 19 January, 1900, AFA; RAB to IAB, 27 June 1900, AFA.

8. See chap. 3, section on technology.

9. IAA to RAB, 17 December 1923, AFA.

10. IAA to RAB, 24 February 1925, AFA; AAA to RAB, 9 March 1925, AFA; AAA to Señor Gerente, Negociaciones Agrícolas Cayalti y Palto, 22 March 1925, AFA; LAA to RAB, 22 May 1925, AFA; IAA to RAB, 11 September 1928, AFA; IAA to RAB y Hermanos, 17 September 1928, AFA.

11. Censo de 1932, AFA.

12. Felipe de Osma, *Informe sobre las huelgas del norte*, 2d ed. (Lima: Biblioteca Peruana de Historia Económica, 1972), pp. 13–14.

13. Lauro A. Curletti, *El problema industrial en el valle de Chicama. Informe del Ministro de Fomento*, 2d ed. (Lima: Biblioteca Peruana de Historia Económica, 1972), p. 12.

14. Contract between Cosme Rojas H. and Enrique Bruning, 15 February 1915, Contratos de la Hacienda Pomalca, 1900–1920, AFA.

15. AH to AH, 18 March 1896, AFA.

16. AH to AH, 13 December 1897, AFA; AH to Señor Jefe del Almacén, 20 November 1900, AFA.

17. AH to AH, 4 January 1898, AFA; AH to AH, 7 January 1899, AFA; AH to AH, 10 January 1899, AFA; AH to AH, 29 November 1900, AFA; AH to Señor Jefe del Almacén, 20 November 1900, AFA.

18. AH to AH, 27 June 1894, AFA; AH to AH, 13 December 1897, AFA; Francisco Pérez-Céspedes to AH, 24 November 1902, AFA.

19. VAT to AH, 5 September 1912, AFA.

20. T. Cañas to AH, 12 September 1908, AFA.

21. VAT to AH, 5 April 1910, AFA; VAT to AH, 13 February 1910, AFA; AH to Carlos E. Gutiérrez, 24 February 1910, AFA.

22. AAB to RAB and BAB, 27 November 1913, AFA.

23. This unrest will be discussed in the following chapter.

24. Liisa Lukkari North, "The Origins and Development of the Peruvian Aprista Party "(Ph.D. diss., University of California, Berkeley, 1973), p. 26. Leguía appointed visitadores de subsistencias to inspect plantation stores for overcharging: see VAT to AH, 21 September 1920, AFA; AAB to VAT, 2 February 1921, AFA. See chap. 7 for

wages. Staples were eventually sold in an *almacén de subsistencias*: see VAT to Señor Gerente, Negociaciones Agrícolas Cayaltí y Palto, 21 June 1921, AFA; table 41.

25. Informe sobre la Hacienda Cayaltí, 1923, 5 October 1923, AFA; LAA to RAB, 23 May 1924, AFA; RAA to RAB, 29 May 1925, AFA; LAA to RAB, 9 January 1926, AFA.

26. RAA to RAB, 29 May 1925, AFA; AAA to RAA, 26 December 1927, AFA.

27. IAA to Señores Aspíllaga Anderson Hermanos S.A., 14 November 1929, AFA; IAA to Señores Aspíllaga Anderson Hermanos S.A., 23 December 1929, AFA; LAA to RAA, 18 November 1929, AFA; LAA to RAA, 25 November 1929, AFA; RAA to IAA and LAA, 20 November 1929, AFA; AAA to RAA, 25 May 1930, AFA; aviso, 9 August 1930, AFA; IAA to M. Asián, 11 August 1930, AFA.

28. Henry E. Dobyns and Paul L. Doughty, *Peru: A Cultural History* (New York: Oxford University Press, 1976), pp. 169–170, 212.

29. Ricardo Palma to AH, 22 September 1909, AFA.

30. AH to AH, 8 February 1900, AFA; AH to AH, 24 November 1906, AFA; Juan M. Vásquez to RAB, 16 July 1907, AFA; VAT to AH, 16 March 1910, AFA; AAB to AH, 15 June 1910, AFA; Ricardo Palma to AH, 4 December 1910, AFA; RAB to AAB and BAB, 12 January 1916, AFA; RAB to AAB and BAB, 23 January 1916, AFA; RAB to AAB and BAB, 25 January 1916, AFA; BAB to AH, 11 April 1916, AFA; VAT to AH, 3 May 1916, AFA.

31. LAA to RAA, 21 October 1930, AFA; LAA to RAA, 22 October 1932, AFA; LAA to RAA, 5 November 1932, AFA.

32. LAA to RAA, 21 October 1930, AFA.

33. AAB to RAB, 30 October 1913, AFA. Also instructive on this point are the following statements from, respectively, Antero Aspíllaga Barrera and Luis Aspíllaga Anderson: "Where there is not health, one cannot have work nor satisfaction for anyone" (AAB to RAB and BAB, 30 October 1913, AFA); "With respect to the orders for medicine, we are controlling this in order to avoid useless and luxurious expenditures, which the doctors are very fond of, and which the company cannot tolerate" (LAA to RAA, 22 September 1924, AFA).

34. AH to AH, 27 March 1888(a), AFA; AH to AH, 29 March 1888, AFA; AH to AH, 31 January 1889, AFA; AH to AH, 3 February 1889, AFA; AH to AH, 21 February 1889, AFA.

35. AH to AH, 23 January 1890(a), AFA; AH to AH, 6 February 1890, AFA; AH to AH, 25 March 1891, AFA; AH to AH, 9 June 1891, AFA; AH to AH, 23 August 1892, AFA; AH to AH, 3 September 1892, AFA; AH to AH, 21 March 1893, AFA; AH to AH, 15 April 1893, AFA; AH to AH, 20 February 1894, AFA; AH to AH, 17 July 1894, AFA; AH to AH, 2 April 1897, AFA; AH to AH, 3 May 1897, AFA; AH to AH, 19 May 1897, AFA; AH to AH, 7 July 1897, AFA; G. López to AH, 12 October 1899, AFA; G. López to AH, 19 October 1899, AFA.

36. AH to AH, 10 June 1901, AFA; VAT to AH, 16 March 1916, AFA; AAB to AH, 15 June 1910, AFA; Ricardo Palma to AH, 4 December 1910, AFA; RAB to AAB and BAB, 12 January 1916, AFA; RAB to AAB and BAB, 23 January 1916, AFA; RAB to AAB and BAB, 25 January 1916, AFA; BAB to AH, 11 April 1916, AFA; VAT to AH, 3 May 1916, AFA.

37. IAA to RAA, 5 June 1932, AFA; RAA to IAA and LAA, 10 June 1932, AFA.

38. C. Medina to AH, 9 September 1912, AFA.

39. N. Salcedo to AH, 9 May 1903, AFA; AH to AH, 20 December 1904, AFA; AH to AH, 15 February 1906, AFA; Francisco Pérez Céspedes to AH, 28 June 1907, AFA; BAB to AAB and RAB, 25 October 1908, AFA; VAT to AH, 21 November 1908, AFA; VAT to AH, 5 December 1908, AFA.

40. AH to AH, 20 December 1904, AFA; AH to AH, 15 February 1906, AFA; Francisco Pérez Céspedes to AH, 28 June 1907, AFA; BAB to AAB and RAB, 25 October 1908, AFA; VAT to AH, 5 December 1908, AFA.

41. AH to AH, 8 February 1900, AFA; AH to AH, 24 November 1906, AFA; Juan M. Vásquez to AH, 16 July 1907, AFA.

42. Juan M. Vásquez to RAB, 14 September 1905, AFA; Juan M. Vásquez to AH, 16 July 1907, AFA; Sebastián Tello to AH, 25 October 1905, AFA.

43. Juan M. Vásquez to AH, 14 October 1908, AFA.

44. C. Medina to AH, 9 September 1912, AFA.

45. Ibid.

46. Ibid.

47. Ibid.

48. Informe de la visita de inspección de la Hacienda Cayaltí por el Señor Don Ramón Aspíllaga, Octubre y Noviembre, 1916, AFA; C. Medina to Señor Gerente, Negociaciones Agrícolas Cayaltí y Palto, 18 February 1921, AFA; VAT to Señor Gerente, Negociaciones Agrícolas Cayaltí y Palto, 13 November 1922, AFA; LAA to RAA, 11 April 1924, AFA.

49. IAA to RAB ("Querido Papá"), 10 January 1926, AFA; AAA to RAB, 3 June 1927, AFA.

50. LAA to RAB, 7 September 1925, AFA; C. Medina to Señor Gerente, Negociaciones Agrícolas Cayaltí y Palto, 28 January 1921, AFA.

51. AAB to VAT, 8 December 1921, AFA.

52. Ricardo Palma to AH, 22 September 1909, AFA; VAT to AH, 8 October 1909, AFA; Ricardo Palma to AH, 1 March 1911, AFA; LAA to RAA, 22 September 1924, AFA; IAA to "Querido Papá y Hermanos," 20 October 1928, AFA; AAB to RAB, 30 October 1913, AFA.

53. AH to AH, 29 June 1901, AFA.

54. Administrador General to RAB, 23 January 1927, AFA.

55. AH to Guillermo Aspíllaga y Taboada, 5 October 1906, AFA.

56. Informe de la visita de inspección de la Hacienda Cayaltí por el Señor Don Ramón Aspíllaga, Octubre y Noviembre, 1916, AFA.

57. VAT to AH, 1 March 1912, AFA.

58. Ibid.

59. Letter dated 12 December 1919, AFA.

60. AAB to RAB and BAB, 11 February 1917, AFA.

61. AAB to RAB and BAB, 11 December 1913, AFA; AAB to RAB and BAB, 11 February 1917, AFA; AH to AH, 13 February 1894, AFA.

62. AH to AH, 30 January 1894, AFA; AH to AH, 3 February 1894, AFA; N. Salcedo to AH, 9 October 1899, AFA; VAT to BAB, 1899 (month and day not given) AFA; Guillermo López to AH, 9 October 1899, AFA; Guillermo López to AH, 12 October 1899, AFA.

63. RAB to AAB and BAB, 30 December 1915, AFA.

64. AH to AH, 22 May 1885, AFA; AH to AH, 23 April 1890, AFA; AH to AH, 19 January 1892, AFA; AH to AH, 1 November 1892, AFA; AH to AH, 24 October 1896, AFA; AH to AH, 25 November 1897, AFA.

65. AH to AH, 8 December 1898, AFA.

66. AH to AH, 7 February 1894, AFA; AH to AH, 13 February 1894, AFA; AH to AH, 12 February 1896, AFA; AH to AH, 29 February 1896, AFA.

67. AH to AH, 29 February 1896, AFA.

68. "Principales obligaciones de los guardianes de la Hacienda, 1928," AFA.

69. N. Salcedo to AH, 4 August 1899, AFA; AH to AH, 29 June 1901, AFA.

70. RAB to AAB and BAB, 7 January 1916, AFA.

71. RAB to AAB and BAB, 11 January 1916, AFA; RAB and AAB and BAB, 15 January 1916, AFA.

72. AAB to RAB and BAB, 3 January 1917, AFA; AAB to RAB and BAB, 11 February 1917, AFA; AH to VAT, 13 November 1917, AFA.

73. Letter dated 12 December 1919, AFA; Informe de la visita de inspección de la Hacienda Cayaltí por el Señor Don Ramón Aspíllaga, Octubre y Noviembre, 1916, AFA.

74. IAA to Señores Aspíllaga Anderson Hermanos S.A., 6 January 1930, AFA.

75. Francisco Pérez Céspedes to AH, 15 February 1908, AFA; VAT to AH, 15 February 1908, AFA; Francisco Pérez Céspedes to AH, 24 February 1908, AFA; AAB to RAB and BAB, 6 July 1908, AFA.

76. Informe de la visita de inspección de la Hacienda Cayaltí por el Señor Don Ramón Aspíllaga, Octubre y Noviembre, 1916, AFA; RAB to AAB and BAB, 25 October 1916, AFA; IAA to RAB, 28 December 1926, AFA.

77. VAT to Señores Gerentes, Negociaciones Agrícolas Cayaltí y Palto, 11 September 1922, AFA.

78. IAA to RAB, 18 September 1923, AFA.

79. AH to AH, 6 January 1900, AFA; AH to AH, 18 December 1906, AFA; "Programa de 1925," AFA.

80. AH to AH, 18 December 1906, AFA; "Programa para las fiestas del año nuevo, 1910," AFA; LAA to RAB, 26 July 1927, AFA.

81. AH to AH, 18 November 1887, AFA.

82. AH to AH, 7 February 1893, AFA; AH to AH, 2 August 1898, AFA.

83. AH to AH, 11 September 1914, AFA.

84. AH to AH, 7 February 1893, AFA.

85. VAT to AH, 25 September 1914, AFA; AH to AH, 22 June 1901, AFA.

86. María Mercedes García to Administración, 17 October 1907, AFA; VAT to Señores Gerentes, Negociaciones Agrícolas Cayaltí y Palto, 15 December 1922, AFA.

87. AH to AH, 18 November 1887, AFA; AH to AH, 20 February 1894(a), AFA.

88. Herbert G. Gutman, *Work, Culture, and Society in Industrializing America. Essays in American Working-Class and Social History* (New York: Knopf, 1976), pp. 20–21; Sidney Pollard, *The Genesis of Modern Management: A Study of the Industrial Revolution in Great Britain* (London: Edward Arnold, 1965), chap. 5.

89. After Ronald Dore, *British Factory-Japanese Factory: The Origins of National Diversity in Industrial Relations* (Berkeley & Los Angeles: University of California Press, 1973), p. 270.

90. Bernardino Copia to Catalino Coronado, 12 November 1918, AFA; Maximiliano Quebara to Catalino Coronado, 16 June 1918, AFA.

91. Quoted in Dore, *British Factory*, p. 407.

92. The main exception to this would be the hiring of Victor and Guillermo Aspíllaga Taboada for staff positions. The relationship of owners with staff is not, however, the real subject of this discussion.

93. Eric J. Hobsbawm, "Custom, Wages and Work-Load," in *Labouring Men: Studies in the History of Labour*, ed. Eric J. Hobsbawm, p. 421 (New York: Anchor, 1967).

94. Joaquín Capelo, *Lima en 1900: estudio crítico y antología* (Lima: Instituto de Estudios Peruanos, 1973), p. 69.

95. United States Bureau of Census, *Historical Statistics of the United States, Colonial Times to 1957* (Washington, D.C., 1960), pp. 180–181.

Chapter 9: Confrontation

1. AAA to RAB, 29 December 1927, AFA.

2. Peter Blanchard, "A Populist Precursor: Guillermo Billinghurst," *Journal of Latin American Studies* 9, no. 2 (1977): 251–273.

3. RAB to AAB, 14 June 1917, AFA.

4. Peter Blanchard, *The Origins of the Peruvian Labor Movement, 1883–1919* (Pittsburgh: University of Pittsburgh Press, 1982).

5. Bill Albert, *An Essay on the Peruvian Sugar Industry, 1880–1920 and the Letters of Ronald Gordon, Administrator of the British Sugar Company in Cañete, 1914–1920* (Norwich: School of Social Studies, University of East Anglia, 1976), pp. 192a–193a.

6. The Aspíllaga correspondence contains ample testimony on this point. Leguía did enjoy the backing of the de la Piedras, the owners of Pomalca. The de la Piedras were relative latecomers to plantation agriculture and were not members of the Civilista party.

7. See the Aspíllaga correspondence for this period.

8. Peter F. Klarén, *Modernization, Dislocation, and Aprismo: Origins of the Peruvian Aprista Party, 1870–1932*, Latin American Monographs, no. 32 (Austin, Tex.: Institute of Latin American Studies, 1973), chap. 2; Albert, *Peruvian Sugar Industry*, pp. 178a–218a.

9. Klarén, *Modernization*.

10. See chap. 3 for land consolidation and technological improvements; AH to VAT, 16 April 1912, AFA; *La Reforma* (8 April 1912); Felipe de Osma, *Informe sobre las huelgas del norte* (Lima: Biblioteca Peruana de Historia Económica, 1972), p. 12.

11. Letter dated 18 April 1912, in Pablo Macera, ed. *Cayaltí 1875–1920: Organización del trabajo en una plantación azucarera del Perú* (Lima: Seminario de Historia Rural Andina, 1973), p. 224.

12. Albert, *Peruvian Sugar Industry*, p. 106a; *La Reforma* (8–11 April 1912; 15 April 1912; 18 April 1912; 19 April 1912).

13. Klarén, *Modernization*, p. 36; Albert, *Peruvian Sugar Industry*, p. 108a.

14. This interpretation is based largely on the reporting of the Trujillo daily *La Reforma*. This paper may be considered a controversial source, because it was

owned by Víctor Larco Herrera, the propietor of the plantation Roma and an adversary of the Gildemeisters. It could be argued that Larco exaggerated strikers' gains to embarrass his German-Peruvian rivals, especially since his plantation had escaped unharmed. However, this would have also involved the risk of publicizing nonexistent advances that could have encouraged his workers to seek equity. False reporting would have also opened the door to lawsuits by the powerful Gildemeisters as well as by the Peruvian and German officials reported as parties to the agreement. Thus, there seems to be more reason to believe the authenticity of the reporting than to dismiss it as inherently biased.

15. *La Reforma* (30 April 1912; 1 May 1912; 6 May 1912).

16. For lengthy discussions of strikes during this period, see Blanchard, *Origins*, chaps. 9 and 10; and Albert, *Peruvian Sugar Industry*, pp. 178a–198a.

17. *La Reforma* (1–2 June 1917; 4 June 1917; 6 June 1917); *La Industria* (4 June 1917); Albert, *Peruvian Sugar Industry*, pp. 187a–188a.

18. Albert, *Peruvian Sugar Industry*, p. 171a.

19. RAB to AAB, 12 July 1917, AFA; RAB to AAB, 17 July 1917, AFA.

20. Klarén, *Modernization*, p. 38; Joaquín Díaz Ahumada, "Las luchas sindicales en el valle de Chicama," in *Imperialismo y el agroperuano* (Lima: Universidad Particular Ricardo Palma, n.d.), pp. 18–20, 25. Díaz Ahumada participated in the 1912, 1917, and 1921 strikes and was an early union organizer.

21. See chap. 2, section on profits.

22. Albert, *Peruvian Sugar Industry*, p. 171a.

23. Ibid., chap. 2.

24. Díaz Ahumada, "Las luchas sindicales," pp. 28–29. Díaz Ahumada presents a full list of demands.

25. Ibid., pp. 29–34. At some point during the ensuing strike, the government also reportedly fed strikers: see Albert, *Peruvian Sugar Industry*, p. 212a.

26. Agustín was the brother of Víctor Raúl Haya de la Torre, founder of the APRA party.

27. Díaz Ahumada, "Las luchas sindicales," pp. 31–32; Klarén, *Modernization*, p. 46.

28. Klarén, *Modernization*, pp. 46–47.

29. Lauro A. Curletti, *El problema industrial en el valle de Chicama. Informe del Ministro de Fomento* (Lima: Biblioteca Peruana de Historia Económica, 1972), pp. 31–33.

30. Albert, *Peruvian Sugar Industry*, p. 217a.

31. Díaz Ahumada, "Las luchas sindicales," pp. 47–54; Albert, *Peruvian Sugar Industry*, pp. 217a–218a.

32. See chap. 3.

33. Klarén, *Modernization*, pp. 123–127.

34. Ibid., pp. 129, 136; Steve Stein, *Populism in Peru: The Emergence of the Masses and the Politics of Social Control* (Madison: University of Wisconsin Press, 1980).

35. Klarén, *Modernization*, chap. 7; Guillermo Thorndike, *El año de la barbarie: Perú 1932*, 3d ed. (Lima: Mosca Azul, 1973); Don J. Leoncio Rodríguez Manffaurt, *Actuación del Capitán Don J. Leoncio Rodríguez M. durante el movimiento revolucionario de Trujillo. Julio de 1932* (Trujillo: Tip. H. Cuba,

1932); Merino Arana, *Historia policial del Perú en la República* (Imprenta del Departamento de Prensa y Publicaciones de la Guardia Civil).

36. IAA to RAA, 28 May 1931(a), AFA.

37. IAA to RAA, 28 May 1931(a), AFA; IAA to RAA, 31 May 1931(a), AFA. It is unknown when sugar workers had begun to celebrate May Day, but this is an important indication that they were beginning to form a class consciousness.

38. The administrator of Pucalá was Edgardo Seoane, the brother of the Aprista leader Manuel Seoane. Ismael believed that Edgardo was also an Aprista and behind many of the disturbances; however, no evidence has been found to support this view.

39. IAA to RAA, 28 May 1931(a), AFA; IAA to RAA, 31 May 1931(a), AFA.

40. RAA to IAA, LAA, GAA, 29 May 1931, AFA.

41. IAA to Señores Aspíllaga Anderson Hnos. S.A., 6 June 1931, AFA.

42. RAA to IAA and LAA, 13 June 1931, AFA.

43. IAA to Señores Aspíllaga Anderson Hnos. S.A., 14 June 1931, AFA; LAA to RAA, 16 June 1931, AFA.

44. IAA to Señores Aspíllaga Anderson Hnos. S.A., 14 June 1931, AFA; IAA to Señores Aspíllaga Anderson Hnos. S.A., 16 June 1931, AFA; IAA to Señores Aspíllaga Anderson Hnos. S.A., 23 June 1931, AFA; RAA to IAA and LAA, 15 June 1931, AFA; RAA to IAA and LAA, 18 June 1931, AFA; RAA to IAA and LAA, 25 June 1931, AFA; LAA to RAA, 16 June 1931, AFA.

45. VAT to AH, 21 April 1912, AFA; VAT to AH, 4 May 1912, AFA.

46. AAB to AH, 13 November 1912, AFA.

47. AH to VAT, 12 September 1916, AFA.

48. VAT to AH, 19 September 1917, AFA.

49. AAB to RAB and BAB, 16 June 1917, AFA; AAB to RAB and BAB, 21 June 1917, AFA; RAB to AAB, 2 July 1917, AFA; RAB to AAB, 12 July 1917, AFA. Also see pp. 173–174.

50. AAB to RAB and BAB, 29 April 1917, AFA.

51. Letter dated 22 July 1919, in Macera, *Cayaltí*, p. 231; letter dated 7 August 1919, AFA; letter dated 28 August 1919, AFA; and Albert, *Peruvian Sugar Industry*, p. 197a.

52. IAA to RAB, 5 October 1923, AFA; IAA to RAB, 8 October 1923, AFA.

53. LAA to RAA, 2 July 1927, AFA; AAA to RAA, 2 July 1927, AFA; LAA to RAA, 7 July 1927, AFA; IAA to RAA, 8 July 1927, AFA; AAA to RAA, 12 July 1927, AFA; LAA to RAA, 2 August 1927, AFA.

54. AAB to VAT, 26 December 1921, AFA.

55. VAT to AAB, 16 December 1920, in Lorenzo Huertas, ed. *Capital burocrático y lucha de clases en el sector agrario (Lambayeque, Perú, 1920–1950)* (Lima: Seminario de Historia Rural Andina, 1974), p. 175; letter dated 10 December 1921, in Huertas, p. 177.

56. IAA to RAA, 28 May 1931, AFA; IAA to RAA, 2 June 1931, AFA; IAA to RAA, 14 June 1931, AFA; IAA to Señores Aspíllaga Anderson Hermanos S.A., 16 June 1931, AFA.

57. Marejildo Izquierdo to editors of *El Trabajador*, 14 June 1931, AFA.

58. Dennis L. Gilbert, *The Oligarchy and the Old Regime in Peru* (Ithaca, N.Y.: Cornell University Dissertation Series on Latin America, 1977), pp. 116–119.

59. Ibid.
60. Denis Sulmont, *El desarrollo de la clase obrera en el Perú* (Lima: Centro de Investigaciones Sociales, Económicas, Políticas y Antropológicas, Pontificia Universidad Católica del Perú, 1974), p. 48.
61. Gilbert, *The Oligarchy*, p. 193.
62. Ibid.
63. Ibid.
64. See the series of letters from the Cayaltí correspondence published in Huertas, *Capital burocrático*, pp. 236–285.
65. Gilbert, *The Oligarchy*, p. 195.
66. Ibid., pp. 195–196.
67. R. Neumann to RAA, 2 December 1950, in Huertas, *Capital burocrático*, pp. 268–289; Orlando Plaza, "Historia del Sindicato de Cayaltí" (B.A. thesis, Pontificia Universidad Católica del Perú, 1971), p. 10.
68. Plaza, "Sindicato de Cayaltí," p. 11. The translation is Gilbert's, *The Oligarchy*, p. 197.
69. Plaza, "Sindicato de Cayaltí," p. 10. The translation is Gilbert's, *The Oligarchy*, p. 197.
70. R. Neumann to RAA, 2 December 1950, in Huertas, *Capital burocrático*, pp. 286–289.

Conclusion
1. Peter F. Klarén, *Modernization, Dislocation, and Aprismo: Origins of the Peruvian Aprista Party, 1870–1932*, Latin American Monographs, no. 32 (Austin, Tex.: Institute of Latin American Studies, 1973), p. 16.
2. On this point, also see Bill Albert, *An Essay on the Peruvian Sugar Industry, 1880–1920 and the Letters of Ronald Gordon, Administrator of the British Sugar Company in Cañete, 1914–1920* (Norwich: School of Social Studies, University of East Anglia, 1976); Rosemary R. Thorp and Geoffrey Bertram, *Peru, 1890–1977: Growth and Policy in an Open Economy* (New York: Columbia University Press, 1978).
3. Thorp and Bertram, *Peru*.
4. Ibid.
5. Paul Sweezy, "A Critique," in *The Transition from Feudalism to Capitalism*, ed. Rodney Hilton, p. 33 (Norfolk: Lowe & Brydone, 1976).
6. Arnold J. Bauer, "Rural Workers in Spanish America: Problems of Peonage and Oppression," *Hispanic American Historical Review* 59, no. 1 (February 1979): 34–64.
7. Juan Pérez de la Riva, *El barracón: Esclavitud y capitalismo en Cuba* (Barcelona: Editorial Crítica, 1975).
8. Hugh Thomas, *Cuba: The Pursuit of Freedom* (New York: Harper & Row, 1971), pp. 186–189.
9. François Bourricaud, *Power and Society in Contemporary Peru*, trans. Paul Stevenson (London: Faber & Faber, 1970), part 2, chap. 1; part 3, chap. 1.
10. Carlos A. Astiz, *Pressure Groups and Power Elites in Peruvian Politics* (Ithaca, N.Y.: Cornell University Press, 1969), p. 106.
11. Douglas E. Horton, *Haciendas and Cooperatives: A Study of Estate*

Organization, Land Reform and New Reform Enterprises in Peru (Ithaca, N.Y.: Cornell University Dissertation Series in Latin America, 1976); Abraham Lowenthal, ed. *The Peruvian Experiment: Continuity and Change under Military Rule* (Princeton: Princeton University Press, 1975).

Index

234   Index